Chattel House Blues

Chattel House Blues

Making of a Democratic Society in Barbados

From Clement Payne to Owen Arthur

Hilary McD Beckles

Ian Randle Publishers
Kingston • Miami

James Currey Publishers
Oxford

First published in Jamaica, 2004 by
Ian Randle Publishers
11 Cunningham Avenue
Box 686, Kingston 6
www.ianrandlepublishers.com

National Library of Jamaica Cataloguing in Publication Data

Beckles, Hilary
Chattel house blues : making of a democratic society : from Clement Payne to Owen Arthur /
     Hilary McD Beckles

     p. ;   cm

     Bibliography : p.

     ISBN 976-637-086-9 (paperback)

1. Barbados – History   2. Democracy – Barbados   3. Barbados – Political and government
I. Title

     972.981   dc21

First Published in the United Kingdom, 2004 by
James Currey Publishers
73 Botley Road
Oxford OX2 0BS
www.jamescurrey.co.uk

ISBN 0-85255-494-X (paperback)

British Library Cataloguing in Publication Data
A cataloguing in publication record is available on request from the British Library

Cover painting "Chattel House Blues" by Jonna Twigg
Book and Cover design by Shelly-Gail Cooper
Printed in the United States of America

To George Lamming, Austin Clarke, Bruce St John,
Timothy Callender, Kamau Brathwaite, the Mighty Gabby,
and all the other artists who showed the way.

For Athol 'T.T.' Lewis and Wynter Crawford,
unsung heroes of the democratic movement.

Table of Contents

Preface and Acknowledgements

The idea of writing this book originated in the context of my participation in the public discourse on political democracy and economic injustice in Barbados during the 1980s and 1990s. Being an advocate for the cause of popular economic enfranchisement in the country invoked the need for historical readings of the economic environment. This political circumstance and the academic challenge were the principal motivational sources.

Much of what is written here, however, first came into being as words spoken during dozens of public lectures delivered in Barbados, the wider Caribbean and beyond. I have sought to maintain the discursive spirit of these social encounters and have employed devices such as the use of extensive quotations from unpublished manuscripts in order to generate a strong sense of immediacy and to keep references to these documents to a minimum. It is a matter of great importance to me that audiences who heard these utterances will recognise them and bear witness to their evolution.

I would wish to thank all my friends and colleagues who supported this project, especially those who insisted that the text be presented as a document for public consumption rather than an academic production.

Dr Alana Johnson and Dr David Browne served as research assistants from 1995-97, and I wish to thank them for excavating dozens of nineteenth and early twentieth century documents that have informed much of the analysis. Dr Henderson Carter and Dr David Browne, at a later date, generously shared with me important documents that informed the tone and texture of my arguments. The three of them have offered excellent encouragement and I wish to thank them sincerely.

Years of discussion and interaction with the work of experts of nineteenth century Barbados, Woodville Marshall, Kortright Davis, Celia Karch, Bonham Richardson, George Belle, John Gilmore, Noel Titus, Anthony Phillips, Karl Watson, Velma Newton, Janice Mayers, Pedro Welch, Trevor Marshall, Robert Morris and Bentley Gibbs, have deepened my understanding of post-slavery reconstruction and the Black struggle for a genuine emancipation.

Works on the twentieth century by Hilbourne Watson, Farley Brathwaite, Glenford Howe, Don Marshall, Wilber Will and Alexander Hoyos, especially, have enabled me to see more clearly historical continuities that inform the 1960s discourse on nationhood.

Finally, I would like to express gratitude to Grace Jutan for working gracefully with unreasonable deadlines on various drafts of this manuscript.

Introduction

Building a Nation with the Grassroots

'Barbados is in revolt against the status quo. Throughout the country thousands of middle class and working class men and women are voicing the most determined protests against poverty and unemployment. These thousands are resolved to put more of the wealth in the colony at the service of the people; these thousands are in deadly earnest; this spirit may well be called NEW DEMOCRACY . . . No longer are the people of this island prepared to entrust their destinies to the representatives of big business.' Wynter Crawford, *Observer*, 27/11/44.

Young nations, such as Barbados, struggling to break free of the colonial scaffold, require a coherent and accurate sense of the past or the living memory. If the present and future are to be places invested with cultural meaning and creativity, the survival activities of ancestors must be discovered and presented as relevant and determining.

At present, there is a call in some quarters for a discursive disconnect of political thinking from the historical process. This should be resisted. One way to proceed is to illustrate the fundamental continuities in the major political projects of development in the twentieth century with the historicised imagination of Caribbean people today. Attempts to downsize the importance of history in the reading of political options can only serve to blur, subvert and weaken any vision that may help to deepen the democratic cause that began with the enslaved Africans' flight from slavery.

The remaking of colonial Barbados as a postmodern nation-state has its political roots buried deep within the past. These roots gave life to great thoughts and actions conceived in the branches of an enchained people in search of liberation and redemption. The nation emerged from the unfathomable depths of slavery, referred to by the enslaved as the 'barbarity times', and came into being along a road signposted by untold suffering and countless deaths. Barbados, the first slave society of the Americas, a place where enslaved Africans and their offspring knew the deepest wounds of the whip, now stands as a monument to a freedom long imagined and painfully pursued.

The journey to nationhood from the plantation mirrored this misery. There were stories about those tortured for thinking about rebellion; those tortured and killed for thinking and talking about freedom; those driven to starvation, destitution and madness for seeking rights and respect after the time when emancipation was meant to assure and restore. But the nation was born. It was a living space that rose from the tomb of colonialism, where some of the world's newest citizens, still shaken by the shackles, are now celebrating while reflecting on where the next step will lead.

In 1937, Clement Payne pulled the fragmented political elements together in order to produce the transforming moment, as did General Bussa and General Green in 1816 and 1876 respectively. Countless men and women in between these times kept alive the feeling of freedom and justice with thousands of recorded and unrecorded acts of personal revolt against the system they knew only collective action could dismantle.

In 1950, Grantley Adams, Moses, and the irrepressible anti-colonialist Wynter Crawford, pioneered the legislative path to universal adult suffrage in Barbados. The following year, in a general election, they ended 324 years of African political exclusion on the island. As a discourse in social justice, this process reached maturity in 1994 when Owen Seymour Arthur, a young man from the chattel house in the plantation tenantry, became prime minister. This event brought closure to the culture of formal institutional denial and exclusion based on class.

This contested past that details the making of the nation has been told and written in many places. The telling is rarely rooted in perspectives that centre centuries of sophisticated grassroots struggle. It is still common to encounter accounts that suggest the driving of democracy from the metropolis, and its bestowal upon the masses by elites at moments of imperial and colonial enlightenment.

Rewriting this history in order to locate the evolving nation-state within the stream of popular agitation and rebellion meant direct confrontation with interest groups that benefited from such an interpretation. But the historical evidence shows compellingly that democracy in Barbados, as a social, political and cultural reality – not yet an economic condition – has its origins principally within working class demands for freedom, justice and equality.

No one expected that such an undertaking would be a simple matter. Some, however, knew that it would be difficult and could be dangerous. Rewriting the history of one's country within the context of a dying colonialism could destroy an academic career in much the same way that Sir Grantley Adams suggested in the 1930s – that to confront the plantation interest was to destroy a political career. There was also the risk of losing a life, because debunking established myths that go as history is to challenge the power of special interest groups.

Historians, like politicians, are generally trained to be professionally cautious and, publicly, most of them are. The case of Barbados is no different from what obtains elsewhere. Few are prepared to critically assess the national usage of power by elites because wisdom suggests that no personal benefits would be derived from the exercise. But historians, perhaps more so than most knowledgeable workers, are well placed to be aware of the methods by which the masses of people are held prisoner by interpretation of the past. Despite their special status, some historians become hired minds, defending those who display their wealth and wield power. Occasionally, they are prepared to bury at birth any vibrant life within the nation that demands greater space.

Afro-Barbadians were able to develop, at an early stage, a mature sense of social responsibility that now constitutes the bedrock of the nation. Yet it was written, understood and taught that the unfolding of human and civil rights during the 100 long years of increased cruelty after Emancipation had to do principally with the increasing liberalism of the planter-merchant elite. This group, it was said, granted concessions gradually to subordinate classes as this was consistent with its growing sense of civil responsibility. Democracy, in this view, descended from above like 'snowflakes falling on canefields'.

It was only a matter of time before another group of historians presented the struggle of the people, showing the intensity of their political leadership and the costs in human life that they paid. In so doing, they established that the forces for democracy from below, at the base of the society, were stronger. Also, that these popular forces were long-term and that they determined the agenda of what we now know as the anti-colonial, democratic tradition.

The production of a historical literature that set out this people-centred culture of change and transformation became a national necessity. The objective was to empower the majority of citizens with the knowledge that their fore-parents were not just passive passengers on the nation-building train, but drivers and engineers, among other things.

Furthermore, it was the historians' duty to protect and defend what had been achieved while continually seeking new ways to deepen and expand democratic rights and freedoms. It was for them to feel a strong and legitimate sense of national ownership and belonging, and to experience the citizenship won as a deeply rooted social and moral fact.

If power can be defined as the ability to interpret events and processes and to have them accepted and implemented, then the evidence suggests that the white elite in Barbados, with its external allies, had enjoyed a virtual literary monopoly of interpretation for over 300 years. The concentration of conceptual power and authority in the hands of this social/racial minority (whose dominance of productive resource ownership and economic decision-making survived the reformist attacks of the mid-twentieth century, Black-led democratic movement), has been greatly enhanced by much of the liberal historiography of post-colonialism.

Independence and nationhood, critical markers in the journey to justice, have not foreclosed on the historical process. In much the same way that emancipation served also to consolidate aspects of the slavery mentality, the birth of the nation (November 30, 1966) witnessed a certain determination by the elite to preserve self-serving vestiges of colonialism. The movement for the economic enfranchisement of Blacks erupted in the 1980s as the next stage in the struggle for democracy.

The workers, politically enfranchised in 1950 with universal adult suffrage, were now rising to an appreciation of their economic rights. Middle class Blacks also demanded access to the high end of the corporate sector and the removal of the race-based obstacles that served to exclude them as entrepreneurs and managers. The coining of the term economic democracy was critical, and the concept moved to centrestage of party political contest during most of 1990.

Clement Payne's vision, then, is almost fully implemented. The civil rights of the masses are respected and defended by strong and effective trade unions and political parties that carry the word 'labour' in their titles. Payne was consistent in his view that strong trade unions are the key to achieving and sustaining workers' enfranchisement. The debate is developing on the issue of popular economic democracy, and there is general agreement that this struggle is the next step in civil rights development that the society is preparing to take. This is where the country's democratic discourse has reached. This text merely seeks to visit the discursive aspects of these twentieth century movements, from Clement Payne to Owen Arthur, and to suggest ways of reading the period beyond.

- *One* -

Freedom and Justice:
Clement Payne's 1937 Revolution

1930: Workers Betrayed, Landed Enfranchisement Denied

In March 1930, the Report of the West Indian Sugar Commission was submitted to the Secretary of State for the Colonies. The Commission dealt comprehensively with the deepening crisis of the sugar economy and the inability of its managers to find strategic solutions. It was particularly sensitive to the recommendations of the 1897 Royal Commission and saw its duties, in part, as a reflective exercise on this earlier investigation.

The 1930 Commission focused on the continuing plight of workers 33 years later and had much to say about production levels, falling wages and the land question. Barbados was singled out as the one colony where planters used wage reduction to increase profitability instead of devising ways to increase yield and productivity. This strategy of squeezing the sugar workers was patterned off the strategy used in the East Indies, in colonies such as Java, where it was considered to be profitable and effective. The Commissioners commented on the relevance of this approach for the West Indies. The report stated that the East Indies had:

> a rate of wages about half the minimum West Indian rate, that enables Java to produce sugar so cheaply. It is not an advantage British West Indian communities need envy, nor are the conditions which afford it such as one would desire to see the West Indies reduced to. The nearest approach to such conditions in the West Indies may perhaps be found in Barbados.

With respect to the recommendation of the 1897 Commission that land be made available to the workers in order to produce a class of commercial small farmers and peasants, the 1930 Report indicated deep concern that no progress had been made in Barbados:

> where progress has not been made we endeavour to indicate the extent and the causes of the failure. We also have, unfortunately, to observe, that where the policy recommended has, for whatever reason, not been pursued, the conditions at the present date appear most disquieting.

The explanation for the Barbadian planters' refusal to accept the recommendations of 1897 was presented as follows:

> It is manifest that where the economy of a community depends practically entirely, as that of Barbados . . . still does, upon a single industry carried on by the employment of wage labourers on estates, the public policy of the class most influential in guiding the Government must almost inevitably incline to this economic view. If they encouraged action which, in their belief, must tend to diminish their labour supply, they would be cutting away the branch upon which they sit. Nevertheless, our survey, after the lapse of thirty-three years, of the conditions prevalent in the West Indies makes it necessary for us to express our strong concurrence in view of Sir H. Norman's Commission.

That view was that landed enfranchisement for Blacks constituted the way forward for the social well-being of the colony. The Commission gave evidence of the success of the land reform policy in other countries and lamented that white Barbadians had steadfastly refused to accept the recommendation. The 1930 Report stated furthermore:

> Such communities as Barbados . . . cannot be salvaged in the event of a collapse of the sugar industry merely by allowing the labouring class to rent provision grounds on estates. Nowhere throughout the British West Indies has this system proved satisfactory. The peasant cultivator, if he is to thrive, must have land which he knows is his own and which he can improve, a homestead in which he can take pride, access by roads, facilities for marketing, and a proper water supply. In St. Vincent some old sugar

estates have been, on the recommendation of Sir H. Norman's Commission, broken up into small holdings, with the result of a most remarkable development in that Island's prosperity, as shown by its exports and its annual public revenue. As another result of their recommendations, the rules for the sale of Crown lands in Trinidad were made more liberal. Smaller holdings were sold at an easier price. This policy had already been adopted by the Government of Jamaica and at the present day facilities are afforded, through Agricultural Loan Banks, for the purchase and breaking-up of suitable large estates. No action, however, nor any attempt at action in this direction, so strongly and so well-advisedly recommended by Sir H. Norman's Commission, was taken in Barbados . . . .

The 1930 Commission's recommendation asserted that Barbados should receive no more support for the plantation sector from the Imperial Government until it moved to implement the land reform as specified in the 1897 Report. The recalcitrant nature of the Barbados planters had incurred the disgust of the commissioners who could not accept the view that Blacks should remain in a state of starvation and hopelessness while subsidised sugar plantations had no future. The report stated:

> In view of the permanence of the menace of the present conditions of sugar marketing to the possibility of maintaining that industry in Barbados and the similar islands, a menace, the early materialisation of which can only be averted by means of some intervention by the Imperial Government, it appears to us that it is a matter of Imperial interest that no assistance of this character should be given by the Imperial Government to the West Indies except upon the understanding that the recommendations of the Royal Commission of 1896-97 are to be seriously taken to heart and embodied in a continuous policy: that is to say, that deliberate steps should be taken, as have been taken for many years past in Jamaica, for placing many more of the population upon a self-supporting basis. The difficulty of embarking upon such a transition in Barbados and other sugar districts (for British Guiana needs a similar policy) is indisputably very great, but a resolute effort should be made to surmount it.

Two commissions had made recommendations for placing 'many more of the population upon a self-supporting basis', and both reports were rejected by the plantocracy. When the commissioners arrived in Barbados on October 17, 1929, the workers had good cause to feel betrayed after the 1897 Royal Commissioners had accepted and advocated their strategic solution to mass starvation and deprivation. There was only change for the worst, and a deep sense of disillusionment pervaded the rural poor who were now preparing to shift to a new form of professional, radical organisation.

The negative report given by the commissioners of 1896-97 on the question of emigration from Barbados was equally, and with a more discouraging effect, applicable. The formal openings for the employment of Barbadian emigrants in foreign countries had, in recent years, become increasingly restricted. Brazil and Venezuela were now closed to them. The demand for seasonal labour in Cuba had ceased. Very few West Indian emigrants were now allowed to enter the United States of America. The unoccupied lands of British Guiana, of which the commissioners of 1897 made mention, could not be regarded as available for Barbadian settlement, while, in the event of the further failure of the sugar industry, there would be no demand anywhere for labourers. Trinidad appeared to offer the most promising site for any migratory settlement of Barbadians. Suitable land existed there and appropriate productive work could be found, but Indian indentured servants had provided adequate labour to the sugar sector. The Trinidad oil industry was highly mechanised and did not promise any large or increasing demands for manual labour.

The 1930 Commission painted a picture of Barbadian workers in a state of structural seige, still entrapped within the bondage devised in the aftermath of the 1838 Abolition Act. A century had passed, during which time, in the views of two successive commissions, planters continued to see workers as cheap serviles rather than members of a free community. The survival of the plantation, the sugar industry and the dictatorship of the sugar planter, all depended on the persistence of this view of the Black community.

The report stated, with respect to the bondage of workers:

One of the results of the tenacity of the system of sugar production in the Island, demanding as exclusive as possible a control of land and of the supply of labour to work it, has been that, until quite recently, there has been hardly any breaking up of estates. The predominant impression produced by travelling through much of Barbados is that the labouring population reside clinging on to the fringes of cane-fields and perched on the banks of the highways. 'Located Labourers', that is, labourers resident on and employed under statutory prescriptions on the estates, are indeed allowed to rent quarter-acre pieces at the rate of £4.16s per acre per annum on condition of their cultivating canes for the estate.

Furthermore, it commented on efforts to block the access by Blacks to land:

So long as the sugar industry is maintained on its present footing this may be the simplest and most effectual means of enabling landless labourers to earn a certain amount of cash by their home labour; though the rental paid and the legal service conditions under which the plots are occupied are prohibitive of any organic development of peasant cultivation or cane farming on the lines on which these are successful and advantageous elsewhere. The independent agriculture of small proprietors or farmers is occasionally to be seen in some outlying districts, but the extent of these is obviously very limited, and most of the land that has been acquired by small purchasers has been bought at exorbitant prices (£60 to £100 an acre) for house plots and not for earning a living by cultivation, and has been paid for by remittances from friends and relations outside the Island. The value placed upon agricultural land is still exceedingly high as compared with the price at which small settlers can buy or rent holdings in other islands.

These remarks were made in order to establish that something peculiar was happening in Barbados and that the Black community found itself barred in all its efforts to achieve a meaningful emancipation. But it is this statement which, finally, placed the tragedy of the landless within the context of the colony's future:

Concurrently with these conditions obstructing the development of any great number of independent cultivators, it was brought out in evidence that no attempt has been made by either the Government or the Agricultural Society from the date of the [1897] West India Royal Commission's Report to this day to organise any kind of popular associations for the encouragement and improvement of peasant and labourers' garden agriculture, such as exist in almost every other civilised country in the world and have been actively promoted in other West Indian islands.

In 1934, when the merchant-planter elite formed the Barbados Producers Export Association (BPEA), the price of sugar collapsed to five shillings per c.w.t. from a level of 26 shillings in 1923. It stayed at the five-shilling level for another three years. Employers reduced wages, cut back on the number of employees and passed on much of the financial grief to the already impoverished labour force. Workers demanded employment and better wages but were confronted with legislation to prevent alliances. With the closing of large scale emigration outlets and increasing pressure upon their organisations and leaders by the State and its supporters, workers were driven on the defensive.

The 1930 Sugar Commission which investigated the effects of low sugar prices on workers spelled out gloom and offered no positive

Table 1
**Death Rates and Infantile Death Rates in Barbados,
British Guiana and Trinidad, 1924-29**

Year	Death Rate Per 1,000 Inhabitants			Death Rate Under One Year Per 1,000 Living Births		
	Barbados	British Guiana	Trinidad	Barbados	British Guiana	Trinidad
1924	29.5	25.6	...	298	165	...
1925	29.5	24.2	29.5	312	155	134
1926	29.6	25.5	28.8	314	159	143
1927	20.2	26.0	17.8	201	158	130
1928	30.1	27.9	18.7	331	185	129
1929	23.7	23.5	18.5	239	146	128

Source: *Report of the Acting Chief Medical Officer* (1929), p. 4.

suggestions. The daily wage of most labourers remained below the one-shilling mark, hardly an improvement since the mid-nineteenth century. With rising levels of inflation after the 1870s, the real income of agricultural workers was slowly eroded. By the mid-1930s, living standards were no higher than at the end of the nineteenth century. At the same time, workers complained that the prevalence of anti-black racist sentiments had increased since the era of Panama migration and that, on the whole, the quality of race relations, already bad, had deteriorated.

By January 1937, workers were on the receiving end of increasing material pressures and severe social discrimination. They also found themselves lacking effective leadership, at either the organisational or intellectual level. Clennell Wickham was now marginalised and Charles Duncan O'Neale had passed on. Grantley Adams, still balancing the defence of colonial liberalism and the parliamentary representation of the Black middle class and the more secure workers added to, rather than removed, the anxiety among the labouring poor. The man who brought sudden, dynamic, revolutionary leadership to the workers was Clement Payne, a young man in his early thirties of Barbadian parentage, though Trinidadian by birth. He arrived at Barbados on March 26, 1937 and, with the assistance of Israel Lovell, a Garveyite, he rapidly established a large following in the Bridgetown area.

A major part of Payne's activities involved organising workers into a strong trade union force in order to counter the power of the corporate merchant-planter elite. Trade unionism was still outlawed, but Payne sought to impress upon his followers the critical importance of confronting 'capitalism' with 'strong trade unions.' He argued that this was the only way to deal with depressed wages, price inflation and victimisation of workers in the workplace. His rhetoric attracted workers in their thousands, especially in the Bridgetown area, who had already benefitted from the politicisation of the Democratic League and the Workingmen's Association.

Payne succeeded in combining the incisive sociopolitical analysis of Wickham with the organisational drive of O'Neale and, in a short period of time, captured the imagination of radicals and the younger generation. He did not confine his fiery speeches to the labour question, but spoke of race relations and cultural suppression in Barbados, the pan-American nature of Garveyism, as well as Italian aggression toward Ethiopia. Ernest Mottley, the black real estate agent and supporter of the planter-merchant elite, stated what Payne's politics were of and that he thought his ideological position was, unlike O'Neale's, communistic.

Payne incurred the wrath of respectable black professionals because he placed the issue of racial and cultural domination at the fore of the old debate about economic domination. In addition, his political agitation centred on the need to defend strike actions that had been proliferating throughout the West Indies. In St Kitts, for example, workers on a sugar estate had rioted in January 1935 over wage levels and money bonuses. The riot was put down by armed police who shot dead three workers and wounded another eight. He brought such information to the attention of Barbadian workers, and also informed them that riots were taking place throughout the islands as a result of similar circumstances. Coal workers in St Lucia and oil workers in Trinidad quickly followed those in St Kitts, and Payne held these events as evidence of the rising consciousness of black West Indians.

Government officials and police authorities had been closely monitoring Payne from his first public meeting in Bridgetown. They had recognised in him a new quality of leadership; one that was aggressive, intellectually forceful and attractive to the younger generation. He was considered dangerous to the social order and had to be removed. The government decided to act by putting Payne on trial for declaring falsely to the immigration authorities on arrival from Trinidad that he was born in Barbados. The objective was to gain a conviction for his deportation. He was convicted on July 22 and, on the evening of July 26, 1937, Payne was clandestinely spirited out of the island by Barbadian police acting in association with their Trinidadian counterparts.

The trial of Payne was a major public event; workers assembled outside the court in their thousands to keep abreast of proceedings. His counsel was Grantley Adams who, though still not committed to worker radicalism, considered that the government was exerting pressure unconstitutionally on the judiciary in order to gain a political victory over workers. On being convicted, Payne led a force of over 5,000 to publicly appeal the decision before the governor. The police refused to let him see the governor, and when he persisted he and a number of his followers were arrested. An order was then issued for his deportation.

On July 26, the Court of Appeal quashed his conviction on the grounds that since he had spent a number of years as an infant in Barbados, he might not have known that he was born in Trinidad. During the course of the day, workers prepared to act on the court's decision by rescuing Payne from police custody, but discovered during the evening that he had already been deported. Angered by the actions of government, workers converted Bridgetown into a riot zone – clashing with police in Golden Square, destroying private and public property. Cars were smashed and public lighting utilities along River Road and Jemmott's Lane were damaged. Armed police managed to control the situation that evening, but the following morning, July 27, rioting flared up once again in Bridgetown and spread into the countryside.

The violent assault by workers on officialdom and its immediate representatives, the police constables, that morning was unexpected. Government had assumed that workers' grievances had been expressed and quelled the previous day and was therefore not politically prepared. Workers had not revolted in this violent manner since the 1876 War of General Green, the Confederation Affair, and the ruling classes saw no reason to believe that it would occur then. Armed with stones, bottles, sticks and such instruments, workers began their attack upon the heart of ruling class power – the commercial district of the city. They smashed office fronts, store windows and overturned cars on Broad Street; they shouted to the 'marooned' white employees in the office of the Barbados Mutual Life Assurance Society – 'you blasted sons of white bitches' and threatened to burn the building. Before doing so, they were attacked by a police detachment who fired blank volleys from their rifles. Properties were also damaged in Bay Street and Probyn Street, most of these before the rebels had crossed Chamberlain Bridge from the Golden Square area and moved across Trafalgar Square into Broad Street.

By midday the police had been instructed to use all possible means to restrain and subdue the workers. The police reported being informed that some of the rebels had been in possession of firearms and were prepared to use them. With bayonets fixed to their rifles and loaded with rounds of ammunition, police detachments confronted rebels in Bridgetown and killed several. This display of naked power threw the unarmed workers on the defensive; groups broke up as individuals fled in fear of their lives.

The police prepared 'Situation Reports' that set out the localised circumstances within the revolt. Two extracts from these reports are indicative.

Report A

1.8.37 Report by Captain Lamb and Mr. Stevenson

Left Central Station at 10 am and proceeded to Codrington Experimental Station. Dr. Saint reported all quiet — no labour troubles.

Redland Plantation

Interviewed Mr. A. Cox concerning a threatening letter. Advised him to ignore it; it was apparently from a religious 'mental' — no labour grievances.

Todd's Plantation
The manager, Mr. Gill, reported that not many had returned to work during the last few days. No trouble at pay out. A few labourers complained about wages being too low.

Poole Plantation
All quiet, no grievances.

Government Industrial School
Mr. Chase said that he had no labour troubles. He had not reduced 'day' wages since crop had ended. Women paid 24 cents. He stressed the fact that the

price of foodstuffs had increased during the past few months and was of the opinion that 24 cents was a minimum wage.

On Thursday morning, hearing that rioters were at Four Square and Sunbury, he called for volunteers to protect the school and all labourers responded. He armed them with sticks and also armed about 25 of the older boys. The mob came from Sunbury to Dodds to a field of potatoes led by one Harding (ex-overseer of Dodds dismissed two or three years ago and now an Island Constable). After a small clash the mob retreated. In this clash one of the boys was holding a rioter and the leader, Harding, said 'crown him' and the boy was struck on the top of his head by an iron bar.

The rioters appeared to be all local people.

Crane
All quiet.

Sanford Plantation
Conditions greatly improved. Mr. L. Smith stated that he would like one more trip round the district with his food lorry after which, he considered that the volunteer detachment was no longer necessary.

The arrests made in the Blades Hill District had caused a general 'wind up', looted goods were being thrown down walls and into the sea, and individuals were voluntarily surrendering at District C.

He expected that all labourers would be resuming work tomorrow.

On Tuesday morning cyclists from St. Michael had been seen inciting labourers.

In one gang of rioters which Mr. Smith had endeavoured to pacify, there were at least three men armed with revolvers, and they obeyed orders from their leader. Several respectable men, such as engineers from Three Houses Factory, were among the mobs.

River Plantation
Mr. Farmer reported no further trouble, conditions improved. Known bad families, Greaves and Grazettes, living in tenantry near.

East Point Plantation
Damage to the house much less than reported – add drawers, one or two jalousies, few chairs, electric wires and some windows. Attempts had been made to open the safe with a metal instrument. Some clothes, all the china and crockery, and all the food had been stolen.

Bath Plantation

No trouble. Labourers content with their wages. Vague rumours that when the Appollo departed and some of the police went ... to Bridgetown, the country districts would arise again ... would be attacked when their rifles were withdrawn.

Newcastle Plantation

Mr. Banfield reported no further trouble, and that when the police patrols had been increased in that area general conditions had greatly improved.

Two men, Thompson and Squires, had said to one another in the course of a conversation that the homes of police constables should be wrecked.

Mr. King of St. Martin's Bay reported that he had been threatened three times. District C was ordered to patrol his house. There was much loot from shops in gullies in that area where it had been thrown by people fearing arrest.

Blackman's Plantation

Mr. G. Hutson reported all quiet, and except for one or two cases, no grievances. He said that many labourers preferred to work for 16 cents day wage than for task work wages when they could earn up to 30 cents per day.

Extensive gambling took place in that area in Blackman's Quarry, and he knew of many cases when good workers lost all their wages to useless unemployables; he believed this to be universal throughout the island.

2.8.37   *Report by Captain Lamb*

At 10 am I left Central Station and proceeded to Sion Hill. There I interviewed Mr. Kellman, a shopkeeper, who also owns about 25 acres of land. He said that all was quiet in that area. On the night of the 28th July at about 9:30 am he had heard two very loud explosions on the Spring Head road above his shop followed by revolver shots which in turn were followed by rifle fire; he learnt that a police car had been attacked by a party of men.

As a small holder he was of the opinion that with the price of sugar as it is, the maximum wages which he could afford to pay were 30 cents a day for men and 20 cents per day for women. There had been no labour discontent in this area.

Dunscombe Plantation

Labourers had come out on strike that morning. Their grievance was the hard ground caused by the drought.

Wage had been raised from 10 cents per 100 cane holes to 12 cents and they had returned to work.

No men from St. Michael had come up to this area.

It was reported that it had been arranged that the riots should commence on Friday, the 30th July, when all the planters were in Bridgetown, but on account of Payne's deportation it was not possible to keep the plan secret.

Car T79 belonging to a man named Knight, who lived behind St. Thomas' Almshouse, was being used to transport a party of armed men round the country. It was a Ford, 1931 model.

Hillaby Village
All quiet and the food sufficient.

Marshall's shop in this village had been burnt by men from outside the district. Two shops had opened and the third was opening tomorrow.

Orange Hill
All quiet and food sufficient.

Four Hills – Mr. Gill
Owing to the drought the ground was too hard to work. There is some unrest in this area, especially towards Indian Ground.

Indian Ground Village
Quiet. Food sufficient.

Mount Prospect
All quiet.

Portland Plantation – Mr. Ward
No labour troubles – paying wages of 12 cents per 100 cane holes.
We had heard that one or two men were missing. Patrols had had a very good influence.

Pleasant Hall Plantation – Mr. F.F.C. Gills
No labour troubles. Paying 10 cents per 100 cane holes. There were rumours of trouble at Josey Hill. A postman named Gilkes was the leader of a gang from Mile and Quarter.

District 'E' Station – Sgt. Yard
All quiet.

Mr. Matthews, who owns two buses which had been placed inside the station for safety after he had been threatened because he refused to transport some potato raiders, was going to run his buses to Boscobel tomorrow.

The areas, Sutherland Hill, Boscobel and Crab Hill, are quiet but are rather sullen, and it is said that they are awaiting their opportunity to make further acts of violence.

Bromefield Estate – Mr. Alleyne
All quiet. No labour troubles.

Cyclists from Bridgetown had been seen in this area on Tuesday morning. He had heard that revolvers were being smuggled into the Island in bundles of old clothing which were sent from other islands.

Sutherland Hill
Shops were opened and village quiet. I spoke to several groups who tended to be truculent.

Content Village
Food alright. Shopkeepers were nervous and appear to be expecting trouble.

Crab Hill Estate
No labour troubles. Wages 10 cents per 100 cane holes.

Harrison's Plantation – Mr. Webster
Labourers had not come out today, saying that they were going to stay at home until they heard from the Governor. Mr. Webster and two other managers, Mr. Husband of Babbs and Mr. Allamby of Bowbon, had been threatened.

The leader of the Sutherland Hill gang, Edwin Greaves, was now in St. Lucy's Almshouse, having been wounded on the morning of the 28th July. I instructed Sgt. Yard, at District 'E', to send patrols to this plantation.

St. Lucy's Rectory – Revd. Alleyne
All quiet. Airplanes had been very effective in dispersing potato raiders.

St. Lucy's Almshouse
I interviewed the two men, Clarence Ifill and Edwin Greaves, who had been wounded on the morning of the 28th July near St. Lucy's Church. Ifill had been hit in both knees. Edwin Greaves had been hit in the left leg just above the ankle, and the leg broken. He had also been hit by at least two bullets in the abdominal region. They both stated that they had been walking up the

Bourbon Road about 10:30 am on the morning of the 28th July by St. Lucy's Church to try to catch a cross country bus to St. Philip (I am not certain of the name of the parish) to see Greaves' brother who had been wounded.

A crowd came streaming across the pasture just behind them. Several police cars drove up the road, one car stopped in from of them and the others behind and the police got out and opened fire on them. They were taken to the Almshouse by the Almshouse cart.

Mr. Yearwood, the Superintendent of the Almshouse, said that two others had been wounded in this affray. One had already been reported and the other was believed to be in the Crab Hill area.

Report B

29.7.37 Report by Captain Lamb

Visited Warren's Factory at 11am this morning. The majority of men had returned to work.

Redman's Village
No food in the shops. Men were interviewed; were afraid to leave vicinity.

Rock Hall Village (above St. Thomas Church)
Shops were open and had a certain amount of food.

Visited District D Police Station where I was informed that Farmers Plantation had not been damaged. At Hillaby one mile from Farmers a shop was looted and burnt last night.

In Westmoreland, Sion Hill and Rock Dundo Villages there was practically no food left. Mr. E. Kellman of Sion Hill said he would send a lorry for food when I informed him that a guard for it would be provided. Labourers were working in the fields along the road and at Whitehall all the Central Road Board's labourers were working on the new road.

On the 27th July, Carlisle Greaves of Sherman's, St. Peter, was wounded by one Bruce Gill who fired three rounds at a crowd from his car.

At District E police station the junior N.C.C. reported that on the 28th July DaCosta O'Neale was found dead on the road 1¼ miles east of District E in the early morning.

On the 28th July it was reported that Rimple Kettle of Boscobel had been found dead in the early morning on Boscobel Road. Last night the whole district was quiet.

Speightstown

Shops are open but food supplies are low. Mr. C.H. P. Jordan is arranging to make two lorry trips tomorrow to Bridgetown for supplies. I informed him that he would be protected.

Welchtown, Farley Hill, villages along the road to Belleplaine in St. Andrew were all quiet and said that there had been no trouble in that area. I informed shopkeepers in these villages that if they combined and sent a lorry to Bridgetown for food a guard would be provided for same.

At District F., Sgt. Thompson reported that on the 28th July at 7:30 am a shop at Hillaby, owner Mr. RDN Maxwell, was burnt. At 11:30 pm a shop at St. Simon's, owner J. A. Tudor, was robbed.

On the 29th July at 12:30 pm a shop at Melvin Hill, owner Mr. C.M. Austin, was stoned. I visited this spot and local inhabitants informed me that it had been attacked by a band of men and youths.

I visited Park's House and Mr. J.A. Haynes informed me that he had had no trouble until at 10:30 am this morning; all the labourers left saying that if they worked they would be attacked. He informed me and Sgt. Thompson of District F also informed me that they had heard that plans had been made to raid a shop at Cane Garden near St. Saviour's Chapel, St. Joseph, tonight.

Labourers left Applewaite Plantation today at 10:30 am being afraid to work.

Report C

31.7.37 Report by Captain Lamb

Leaving Central Station at about 3 pm today I proceeded to Rices, St. Philip via Worthing and Oistins. At Rices I met Mr. Fields, the owner of the building in which is situated the shop of Martin Doorly, which was looted on the 30th July. He informed me that it had been done by a gang of about 16 men from the Crane district and that Mr. Corbin of Martin Doorly had a list of names. Since the incident the gang had been very quiet, due to the shooting of one member by the police, who happened to arrive as the loot was being removed.

Crane Hotel

All was quiet. Mr. Lamming had heard a rumour that the hotel was going to be raided again.

Statement by Mr. Farmer of River Plantation, St. Philip:

On the night of the 28th July, my overseer, Mr. H.O. Clarke reported that a crowd of people had broken up my house at Coles, St. Philip, and that they had stolen 10 sheep and 28 pure bred leghorn fowls. He reported the names of a few taking part in the raid:

> *George Alleyne*
> *Harmon Sealy*
> *Olly Brathwaite*
> *Lily Brathwaite*
> *Ernestine Pollard*

As far as he knew all those taking part in the raid were local men.
Fred Squires, the watchman, said that one man had fired at him with a revolver; other local inhabitants had heard shots. Amongst other articles, a portable Colombia gramophone and an Optimist lantern had been stolen.

East Point Lighthouse
The keeper reported that Olly Brathwaite, who had been loitering around the lighthouse last night, had been arrested with his daughter, in connection with the looting of Mr. Marshall's house. I advised the keeper to place the chimney's wilks, etc of the light, inside the base of the tower with a reserve of paraffin oil. The building in which they were, could easily be set alight and contained two large paraffin oil containers.

Clifton Hall Plantation
Mr. C. Haynes reported no further trouble to burn the canes and injure stock had been made, chiefly by one Mapp of Bathsheba.

Foster Lodge Plantation
Here threats had also been heard. Beverley White of Martin Bay, St. John, a relative of the man who had been wounded when Mr. Clarke, the overseer, had fired at the mob on the 28th July, was one of the local ringleaders. He was often seen driving a motor car J27.

Sgt. Thompson of District F reported all quiet. He had investigated Beverley White's movements and found that he often drove past Newcastle on his way to see his lady friend.

Report D

29.7.37 From: Headquarters Volunteer Force

Report by Captain Evelyn from St. Philip

He finds conditions up there fairly quiet. Acts of rowdyism are being carried out by the younger men only. He also finds a distinct shortage of provisions obtainable at shops (this in the case of every shop that he visited). He finds that the people cannot buy food and that the shopkeepers cannot be supplied from Bridgetown. There is a general desire to get supplies from Bridgetown and the people are willing to buy them. In some cases shops have been raided and everything taken away. No raids in Christ Church but there is a shortage of provisions in shops which is getting gradually worse.

Report of Captain Williams

He is operating on No. 1 Highway and has found great shortage of provisions in all shops visited. There has been looting of a minor nature in places. No provisions can be obtained from Bridgetown and the people are hungry. Both officers consider that there is urgent need of supplies.

Report of Captain C. R. Armstrong

Clarke's big shop has little foodstuff left and there is a large number of people to be supplied. When his supply runs out there may be trouble. People are anxious to buy.

Bowmanston Pumping Station

Report by a member of the Volunteer Force who visited this station. The attitude of the staff is 'why should they stop there and work when they cannot get food'.

Hungry workers then responded by looting potato fields, plantation stocks and by threatening white plantation personnel. In St Lucy and St Andrew, workers were determined to appropriate as much food as possible from the plantations. In these parishes, planters enlisted specially armed constables to restrain workers. Special constables shot many persons suspected of looting. By the morning of July 30, the revolt was crushed by armed forces, and calm was restored to both town and country. No Whites were killed, but 14 Blacks were reported to have lost their lives and 47 were injured. Over 500 persons were arrested; many were tried, convicted and imprisoned after receiving, in some cases, severe beatings from the police and special constables.

Table 2
List of Alleged Rioters

NAME	AGE	OCCUPATION	ADDRESS
Iroine Broody	42	Cooper	Reid Street, City
Joseph Rollock	33	Labourer	Water Hall
Clarice Brooks	26	Washer	Mason Hall Street
Alexander	26	Labourer	Rock Hall, St John
Collymore	14	Labourer	Searles Land – throwing stones
John Bailey	28	Labourer	Martin's Bay, St John
Dudley White	27	Labourer	Bull's Alley
Seymour Walker	22	Cooper	Carrington's Village
Leroy Cumberbatch	20	Mechanic	Nurse Land
Fitzgerald Burgess	30	Labourer	Carrington's Village
Horace Lovell	20	-	Chelston Gap
Clifford Francis	43	Hawker	Cunchs Alley
Mortimer Skeete	30	Shopkeeper	Tweedside Road
Henry Goodman	17	Apprentice	St Christopher, Christ Church
Clyde Griffith	19	Gardener	Lightfoot Land
Frome Jordan	24	Chauffeur	-
Gordon Small	25	Domestic Servant	Suttle Street
Ivy Thompson	25	Labourer	Halls Road
Oliver Phillips	21	Porter	-
Whitfield Rawline	-	Porter	Suttle Street
Eric Harris	22	Porter	Westbury Road
Wilbert Harewood	19	Baker	Reid Street
Emanuel Gabriel	16	Labourer	Eagle Hall
Seymour Small	35	-	Cheapside
Donald Dyal	23	Porter	Barbarees Hill
Herbert Williams	27	Domestic Servant	Dash Gap
Lydia Osbourne	31	Domestic Servant	Chapman Lane
Delphine Jordan	28	Domestic Servant	Suttle Street
Elmina Brathwaite	22	Domestic Servant	Suttle Street
Daphne Harris	23	Domestic Servant	Suttle Street
Agatha Lewis	25	Labourer	Bull's Alley
Reginald Taitt	28	Labourer	Beckles Hill
Simeon Barrow	21	Labourer	Richmond Gap
Sydney Dottin	20	Porter	6th Ave, New Orleans

NAME	AGE	OCCUPATION	ADDRESS
Clyde Carew	29	Hawker	Suttle Street
Louise Sobers	22	Domestic Servant	Reid Street
Ernesta Griffith	20	Domestic Servant	Watkins Alley
Doris Callender	27	Domestic Servant	Bull's Alley
Leotta Glynton	17	Tailor	Half Moon Forte, St Lucy
Egbert Moore	20	Labourer	Jackson
Vernon Price	26	Domestic Servant	-
Irene Agard	23	Boatman	Green Field
Charles Downer	24	Labourer	Black Rock
Joseph Griffith	19	Labourer	Church Village
Delbert Bates	22	Labourer	Church Village
Leon Bascombe	32	-	Lucas Street
Olric Grant	39	Chauffeur	Martindale's Road
Fitzgerald Chase	34	Carpenter	Baxter's Road (£1000 bond)
Israel Lovell	26	Labourer	Bush Hall (£500 bond)
Darnley Alleyne	17	-	Quarry Road, Bank Hall
Stacey Cadogan	15	Labourer	Spooner's Hill — damage to T.R. Evans store
Henry Hunte	20	Labourer	Hinckson Gap
Sidney Phillips	19	Labourer	Martindale's Road — damage to Mutual Building
Byron Holder	26	Porter	Jordan's Land — unlawful and malicious damage to Vauxhall Service Station
James Barrow (alias Ten Pounds)	36	Labourer	Richmond Gap
George Alleyne	20	Labourer	Suttle Street
Lawrence Corbin	22	Lighterman	Bank Hall
Westford Hamblin	16	Lighterman	Jessamy Lane
St Andrew Greaves	18	-	Melrose, St Thomas — malicious damage to C.F. Harrison's glass case
Livingstone Hank	20	Labourer	Chapman Lane
		Labourer	Lightfoot Lane — damage to car M202, the property of Dr King
Vernon Elcock	14	Labourer	Lightfoot Lane – (1) damage to a dish and food, the property of Eunice Proverbs (2) armed with an offensive weapon Carrington's Village
Joseph Babb	14	Cooper	Arthur Alley
Holborn Bailey	22	Barber	Arthur Hill
Leroy Cumberbatch	34	Domestic Servant	Dunlow Lane
Joseph Reece	18	Boatman	Jessamy Lane
Verona Phillips	27	Domestic Servant	Westbury Road
Darndey Yearwood	17	Boatman	Peterkin Land
Eunice Harris	20	Domestic	Church Village
Carlos Harris	31	Lighterman	Conch's Alley
Edna Spencer (alias Young Kid)	22	Fisherman	Passage Road — wilful and malicious damage to a motor van, the property of Messrs Johnson and Redman
Winfield Brathwaite	18	Boatman	Martindale's Road — damage to a street lamp, property of the Barbados Gas Company

Leslie Trotman	17	Boatman	Church Village – damage to a show case, the property of Cole's Garage, Bay Street
Monteith Russel	27	Seller	Passage Road – damage to Mr C. F. Harrison's glass case
Dorson Herbert	40	Tailor	Intimidating bus driver
Fitz Weekes	32	Cooper	-
Charles Barrow (alias Talkie)	36	-	-
Lawrence 'Gigga' Johnson	-	-	-

With the removal of Payne from the colony, the working classes was not left leaderless. Payne had been effective within the short space of time precisely because he acted in conjunction with other working class leaders and used existing organisational structures. In his absence, Israel Lovell, who had been critical to the development of the Garveyite movement, came to the fore. It was Lovell who led the agitation against the government during the Payne trial, but it was Ulric Grant who was immortalised for making the statement that 'there was no justice in Coleridge Street' [location of the court] for which the judge in sentencing him for sedition was excessively harsh.

In an attempt to keep the Payne movement alive, Lovell often told workers assembled in Golden Square that he could not be deported, that he was not afraid of police or courts, and that he was prepared to die in the process of building a worker's movement to decolonise the island. He also told workers that the successful criminalisation of Payne by the government was the result of workers' organisational deficiency. In response to one statement about workers and praedial larceny, he stated 'we cannot steal from the white man because, if we take anything, it would be only some of what they have stolen from our fore parents for the past two hundred and fifty years'.

The political speeches of Lovell were steeped in the history of economic and social relations between workers and employers in the colony. He was aware of the need to bring historical awareness to workers so as to mobilise them into conscious, determined action. In one speech he stated: 'we make the wealth of this country and get nothing in return.

Our slave fathers were in a better condition than we are today. The world is against us, so let us unite in mass formation and stand up like men'. These utterances clearly reflected the Garveyite nature of his ideology and illustrated the fact that, with Payne's removal during the trial, the Universal Negro Improvement Association (UNIA) had assumed the leadership of the workers' movement temporarily.

Events which followed immediately after the rebellion established the nature of the reformist leadership which would dominate the labour movement for the next two decades or so. The Deane Commission of Enquiry was established by the governor to investigate and report on the origins, causes and nature of the rebellion. For several sittings after the rebellion, the Assembly did not discuss the matter, and many middle class black politicians distanced themselves from it altogether. As the defence counsel for Payne, Adams was concerned, as were Chrissie Brathwaite, J.E.T. Brancker and Hilton Vaughan, that government officials would attempt to link him in some causal way to the event. When the Deane Commission began to hear evidence for the first time on Friday, August 13, 1937, Adams was the first witness. There, he espoused the view that the 'riot' was the result of rapidly deteriorating social and economic conditions among workers and that liberal reforms could restore healthier social relations.

For Adams, such statements to the Deane Commission were insufficient to enhance his role as the most forceful black Parliamentary reformer, and in September he sought a meeting with Governor Young to inform him that he was going to England on personal business and that he was not 'running away' from the situation. He was given some assurance by the governor that there was no official suspicion of his involvement in the rebellion and that he was still held in some confidence by the Executive. While in England, Adams sought an audience with the Colonial Secretary. Governor Young informed the Colonial Secretary that such a meeting would be of service to Adams 'politically', which might explain the two months that Adams was kept waiting by the Colonial Secretary.

Table 3
Persons convicted at the November 1937 assizes, arising out of the disturbances in 1937

OFFENCE	CONVICTED		SENTENCE
	Male	*Female*	
Assaulting police officer and causing grievous body harm	5	-	10 years P.S. (in each case)
Assaulting peace officer and riotous assembly	11	10	From 3 years to 9 months
Aggravated assault with intent to rob	6	-	From 5 years P.S. to 12 months (and five strokes with the 'cat')
Burglary	3	5	From 5 years P.S. to 12 months recognizance
Bodily harm	2	-	One 18 months hard labour and one 2 years recognizance
Grievous bodily harm and unlawful assembly	4	-	From 4 years P.S. to 12 months H.L.
Grievous bodily harm	1	-	3 years P.S.
Larceny	8	-	From 3 years P.S. to 9 months; one on 2 years recognizance
Larceny and riotous assembly	4	-	18 months hard labour
Malicious damage	13	1	From 2 years H.L. to 9 months
Praedial larceny	33	4	From 2 years to 3 months. One on two years recognizance
Robbery	1	1	One 12 months, hard labour and one 6 months recognizance
Robbery with violence	1	-	18 months and 6 strokes
Robbery with aggravation	2	-	18 months hard labour
Riotous assembly and malicious damage to property	9	2	from 4 years P.S. to 3 months hard labour
Shop-breaking and larceny	111	39	From 7 years P.S. to 3 months hard labour; 20 on recognizance varying from 2 years to 12 months
Unlawful assembly and demanding money with menace	4	2	From 2 years to 9 months
Unlawful assembly	29	2	From 4 years to 3 months; five on recognizance from 2 years to 18 months
Unlawful assembly and inciting to riot	1	-	10 years
Sedition	4	-	10 years, 5 years, 5 years, 9 months
Wounding	4	-	Three received 5 years P.S. and one 18 months and 8 strokes

Adams believed that his role as a social reformer could be expanded only by a close working association with the Colonial Office. As such, he did not depart from England until he had won the confidence and support of most high ranking colonial officials. Colonial Secretary Ormsby-Gore wrote after his first meeting with Adams: 'I saw Mr. Adams and liked him'. He was considered the kind of man the Colonial Office could trust to reform colonial politics in order to undermine the radical socialist alternative. While in England, Adams had also cemented a supportive relation with the Fabian Movement, Labour Party officials and the well-known and respected colonial reformer, Arthur Creech Jones, who became the Secretary of State for the Colonies in Atlee's post war labour government. Adams returned to Barbados fortified with imperial metropolitan support, which he used assertively over the next decade in order to suppress the left wing of the labour movement. He emerged the principal labour leader in Barbados. Fully invested with the support at home and enjoying the confidence of the British labour movement, Adams triumphed as the peoples' 'Moses', a title he carried for the rest of his political career.

- *Two* -

Democracy from Below:
Political Enfranchisement,
1937-1950

*G*rantley Adams espoused the view that the 'riot' in 1937 was the result of rapidly deteriorating social and economic conditions among workers, and that liberal reforms could restore healthier social relations. The Deane Commission of Enquiry into the rebellion also heard that:

> the audiences which Payne attracted at his open air meetings were composed largely of the young and irresponsible members of the community of Bridgetown . . . whose enthusiasm was easily fired by the prospect held out to them of getting more money and the vapid language of his speeches.

This perception of the generality of Payne's followers was shared, in part, by sections of the more privileged black community which had supported the defunct but respectable Democratic League.

Conservative Blacks also condemned workers who resorted to violence and armed confrontation. Adams was aware of the need to mobilise and direct the upsurge of political enthusiasm and energy released as a result of the disturbances, and some of his ardent followers set about the task of forming an organisation to lead and represent working class opinion. The body which was launched in October 1938 to achieve this end was the Barbados Labour Party – a political organisation designed to 'provide political expression for the island's law-abiding inhabitants', as distinct from the so-called 'lawless' poor among whom Payne was alleged to have found extensive support. This organisation soon changed its name to the Barbados Progressive League.

The Progressive League was, in a general way, within the tradition of the Democratic League; it was essentially a middle class-led organisation vying for a mass base in order to confront and eventually reduce the oligarchical political power of the consolidated merchant-planter elite. Logically, therefore, it was composed partly of former Democratic League Assemblymen and followers, and some new radical activists and liberal professionals. Of the former group, C.A. (Chrissie) Brathwaite and J.A. Martineau were most prominent. Brathwaite was a black, small entrepreneur who had made headway in the real-estate business and owned a store in Bridgetown; Martineau, also black, was a beverage producer with a secure financial standing.

The League's ranks were also strengthened by Wynter Crawford, an anti-colonial activist with an interest in the publishing business whose political views, though to the left of Adams, were not as radical as those of Payne or Marcus Garvey. There was also Edwy Talma, a self-defined liberal like Adams, and the Garveyite, Herbert Scale. Brathwaite was selected president Talma, general secretary (after Crawford's refusal) Martineau, treasurer, and Adams, vice-president. Seale, who was appointed assistant to Talma, was soon made general secretary in order to exploit his organising skills.

Within its first year, the League was torn by ideological conflict over the question of working class representation and leadership. The main division that surfaced involved Adams on the right, Seale and his supporters on the left. Both men had substantial support within the League; Adams, unlike Seale, had support within officialdom and, fresh from his English political tour where he had solicited much influence within the Colonial Office, the cards seemed stacked against Seale even though he was closer to the grass roots. Seale had already identified with the political ideas which Payne had sought to bring to the Barbadian worker – firm, aggressive trade unionism within the black consciousness programme as outlined by Garvey. Adams was the 'gradualist' liberal reformer, the political moderate who believed that the workers' main grievances were economic in nature.

Adams, then, became publicly critical of Seale's radicalism, as he had been critical of Wickham and O'Neale during the 1927 dock-workers' strike. He accused Seale of confrontation politics, though he accepted that Seale had been the most active campaigner in terms of taking the League's programme to the working classes and mobilising large crowds for public meetings. For Seale, the liberal element within the League was retarding the struggle for workers' rights; Adams believed that Seale was making 'things move too fast, without at the same time securing a foundation'.

Adams' strategy for social reform, like Samuel Jackman Prescod's a century earlier, was to tap into the marginalised liberal element within the empowered merchant-planter class and encourage them to see that making legislative concessions to workers was in their long-term interest. Seale wanted workers' power consolidated in strong trade unions so as to be able to dictate terms of employment that workers could accept. Within the labour movement, Seale's followers accused Adams of softening worker agitation, while Adams argued that Seale was creating a climate of hostility that could only have adverse effects on the workers themselves.

These debates in 1939 took place within the context of a large number of cane fires, unauthorised strikes and widespread militancy among workers. Seale was instrumental in the organisation of the February 21, 1939 general strike that sought to increase wage levels in the sugar and urban-based industries. It has been suggested that Seale and Cox were concerned principally with creating the context for toppling the president and vice-president of the League, and to bring firmer leadership to the labour movement. Workers in the sugar industry, on the docks and in the omnibus company, were the most militant.

Adams' response was to win support within government, the merchant community and the planter class for a condemnation of the strike, including Seale's participation and leadership. In a speech on March 1, 1939 in Queen's Park, Adams outlined his approach as follows:

. . . we have the government willing to assist us, we have an influential body of merchants willing to go thoroughly into the facts and figures connected with workers in Bridgetown. We give them the assurance that we as your officers of the Progressive League will keep the workers in check, and tell them how stupid, apart from being criminal, it is to strike when negotiations are the correct way to improve conditions.

Adams' supporters outside the League also pressed for Seale's removal from the executive of the League. He succeeded also in obtaining effective support within the executive in order to isolate Seale by condemning the strike action. The *Barbados Advocate* reported:

The Progressive League has done a service to labour and to the community by resolutely condemning the unauthorised strikes that occurred in the city on Monday . . . .The Executive Officers of the League, Mr. C.H. Adams, Mr. C. A. Brathwaite, and Dr. H.G. Cummins acted in a manner that is in the best traditions of Trade Union Leadership. . . . It is gratifying therefore to find its leaders emphasizing that the unauthorised strikes were calculated to harm the cause of the Progressive League and of Trade Unionism in Barbados. The 'Advocate' is prepared to lend its wholehearted support to all those who are resolved to give labour such responsible guidance. On 4th March it was reported that Seale had been forced to resign from the League's executive committee.

But Adams was not satisfied with this victory. He was determined to overturn a decision the executive had made to offer Seale a $550 honorarium for his outstanding services. He went to the League's membership and accused the executive of plotting to squander their money on Seale, the adventurist; this time he won his biggest victory — the resignation of the executive committee. When the committee was reconstituted by elections in July, Adams was the new president, Talma, his loyalist, was treasurer.

The new members were Barry Springer (vice-president) and C.A. Nurse (general secretary), also Adams loyalists. Both Brathwaite and Martineau were removed. Seale was pushed into the background along with the radical workers he had worked with. The surviving veteran element of the Democratic League was purged and Adams' power within the organisation seemed unlimited.

The ability of the Progressive League to mobilise a mass following within a year of its formation had to do with Herbert Seale's promotion of it as an organisation committed to labour solidarity, political agitation and social welfare considerations. The tripartite nature of its programme attempted to cover most aspects of working class demands. The slogan of the League, 'Three units, one arm, raising the living standard for the working classes', reflected these distinct but related dimensions of its programme.

Almost from its inception, the executive of the League vigorously lobbied government officials for the right to represent working class interests before the Royal Commission appointed 'to investigate social and economic conditions in the West Indies'. In this objective it succeeded, and Adams became its principal spokesman before the Commission that arrived in Barbados on Saturday, January 14, 1939. Lord Moyne, the chairman of the Commission, arrived in Barbados the following week, and the exchange between himself and Adams not only influenced the conclusions of the Commission considerably, but illustrated clearly the political interests of Adams and his leadership of the League.

Adams went to great lengths to convince the Commission that neither he nor his colleagues were communists or supporters of such organisations, but were socialists committed to an equitable distribution of economic resources and the liberalisation of social institutions. In full awareness of the fact that the sugar plantation system represented the basis of merchant-planter oligarchical conservatism and liberalism, Adams focussed upon the need to reconstitute the ownership of the sugar industry as the key to sociopolitical transformation. He argued for the partial nationalisation of the industry as a prerequisite for social reform, a view not shared by Lord Moyne.

Adams was soon to rethink his ideas about containing planter-merchant oligarchical power by undermining their monopolistic ownership of the sugar industry. In accounting for Adams backing away from structural change within the industry, Gordon Lewis wrote:

The Adams leadership apparently accepted the widespread Barbadian belief that a radical stance on the sugar question destroys a political career; it apparently also accepted the belief, sedulously spread by the plantocracy, that a nationalisation policy would lead to economic disaster and social chaos.

By 1940, the League was no longer seriously concerned with the question of nationalisation.

The West Indies Labour Congress of 1938 promoted nationalisation as a manifesto issue for most labour organisations. But Adams had sensed that the Moyne Commission and the British government were not supportive of a strategy for socioeconomic reform. Since he had decided that it would be possible to push meaningful labour reforms through the House only if he stayed close to executive power, Adams opted instead for a strategy of 'responsible' dialogue with the landed elite in the hope of gaining concessions for labour.

By the end of 1940 the economic lobby within the League was placed in the forefront of its reform strategy. The friendly society unit and the political wing, which were designed to mobilise the limited electorate (3.5 per cent of the population in 1940) in order to win seats in the House, receded temporarily into the background. The Trade Disputes Act of June 12, 1939 and the Trade Union Act of August 1, 1940, both recommended by the Moyne Commission, created the legislative context within which trade unionism could function constitutionally. On October 4, 1941, the Barbados Workers' Union was formed – the outgrowth of a number of committees within the League that had dealt with the question of workmen's compensation and which agitated for a wage board to assist the process of legalising wage agreements.

Adams' dominance of the labour movement during this period was reflected in his appointment as president of the Union, as well as his appointment by the governor to the executive council as the workers' representative for the 1942-44 session. During the 1940s, when the legislative foundations for effective trade unionism were established, his style of leadership and political ideas were stamped on most important proceedings. That the Trade Union Act had not given workers the right to picket as an important instrument in bargaining illustrated, however, the moderate nature of his leadership.

The Workmen's Compensation Act of 1943 was an important victory for the League, though, like the Trade Union Act, workers found themselves entrapped in a web of conditions, provisions and limitations. Meanwhile, the employers were also making great strides towards the establishment of protective organisations in order to combat labour combination. On May 11, 1945, the Shipping and Mercantile Association was formed. This was followed by the establishment of the Sugar Producers' Federation, the Bus Owners' Association and the Barbados Hackney and Livery Car Owners' Association on December 8, 1945, April 16, 1947 and October 9, 1948, respectively.

Despite the limited franchise, the political wing of the League succeeded in mobilising sufficient votes to win seats in the Assembly for five of the six candidates proposed in 1940. Adams and Crawford had already parted company, and Crawford contested the election as an independent after leaving the League. He won the St Philip seat with a handsome majority. In 1941, Adams, Hugh Springer and Dr H.G. Cummins were sitting in the legislature on behalf of the League, and J.T.C. Ramsay, a known grass roots politician, had won a by-election and was sitting in the House. It was this group which pioneered the legislative labour reforms of the early 1940s consistent with many of the suggestions of the Moyne Commission.

The League's biggest challenge, however, came in April and May 1943 when the House debated the Representation of the People Bill – a measure designed to extend the franchise to a larger section of the labouring population, also recommended by the Moyne Commission. The ruling elite showed its opposition to the measure from the outset. Indeed, Crawford, on the left of Adams, stated that the government's bill was brought to the House with much imperial support, which weighed against the real preference of the elite for a reduction rather than an increase of the franchise.

Adams and Crawford agreed, however, to demand adult suffrage (already won in Jamaica) instead of the government's proposed reduction of the income qualification to £30. The bill was defeated and the motion to amend by reducing the income qualification to £25 was passed on 4th May. It became law as the Representation of the People Act, 1943. The number of persons now able to vote increased by some 510 per cent, and women, for the first time in the colony's history, got the franchise. These were important, though limited, developments in the rise of democratic rights within the colony, and represented triumphs for organised labour.

The franchise extension of 1943 meant that the 1944 general election would take place within larger political dimensions. By this time, the political leadership of the labour movement was divided, with Adams and Crawford representing the two main contending factions. Contesting the elections were Adams' Progressive League, Crawford's newly formed West Indian National Congress Party, and the planters' political party, the Electors' Association. It was an aggressively fought election; never before had the ideological divisions within the island's politics been so clearly articulated and exposed for public discourse.

The conservative and right wing policies of the Electors' Association reflected the determined stance of the planter elite to hold on to political power, while the Congress Party, rooted within radical elements of the working class, sought to break planter-merchant political leadership and advance towards socialist government. The Progressive League, critical of both these right and left parties, pledged itself to labour reforms, social welfare policies and a gradualist approach in the search for liberal political democracy.

The election was fought over many of the issues that had surfaced during the 1937 workers' rebellion and the investigation thereafter. The Congress Party was most incisive in its evaluation of those events, and its campaign revived memories of Clement Payne's movement. It made no compromises in its self-assertion as the radical wing of the labour movement, and Crawford in particular suggested that both Adams and the Electors' Association were involved in plots to undermine the workers' search for power and to deflect the movement from socialism.

Throughout the country, the Congress Party called for adult suffrage, a government nationalisation programme, compulsory education, free books and hot lunches for school children, a national health and unemployment scheme, state ownership of important parts of the agricultural sector and the dis-establishment of the still influential Anglican Church. This party emerged during the campaign as the radical vanguard of the labour movement, imposing a major psychological blow to Adams and the Progressive League. Its manifesto called upon workers to 'vote for a new Barbados' and the *Barbados Observer*, the Party newspaper edited by Crawford, carried the messages: 'Forward to a People's Victory' and 'Bring Socialism to Barbados'.

The *Barbados Advocate* carried the programme of the Electors' Association, while the *Barbados Observer* was particularly venomous in its attack upon the planters' party. The *Barbados Observer* of Saturday, November 4, 1944 carried an article which illustrated what the radicals thought of the Electors' Association:

> . . . Throughout the history of this island, it has been dominated by a small and selfish clique and it is indeed remarkable that now, this clan senses that it has reached a crisis, it has actually had the shamelessness and the temerity to publicly appeal to the people of this island and ask them to help them consolidate their weakening position, for sheer presumptuous impudence it is unparalleled. It is an absolute insult to the intelligence of the people. Only the congenital idiots among the masses will vote for the candidates of the Electors' Association.

Two weeks later, November 27, the *Observer,* by way of deepening its political critique of the ruling class, carried a column which stated:

> Barbados is in revolt against the status quo. Throughout the country thousands of middle and working class men and women are voicing the most determined protests against poverty and unemployment. These thousands are resolved to put more of the wealth in the colony at the service of the people; these thousands are in deadly earnest, this spirit may well be called NEW DEMOCRACY . . . No longer are the people of this

island prepared to entrust their destinies to the representatives of big business.

When the votes were counted later that day the Congress Party had won eight seats, the League seven seats and the Electors' Association eight seats.

These results represented, at least in theory, a resounding victory for the labour movement over the traditional planter-merchant political forces. Crawford spoke of the end of the planter-government and the triumph of the progressive democratic forces while the leadership of the Electors' Association began to prepare a strategy for the protection of its members' economic and social interests.

The development of party politics and the ideological nature of the 1944 general election exposed fully the undemocratic nature of the governmental structure. With a considerably enlarged electorate sending representatives to the Assembly, the system of government in which an executive governor was held fully responsible for political administration seemed contrary to the principle of democratic representation. If power was to reside in the Assembly, it seemed clear that responsibility for government should likewise be found there.

In 1946, Governor Bushe emerged as the agent who sought to attach responsibility for government to the Assembly's determination to hold political power. He proposed a system of government whereby membership of the executive committee would reflect the distributions of seats held by political parties within the Assembly. Such a system of power-sharing had already been suggested by radicals within the labour movement as a democratic solution. The Congress Party had never been comfortable with the system whereby the governor arbitrarily selected the members of the powerful Executive Committee. In this sense, then, the Bushe reform represented a partial victory for the labour movement.

The basis of this constitutional reform was that the officer in charge of governmental administration would approach the parliamentary leader of the political party which held a majority in the House and request that such a person recommend parliamentary members to sit on the Executive

Committee. Constituted in this manner the Executive Committee would then be held responsible for government programmes. Individual members would be placed in charge of sections of government business, with responsibility for policies. In effect, this was the beginning of what became known as 'semi-ministerial' government. Bushe also proposed that, since Attorney-General E.K. Walcott was an active member of the Electors' Association, he should not be considered the government's spokesman in the House. Bushe suggested that this role should be performed by the majority leader. This system of government eventually led to the establishment of cabinet government in 1954.

The Congress Party, in particular, stood to benefit from the new system of government. But since the 1944 election victory, Governor Bushe had decided that the Congress leadership was too radical and therefore not fit to be represented on the Executive Committee; as a result, he gave preference to the Progressive League in the persons of Adams and his loyalist Hugh Springer. Not surprisingly, when the Assembly debated a motion for the increase of the govenor's salary that year, Crawford voted against it while Adams and Springer voted in favour. Governor Bushe expressed his preference for Adams as a labour leader and made no secret of his disapproval of Crawford and the socialist, anti-imperialist Congress Party. At the same time, he reported to the Colonial Office on the disunity within the leadership of the labour movement and the implications this had for the constitutional reform he proposed. The Whites, he stated, were generally opposed to any measure that would strengthen the political hand of the Blacks, while the latter, he added, 'are divided among themselves, suspicious of one another, and apparently incapable of any concerted or constructive action'.

The experiment in semi-responsible government, Bushe reported to Whitehall, could be effective as long as 'the progressive leaders', whom he did not 'trust', could be persuaded to be 'moderate'. While he was being assured by Adams that moderation would prevail, the labour scene was increasingly characterised by unofficial strikes and an almost unending series of cane fires; these developments, according to the governor, reflected the growing militancy of grass roots political activists. The full details of Bushe's plan for governmental reform were finally presented to the legislature on October 1, 1946. It represented the beginning of the end of traditional executive government and the first part of the victory for the principle of popular representative government. In political terms, it meant the seizing of legislative power from the planter oligarchy and a major triumph for the labour movement.

The general election of 1946 presented the first opportunity to witness the functioning of the Bushe reforms. This election was contested by the same political parties as in 1944. The League was now reconstituted and renamed the Barbados Labour Party. It was also an aggressively fought election, with ideological differences held out to the electorate and bitter attacks levelled at opposition leaders and parties. The departing Governor Bushe was also caught within the electioneering crossfire. The Barbados Labour Party, through its organ the *Beacon*, praised him as the kind of progressive governor the island had always needed. He was described as a historic figure committed to the development of the island's national interests.

The Congress Party, on the other hand, held an opposing view of Governor Bushe. Crawford, in particular, had observed how Bushe had favoured the Adams faction, a reflection of the Colonial Office's preference for the brand of politics they espoused. The *Observer* accused Bushe of blocking the progressive policies of the Congress and declared that he had conspired with Adams to keep Congress members off the Executive Committee. Furthermore, the Congress Party accused Bushe of fostering the development of an accommodationist labour movement with the assistance of Adams and the Electors' Association as part of a strategy to suppress worker radicalism, slow down the pace of decolonisation and derail the movement toward socialism.

The basis of Crawford's charge was the fact that, during the 1945 Congress-led sugar workers' struggle for wage increases, the Progressive League, led by Adams and Springer, moved into a reactionary alliance with the Electors' Association in order to break Congress' unionisation of the sugar workers – all with the full support of the Governor's

Executive. The Congress Party, then, though with the most seats in the House, was under-represented on the Executive Committee since, in the words of Bushe, there was no member of that party whom he could 'consider' for selection.

The election results reflected, in part, the nature of the organised pressure exerted upon the Congress Party. The Barbados Labour Party won nine seats, Congress seven and the Electors' Association eight, and one independent candidate was returned. According to the rules of the Bushe reform, Adams, as leader of the Barbados Labour Party, was called upon to lead the government in the House and to nominate four candidates for the Executive Committee. The names submitted by Adams, in addition to his own, were Hugh Springer from the Barbados Labour Party and Crawford and H.D. Blackman from the Congress Party.

The Barbados Labour Party, however, had no working majority in the House and was forced into a coalition with the Congress Party in order to push through reform legislation. It was an uncomfortable coalition from the beginning. Crawford was not impressed by Adams' special relationship with the Colonial Office, nor his accommodationist attitudes towards the conservative Electors' Association. He wanted rapid socioeconomic changes, but Adams, as in the late 1930s, wanted moderate reforms to proceed slowly and without political acrimony. Some members on the Congress backbenches were also not fully committed to the alliance with Adams' Labour Party, and took the opportunity to vote against measures agreed upon in the Executive Committee by Crawford and Blackman.

Meanwhile, as the coalition showed signs of disintegration, Adams initiated a number of political measures designed to split the Congress Party. By October 1947, Crawford had resigned from the Executive Committee but Adams succeeded in countering this move by enticing three of Congress' prominent leaders to cross the floor and join the Barbados Labour Party; these were C.E. Talma, A.E. Lewis and H.D. Blackman. The Barbados Labour Party now had a total of 12 seats in the House, though this was soon reduced to eleven when Hugh Springer removed himself from politics to become the first Registrar of the University of the West Indies (established in Jamaica in 1948). In this year, the Barbados Labour Party won the general election, taking 12 of the 24 seats. Adams' dominance of the parliamentary labour movement was now consolidated.

Within the House, Adams resolved the problem of not having, once again, a working majority by enticing another Congress member, D.D. Garner, to cross the floor and join the Barbados Labour Party. He also engineered the appointment of a Barbados Labour Party member, K.N. Husbands, to the Speakership. But legislative reforms were still being frustrated by the power of the Executive (which remained intact under the Bushe experiment) and the non-cooperation of the Legislative Council, which was still dominated by the conservative members of the planter oligarchy. In 1949, the Barbados Labour Party won the debate on a motion within the House that called for the restriction of the power of the Legislative Council; the House voted in accordance. The next major hurdle for the Barbados Labour Party was the attainment of universal adult suffrage and the abolition of property requirements for membership of the House of Assembly.

By early 1950, Adams – now with a majority in the House – took the opportune initiative of introducing a bill to amend the Representation of the People Act of 1901. For him, this was the beginning of the final phase in the rise of liberal democracy, and the basis of the undoing of the planter elite's political control over the legislature. The measure was also timed to take advantage of problems within the Congress Party and win, for the Labour Party and himself, the recognition of delivering the vote to the masses – an achievement with which they would possess a distinct advantage over other parties in the forthcoming general election.

The Electors' Association and the Congress Party found the unpredictable nature of Adams' political tactics and the forcefulness of his intellect difficult to counter. He introduced the bill merely as a measure designed to expand and deepen the process of democratisation, an objective that had the general support of the British government and even some conservative members of the Electors' Association. In his opening remarks he stated:

> Mr. Speaker, – This is a Bill which one might say is a Bill of very great importance. I think that all honourable members and members of the general public who are not still labouring under the delusion that you can have a democracy and at the same time have limited powers of the expression of will by the people who form that democracy, will agree with a Bill of this sort the chief object of which is to give the right to every adult member of the population to vote for members of the General Assembly.

Recognising that Adams had succeeded in seizing the full support of the House for adult suffrage reform, Crawford stated:

> Mr. Speaker, – I think it is unnecessary in a Chamber constituted as this is at present and at this time in our history to labour the desirability of granting adult suffrage. It is now more or less generally conceded by the people in this island who are in line with general democratic thought that every single taxpayer whether he or she pays direct or indirect taxation is entitled to some say in the election of people to control the affairs of the colony.

J.H. Wilkinson, the veteran leader of the Electors' Association replied:

> Mr. Speaker, – I am very glad to hear the honourable senior member for St. Joseph [Adams] say in respect of this bill that there is no Party question ... We believe that there should be adult Suffrage.

The bill was passed and, in April 1950, property or income requirements for both voting and House membership were removed. The electorate, which had stood at near 30,000 in 1948, was now near 100,000. Three political parties immediately began their campaigns to woo the enlarged electorate for the general election the following year. Open air meetings, loud music and rallies became the order of the day. Food and money were also being offered to potential electors in return for their vote. Adams advised workers not to corrupt their newly won franchise by accepting the bribes of money and rum from the Electors' Association. Crawford on the other hand, urged thus:

> On Election Day, vote right. If money is offered to you for your vote, TAKE IT. You need it. They owe it to you! But don't let that prevent you from VOTING RIGHT. Remember the Ballot is secret. No one can know how you vote except yourself and God!

Finally, the masses of people had been politically enfranchised. Adams' leadership had secured for them the political power they had pursued through party politics since the mid-nineteenth century when Prescod had given them some hope of inclusion. The Adult Suffrage Law of 1950 constituted 'Emancipation from Below'. The process was set in train by the Payne Revolution of 1937 and led by Adams and Crawford. It had taken over a century to achieve, since emancipation from chattel slavery. It was a torrid century in which workers never lost sight of their vision for democratic participation. The political struggle had isolated the issue of the right to vote. The next stage of the struggle for justice would revolve around the quest for what is now called 'Economic Democracy'.

- *Three* -

Children of 1937:
Economic Divide and Labour Politics

$\mathscr{B}$lack economic enfranchisement resided at the core of Clement Payne's political campaign in 1937. In dozens of speeches he explained the relations between planter-merchant economic domination and mass poverty; between racism and economic injustice. He also emphasised the relations between the consolidation of wealth in the hands of a minority elite and the distortion, stagnation and suffocation of the national economy. For Payne, the seizure of government by democratic forces was a necessary precondition for the removal of such inefficient and unjust economic relations, hence his call for political enfranchisement as a prelude to economic enfranchisement.

Payne understood clearly the economic limitations and the social attitudes of what he called the 'capitalistic elements' in the Bridgetown 'merchant houses'. As such, he focused upon the need for 'economic liberation', at all times targeting political mobilisation, popular education and labour unions as the vehicles for its attainment. The impact of his vision upon the political leadership of the immediate post-revolution period was profound. The matter of black economic enfranchisement stayed at the fore of political issues, though it appeared from time to time that the quest for political enfranchisement transcended all other considerations. Grantley Adams told the Moyne Commission:

> I suggest that the plantation system is basically the cause of our trouble, and I think that the system which has survived in Barbados for three

hundred years, of having a small, narrow, wealthy class and a mass of cheap labour on the other side, should be abolished.

He called for the nationalisation and redistribution of land, cooperative production and distribution, and similar reforms as the instrument to effect black economic enfranchisement within the context of the agricultural economy. At this stage Adams was prepared to deal with structural injustices within the economy in addition to political reform.

During the 1940s, however, Adams retreated from this position. At the same time, Crawford argued that the economic enfranchisement of Blacks required not only liberal political adjustments, but the movement toward socialist policies. 'Bring Socialism to Barbados' was the rallying cry of the Congress Party during the 1940s. Crawford, then, unlike Adams, saw socialist reforms as necessary for blacks to attain economic justice. In a November 1944 editorial of the *Observer* (Congress organ) Crawford stated:

> Barbados is in revolt against the status quo. Throughout the country thousands of middle and working class men and women are voicing the most determined protests against poverty and unemployment. These thousands are resolved to put more of the wealth in the colony at the service of the people; these thousands are in deadly earnest; this spirit may well be called NEW DEMOCRACY. No longer are the people of this island prepared to entrust their destination to the representatives of big business.

The call of Congress for a 'New Democracy' was unmistakably the beginning of the move towards 'Economic Democracy' – the highest form within the historic civil rights movement. This was a critical moment within the struggle. Congress sought economic enfranchisement as a central policy issue while the Labour Party held on to the vision that, by seeking first the political estate for the workers, their share of the economic cake would be guaranteed subsequently. Between 1944 and 1950, the political and economic enfranchisement of Blacks dominated national politics. Issues such as land reform, outlawing racial discrimination in the private sector and white control of the capital and equity markets figured prominently in public political discourse.

Between 1955 and 1961 the newly formed Democratic Labour Party (DLP), rising from the ideological ashes of the Congress party, retreated from this tradition and sought less to integrate Blacks in the mainstream of the economy than to internationalise its scope. Successive debate over the sugar industry, for example, degenerated into questions about management and organisation, rather than ownership and control. Also, to questions of economic development, the DLP sought answers not in terms of black economic enfranchisement but in tourism expansion, labour emigration and sugar subsidies. Its electoral success in 1961, then, did not result in a return to the Congress' 1940s policy of black economic enfranchisement.

In order to loosen the white commercial elite's hold over policy, Errol Barrow's strategy as leader of the DLP between 1961 and 1966 was to diversify the economy away from sugar and the distributive trades by expanding tourism and manufacturing. He succeeded with his diversification bid, but did not achieve a corresponding weakening of the planter-merchant corporate control over the economy and development policy. In fact, during the first term of the DLP, it was business as usual and the economic base of the white community increased substantially. Also, an examination of the centre of its economic power, the conglomerate Barbados Shipping and Trading company (Big Six) simply confirms that this elite group had grown in strength while black business remained marginalised and without a corporate presence.

Yet, because of the endemic nature of the black economic enfranchisement movement, the parliamentary debate surrounding Barrow's leadership of the country into Independence in 1966 was characterised by constant references to the market alienation of Blacks and white corporate domination. White corporate chiefs, such as K.R. Hunte, were accused of holding back the process of black economic development by 'bribery and corruption'. The Barbados Shipping and Trading (Big Six) was singled out for special reference. The Hon. A. DaCosta Edwards told the House:

Some of us have a mind that we must be the slaves of the Big Six of this country . . . . They come here and fight the cause of the Big Six today, and tomorrow they are kicked in their rear parts by the same people whose cause they have come to the House and championed. . . . Black people like myself can say that they are championing the cause of this business community and the plantocracy, when other coloured people in this country have had to fight against those people for years! The entire coloured community of this country is aware of the struggle which has been fought against capitalism and the keeping down of the of the masses of this country . . . . We want to make every Barbadian feel that this is a country which belongs to him, and it does not belong to six groups of people who have been for years dominating this country.

No one in the parliamentary debate over independence articulated the concept of black economic enfranchisement as clearly as Frank Walcott, independent member for St Peter. Walcott linked issues such as racial subjection, economic injustice, black corporate marginalisation and white power in a manner that echoed the position of Congress during the 1940s. His call for economic democracy was put as follows:

We want to see the economic and financial translation of this community so reflected that [black] people would be in the hierarchy of business houses in Broad Street . . . . Neither Musson and DaCosta nor A.S. Bryden nor any of these big firms have seen fit yet to elevate a black man to the Board of Directors. I am not talking about somebody that would pass for white, or if you told him he was black he would charge you for slander; I am talking about the unmistakable black man with ability. . . . The plural society we live in must undertake a role that is consonant with the society itself; all of this nonsense that if you put a black man in a high position he will carry away your money or carry out your secrets must go by the board. The time has come in Barbados when ... among the races there must be a common understanding that both of them have a right not only to live, but to enjoy and acquire any position in this country that the wealth will provide.

Crawford, however, could not allow the debate over Independence to pass without reflecting on the predicament inherent in his long political career. He told the House:

There was a time when the white people in this country had political power; they lost it. It was taken from them and they relinquished it with sorrow and they cried. Now they have economic power. There is no power to take economic power from people which we do not have. We have internal self-government, and any action which the government wants to take to distribute the wealth more equally in this island, they can take it.

The question was, according to Crawford, now that Blacks have the government and the law, did they possess the will to ensure that the majority gain the economic franchise as proof of economic democratisation? The issue of the political will of the black leader was placed at the fore. Did they have the will, the courage? Could they fight for economic enfranchisement with the same degree of determination with which they fought for political enfranchisement?

Woodville Marshall provided part of the answer to this question in a paper entitled 'Is there a future for black business?' presented at Yoruba House in 1979. He stated that when the Blacks eventually gained enough political power by the 1940s and 1950s to affect social and economic policies (and therefore continue the revolution) it almost seems as though there was no clear idea about what to do with the questions of economic resources, and so the old economic order and its injustices persisted.

If the politically enfranchised Blacks knew not how or lacked the will to economically enfranchise their communities, the white elite knew precisely what was necessary to preserve their dominant position. According to Rex Nettleford, everywhere they established interlocking networks of interest groups, in and out of political parties, but all rooted within the economic environment, to ensure that their control and direction of economic life was not 'eroded either by new comers emerging from the "cane piece" or by meddling governments elected by those in the cane piece'.

The transfer of power from colony to self-government, then, as Cecelia Karch has noted 'was not accompanied by a challenge to the control of the economy by a small, cohesive, white elite'. Though class relations and race relations were modified with black political administration since the 1950s, Karch noted, 'the basic division within the society continues to be a dichotomy between black and white'. Even in tourism, the plank of the post-independence economy, the leading instrument of modernisation according to state policy, where 'control is local, it is white'. In fact, according to Karch, 'it is the white section of the population that has benefitted from diversification in much the same manner that the transformation to the corporate plantation economy favoured them earlier in the century'. With these conclusions, Karch emphasised that 'the persistence of the racial factor in inequitable structures of ownership and control alerts us to the necessity of examining the importance of race in the maintenance of the economic order'. This is how national poet, Bruce St John puts it:

We got democracy!
Man shut you mout.
We en got democracy?

Who in de assembly now?
Who sheltering who now?
Backra telling me wuh to eat,
Backra telling me wuh to wear,
Backra telling me wuh to live in,
Backra telling me when.

Backra out o' de assembly,
But Backra mekking 'e money!

Slave got government,
Slave got opposition,
Slave defending labour,
Slave opposing labour,

Who defending backra?
Backra mekking money!
Money without Assembly?

Slave making joke.
(Bruce St John, 'Political Progress')

The Barbados Labour Party: Disunity and Decline

The victory of the Barbados Labour Party in the 1951 election which established the formidable power of Adams over the organised labour movement, also carried within it the seeds of internal opposition to his leadership. Once again, Adams found himself having to perform the role of containing political radicalism, both within the Barbados Workers Union and the Barbados Labour Party. This time, his chief assistant would not be Hugh Springer, now at the University of the West Indies, but Frank Walcott, the general secretary of the Barbados Workers Union of which he was president. Walcott agreed with Adams on the removal of radicals from the Union, the so-called 'Iron curtain group'. He was less supportive of Adams' determination to purge the Labour Party of its progressive element. Errol Barrow was undoubtedly the leading opponent of Adams' leadership within the party and, not surprisingly, Walcott frequently attacked him in the House for his dissension. Crawford, meanwhile, used his editorship of the *Observer* to exploit such clashes and to urge Barrow to leave the party.

Adams' response to radical elements within the party and the Workers Union was to urge rank and file members not to embrace communists and extremists, and to reject their attempts to create internal strife within the labour movement. At a public meeting held by the Barbados Labour Party and the Barbados Workers Union in Queen's Park on the evening of July 24, 1952, at which Jamaica's Norman Manley and Grenada's T.A. Marryshow were guest speakers, Adams reminded workers that Trinidad was once in the vanguard of the Caribbean Labour Movement, but now they were at the 'bottom of the ladder' because 'its lieutenants began fighting each other'. Manley's speech was reported as being strongly anti-imperialistic while Adams' called for moderation and loyalty, a division which the *Observer* described as being akin to 'the forefront of the jackass going up the hill while the hind part persists in going back down'. Adams also expressed his dissatisfaction that two labour radicals, Farrell, president of the Electric Company Workers Division of the Union, and Layne of the Rediffusion Company, were both elected to the Executive Council. He warned that as he had purged the Progressive League of such radicals over a decade ago, it was his intention to do likewise with the Barbados Workers Union and the Barbados Labour Party.

Such utterances added to the flames of opposition within the party. During the year, Barrow was reported as making frequent critical comments on Adams' growing conservatism and illustrating that he had the intellectual capacity and stamina to cope with Adams' assaults. Adams was frequently out of the island during this time, and Walcott was left in charge of the government, with the responsibility of keeping the radical faction in check. The debate over a motion to nationalise Barbados Rediffusion Limited in August 1952 was the first major occasion in which the party's division surfaced. Adams was out of the island and Walcott, speaking on behalf of the government, opposed the motion on the ground that it would endanger the economy by repelling potential foreign investors. The government lost the vote by 7 to 3; voting in favour were 6 members of the Barbados Labour Party – Miller, Mapp, Barrow, Talma, Holder and Brancker – and Crawford of the Congress. Voting for the government were Walcott, J.C. Mottley, a Congress member, and H.A. Vaughan, the St John independent. M.E. Cox, the only other member of the Executive Committee who was present, did not give Walcott any support. The press wasted no time in popularising the political divisions within the government and suggested that Barrow had piloted the action in order to embarrass Mr Adams and impress the electorate.

Talk of political crisis and an early general election was common place by the end of the year, and Barrow was seen as the most able leader of the anti-Adams faction. Even F.S. 'Sleepy' Smith, a young barrister, popular with the working classes, who had showed a fondness for worker agitation, and who was reputedly being groomed by Adams to replace Walcott as general secretary of the Workers Union, now began to identify more closely with Barrow. During August, while the Workers Union was tied up with the organisation of parish beauty shows prior to the election of 'Miss Barbados', some workers had broken away and organised themselves into a new political party, the Barbados United Party. This organisation was led by Grafton Clarke, a builder, and in its own words was dedicated to the protection of workers' interests while the Barbados Labour Party's reform mandate was being crippled by internal ideological crisis.

Adams, however, persisted with his strategy of seeking membership support for the removal of radicals from the Workers Union and silencing dissenters within the Labour Party. On Labour Day, October 6, 1952, he based his speech at the Workers Union headquarters on a warning to workers that 'it was not all roses in the garden' and that they should be prepared to pluck out 'undesirable weeds.' He referred to the radical faction within the party as 'rebels' on the verge of committing 'suicide', and concluded his speech by reminding them that 'every lion in the forest which seemed to be sleeping, might not be sleeping, but only peeping'. While chastising the dock workers for their go-slow at the harbour, which, in his opinion was damaging the island's commercial interest, he interjected news of a report which reached him that R. Mapp, L. Williams, A.E. Lewis, E. Barrow, and C. Tudor had held a private meeting which resolved to impress upon him that if the same Lewis and Barrow were not placed on the Executive Committee they would secede from the Labour Party and set up their own.

Adams' response, not surprisingly, was that the radicals were unrealistic about the political possibilities in Barbados, and that their adoption of a rigid anti-colonial stance was not carefully thought out. Adams countered, by declaring at a meeting of the Party caucus on October 19, 1952, that he offered Mr Barrow a place on the Executive Committee but he declined to accept owing to his commitments at the Bar. He then concluded by stating, according to an official report, that 'the malcontents could resign whenever they wanted to do so', and that he intended, in the event of the Five Year Plan being defeated in the House of Assembly, to call a general election to obtain electoral support to purge them from the party.

Colonial officials in Barbados recognised that there were some ideological differences between Adams and the radicals of the party, but admitted that these differences were inflamed by two aspects of Adams' political style. First, his strategy of frequently leaving the island so as to slow down the pace of social reform and keeping 'the backbenchers of his Party at arms' length. Second, that 'he shares the knack of Sir Robert Walpole for driving young men into opposition'. As Adams expected, however, it was the debate over the Five Year Plan in late October which provided the context for the departure of the radical wing of the party.

Adams introduced the Five Year Plan on October 28, 1952 in a speech of four hours duration. Lewis, Vaughan, Crawford and Allder attacked its provisions and omissions, especially the absence of a provision for a deep water harbour. Taxation provisions were attacked by the right and left; the former described the plan as 'Russian', designed 'to soak the rich' while the latter said it was designed to 'drown the poor'. One important outcome of the debate was the resignation of Tudor. In his letter of resignation he is said to have stated that he disagreed so profoundly with the leadership of the government on general policy, and particularly on financial policy, that it would be intolerant for him to loyally abide by its decisions. He is also reported to have stated that 'he was in no way interested in organising or being a member of any third party or group'.

Meanwhile, Adams' politics continued to be concerned with attacks upon the left in both the Union and party. He also sought to dissociate his leadership of the Workers Union from the Marxist element within the Caribbean Labour Council (CLC) particularly Richard Hart in Jamaica and Dr Jagan in British Guiana. On November 14, 1952, he held a meeting in Queen's Park in order to attack the critics of his Five Year Plan as well as Jagan and Hart who had been in Barbados on CLC business. He began by stating that he was running out of tolerance with these radicals and that he would not 'allow the labour Movement in Barbados to be wrecked by people who were in their diapers when it started'. The trade unionists, Farrell and Layne, were denounced as communist sympathisers; he stated that he regretted that F.S. 'Sleepy' Smith had joined the 'rebels and renegades', but added that he thought Smith 'did not know any better and had been misled'. Barrow and Tudor were hardly mentioned, but he was particularly bitter in his criticism of Lewis.

On Monday, November 17, at a meeting of the Executive Council of the Workers Union, Adams successfully won a motion to expel Layne and Farrell, but he was forced to use his casting vote because of a three-way split. He did, however, refrain from seeking the expulsion of Lewis from the Barbados Labour Party since he was not 'prepared to play Mr. Lewis' game and present him with a martyr's crown'. Adams, then, had succeeded in purging the union's executive of radicals and, with Walcott's support, consolidated his hold over the union. By August 1953, he had taken the union out of the CLC, now described by him as 'the chief instrument of the communist front organisation in the area'.

He was, however, less successful in silencing the 'rebels' within the party. The pending implementation of the ministerial system, however, was clearly going to accelerate the pace of the party's fragmentation. Adams was reported to be preparing Talma to be his replacement as president of the union following his resignation on becoming chief minister of Barbados. When, in February 1954, however, he refused to offer Walcott, or any of the radicals within the party a government ministry, Walcott, angered by the personal rejection, went on the offensive. He emerged as a bitter critic of Adams and succeeded in substantially reducing the union's support for the government. This was a critical blow for Adams' leadership. The following month, Barrow resigned from the party and publicly dissociated himself from the government. Tudor, in the same year, returned to the House after winning a by-election in St Lucy as an independent anti-Adams candidate. The rift had taken place, and the party's leading agitators were now officially its opposition.

Rise of the Democratic Labour Party and the Federation Crisis

The political leadership of Adams had been a long crusade against radical left-wing forces within the island. The departure of Barrow from the Labour Party allowed for progressive persons and groups to rally around him as leader of these forces. There had been no structural changes within the economy and society during Adams' reign as head of the organised Labour Movement, though he had left behind him a trail of alienated radical leaders. Barrow, Tudor and Smith were not prepared to offer support and Adams seemed more vulnerable than ever.

Under the political leadership of Barrow, the Democratic Labour Party (DLP) was formally established on April 27, 1955. It was the long awaited organisation which would counter Adams' control of the Labour Movement. It comprised politicians already within the Assembly and many grass root activists within the trade unions. Within the House, its chartered membership included Allder, Barrow, Tudor and Lewis and, for the 1956 general election, Crawford and Brancker of the defunct Congress Party joined its ranks. Formed within one year of the forthcoming general election, the party hardly had sufficient time to fully develop its electoral image, though its leaders were experienced campaigners.

The broad front of the DLP campaign was socialist in theory, characterised by a demand for a reduction in the degree of social inequality; democratisation of resource ownership, socialist reforms in the areas of education, public health, and social security, and diversification of the economy away from the plantation-mercantile axis. With Adams preparing for a major onslaught upon what he termed the band of 'rebels and renegades', the party sought to hold some ground at its first electoral encounter; taking the government was then considered rather unlikely. The DLP sought to sensitise the electorate to the lack of a developmental vision for the country within the Barbados Labour Party, and to attribute this to the colonial mentality which Adams refused to eradicate from government.

The 1956 general election saw some major changes in the island's political culture. Crawford, who had led the Congress Party in defence of workers' interests since the 1940s, was now a frontline DLP campaigner. The Electors' Association, now renamed the Progressive Conservative Party, in the absence of the radical Congress Party, considered its chances of gaining an improved electoral position against the 'in crisis' Barbados Labour Party and the new Democratic Labour Party to be rather good. The campaign was fought with as much acrimony and bitterness as that of 1951. The results, however, were hardly surprising. The Barbados Labour Party won 15 seats, the Democratic Labour Party won 4, and the Progressive Conservative Party, 4. There were two surprise results, and one significant indication; of the former, Barrow lost his St George seat, though he was to re-enter the House after winning a St John by-election in 1958, and Walcott won a seat as an independent. Of the latter, the Barbados Labour Party suffered an erosion of its popular support – taking only 49 per cent of the popular vote while the Democratic Labour Party emerged with 20 per cent.

While the Democratic Labour Party was making a firm impression upon the Barbados electorate, and the political system in general, Adams had been preparing to integrate the island into the proposed Federation of the British West Indies. The idea of West Indian federation had been the subject of a major conference in Dominica in 1932 at which Barbados was represented. The leading advocates of the political union had been Grenada's Marryshow and Trinidad's Captain Cipriani, though it was not until the 1947 conference at Montego Bay in Jamaica that Barbados appeared to have been a keen participant. Indeed, the Barbados Labour Party was one of the leading organisation supporters of Federation, and Adams had seen in it the ultimate political development for the region. Since 1947, federation discussions and negotiations were frequent. Adams had placed them as top priorities of his party during the early 1950s, alongside the movement towards ministerial government with a cabinet system. Finally, in 1956 at the London Conference, it was decided to establish the federation as soon as technical, administrative and constitutional difficulties were resolved.

The decision made by the 1957 conference in Jamaica to locate the federal capital in Trinidad was not well accepted in all the territories. Eric Williams, pleased with having the capital in his country, soon began to cool on the federal structure when Manley in Jamaica opposed the suggestion that the federal government should have extensive powers in finance, taxation and planning. Adams, however, the leading constitutional architect of the federation, was soon embroiled in a wide range of jurisdictional disagreements which were having an impact upon the domestic politics of particular countries. While in 1958 he succeeded in implementing the Cabinet system of government in Barbados and emerged as premier, the matter of federal elections seemed to have been given higher priority on his political agenda.

The election of a federal government in March 1958 represented a major landmark in the development of Barbadian politics. Five seats in the federal Assembly were allocated to Barbados, and these were contested by the three political parties. The results were favourable to Adams, and represented an indication of increased support for his brand of politics. None of the four Democratic Labour Party candidates were returned, with Barrow and Tudor suffering defeats along with Frank Walcott, the independent candidate. The Barbados Labour Party entered five candidates, and four of these – Adams, Ward, Vaughan and Rocheford – were returned. The renamed Progressive Conservative Party, the Barbados National Party, entered two candidates, one of whom was returned – Florence Daysch. Later in the year, Adams became prime minister of the Federation of the West Indies and departed for Trinidad, the capital site. His removal from the scene of Barbadian politics had massive implications for the Barbados Labour Party.

By 1960, the federal structure was shaking at its foundations. The government was considerably weakened because the People's National Movement in Trinidad and the People's National Party in Jamaica, both firm conceptual supporters of federalism, had not won seats in the 1958 federal election. Adams was frequently forced to rely upon the 'independent' vote of Florence Daysch of Barbados in order to strengthen the hand of the ruling West Indies Federal Party. Meanwhile, the Democratic Labour Party in Barbados was taking advantage of Adams' absence and eroding the popularity of the Barbados Labour Party government now under the leadership of Dr Cummins. The new premier and leader of the party had been chosen by Adams over the more radical and popular leader, Cox. As the Federation stumbled towards collapse, the Barbados Labour Party government diminished in credibility, and the foundations of Adams' political career no longer seemed firm.

The government had emerged from the 1958 sugar crisis with a damaged image within the labour movement. In fact, it had not supported the sugar workers in their protracted wage negotiations, and the opposition Democratic Labour Party was able to get some mileage in labelling it as anti-worker and representative of vested elite interests. Crawford, who from his Congress days, had built up a large following within the sugar belt, and Barrow, whose radical oratory was attracting workers across the country, took the opportunity to launch a major assault upon the government at a massively attended Queen's Park meeting. Dr Cummins' subsequent attempts to restore the popularity of the government failed miserably as the ruling party showed further signs of internal division and dissatisfaction with Adams' attempt to manipulate policy from behind. Furthermore, the Barbados Workers Union had now revealed itself as being fundamentally opposed to the government for its weakness on matters concerning labour, with Frank Walcott in particular, now determined to see the end of the Adams era.

The Democratic Labour Party approached the election of 1961 in a positive and optimistic mood. It had rooted itself firmly among the rural poor, the black middle classes and the youth. With its manifesto declaring 'operation takeover', the party was encouraged by Walcott's decision to throw the weight of the Barbados Workers Union behind it. The party's candidates vilified the moderate and limited labour reforms which the Barbados Labour Party had implemented since the 1940s, and argued that the government's lack of an effective industrialisation programme had to do with the stranglehold which the planter-merchant elite had over its policy. In addition, they argued that the high levels of unemployment, inadequate workmen's compensation and poor social security facilities resulted from the same root, and that the government was not capable of the kind of economic modernisation which was now required to get the country moving. Adams, because of his duties as prime minister of the federation, could not participate in the election campaign until the very final stages, but by then it seemed that the anti-government swing had already taken place. To make matters worse for Adams, in September 1961 Norman Manley had been defeated by the anti-federal Alexander Bustamante in the federation referendum; Jamaica was out and Trinidad announced its intention of following suit.

The general election of December 5, 1961 took the Barbados Labour Party out of the office with a clean sweep. There were few surprises. Even the conservative Barbados National Party, in constituencies where it fielded no candidates, urged electors to support the Democratic Labour Party. Only five of the 22 Barbados Labour Party candidates were returned compared with 14 of the Democratic Labour Party's 16. The Barbados National Party won 4 seats and one seat was secured by an independent; five of the six incumbent government ministers, including Premier Cummins, lost their seats. On December 6, 1961, Errol Barrow, the 39 year old lawyer-economist emerged as the premier of Barbados, replacing the 70-year-old Dr Cummins and putting an end to the local political career of Grantley Adams. Trinidad withdrew from the federation in January 1962 and, on May 31, 1962, the West Indies Federation was constitutionally dissolved.

Independence and Nationalism

The economic aspects of the Democratic Labour Party's manifesto in the 1961 election suggested that it was a moderate party. Its policy on nationalisation was cautious and limited to minimum government ownership of public utilities; it stressed government partnership with the private sector rather than ownership. On the social aspects of reform policies, candidates emphasised that, even though there had been significant legislation in the previous two decades, the Adams government had done little to modernise the nature of work relations and workers were still intimidated by employers in the workplace on a daily basis. The Democratic Labour Party, therefore, expressed a commitment to social change by placing, at least in theory, the social security of the worker at the core of its political philosophy.

Barrow's mandate for social change and economic development was not frustrated by his having to take Barbados through the final stages of the Federation's gradual demise. Pressure was brought to bear on his government to encourage it to become the core of a revised federation with the Leeward and Windward Antilles – the so-called 'Little Seven'. The British government had promised, though not as firmly as Barrow would have liked, to provide financial support for the implementation of the reduced federation, while pro-federation economists spoke of the economic benefits to be derived by Barbados in the areas of markets for manufactures, transport and commercial development. Barrow, Vere Bird of Antigua and other leaders held talks on various occasions and arrived at the conclusion that the federation of the remaining eight islands should be attempted. This decision was communicated to the British Colonial Office. Barrow, however, insisted on two major points; firstly that the British government should establish an investment programme for the less economically developed islands; and, secondly, that independence for the region be given immediate priority. In June 1962, the new federal structure was placed before the islands' legislatures; Barbados was to be the capital site. In February, 1963, all political parties in Barbados voted unanimously to support the new federal structure, illustrating the degree of popular commitment to political integration.

During the latter part of 1963, however, difficulties with the federal structure began to emerge, most of which were linked to Britain's refusal to act quickly and with resolve in matters of investment and financial assistance. The 'mother' country, furthermore, categorically stated its refusal to commit itself to an aid-package for more than five years and told the regions leaders outright that they would have to attract funds from elsewhere. The response in Barbados to this development was that the British government since the mid-1950s had been attempting to pass down the line its economic responsibility to the lesser developed islands, first to Jamaica, then Trinidad, now Barbados.

Political differences between the regions' leaders were magnified in this context of economic uncertainty and insecurity. Some disputes became personal and Barrow showed little restraint in adjudging some leaders as careerist, 'pettifogging politicians', not fit to be managing the people's affairs. Rumours that Barrow intended to be dictatorial in relation to the federation were widespread within the other islands.

Barrow, meanwhile, was expressing more concern for Barbadian independence, as he believed that the federal structure was doomed once Britain persisted in 'dragging its feet' on the question of financial support. One by one, countries began to dissociate themselves from the revised federation, first Grenada, then Antigua and Montserrat. Negotiations continued to make little headway into 1965. By this time Barrow publicly declared his determination to press for unilateral independence for Barbados – a decision which led to the resignation of Crawford, the deputy premier, a long standing federalist.

When Barrow's government approached the British government with its independence plan, it did so after consolidating its position in the country and after gaining an unprecedented level of popular political support. Since coming to office, the Democratic Labour Party had done much to modernise the country's economic structure, particularly in terms of its extensive infrastructural development plan. The government was attracted to the 'Puerto Rican model' of industrialisation as outlined by economist Arthur Lewis, which emphasised the central role of foreign investment. In addition, the decision to provide free secondary education in government-assisted schools from January 1962 represented an investment in the country's youth without which industrialisation plans were considered futile. Commitment to the educational development of the population considerably improved the government's image locally and overseas. This image was reinforced by the establishment of a Barbados campus of the University of the West Indies in October 1963. These developments were matched by strides taken in the modernisation of industrial relations. Peaceful picketing was legalised and provisions were made for workers to receive, under certain conditions, severance pay and injury compensation. These advances in socioeconomic relations were predicated on the assumption that the island's economic expansion would be based upon an industrialisation model rather than persistent plantation economy – a significant departure in the political conception of development strategy.

- *Four* -

Nursing Colonial Wounds:
The Health of the Working Class in 1937

The working class in 1937 was in a destitute condition. It was a tragic case of body and soul occupying the lowest rungs of the structures of social existence. A biography of Dame Nita Barrow confirmed what had long been conjectured about the consequences of this condition with respect to political action. The 1937 workers revolt against colonial domination was an act of desperation against the century of landless freedom. The uprising had the immediate effect of restructuring imperial policy, advancing nationalist ideological processes and enabling the privileged minority black middle class to seize an opportunity to advance its agenda of accessing professional careers.

There was nothing particularly surprising about this social development. What was striking, however, was the alacrity with which the moderately propertied, formally educated, but racially oppressed minority moved to empower itself in the aftermath of Clement Payne's struggle for social justice for the poor. Before the ashes of the workers' violent assault upon colonialism had settled, the middle-class professional revolution was well underway.

The acceleration of the process of class formation was punctuated by specific imperial legislative moments and propelled by a complex array of anti-colonial tendencies that collectively illustrate the tensions of race and class within the white supremacy superstructure of colonial society. Seeking to situate Nita Barrow and her family within the context of Clement Payne's Barbados, her biographer drew attention to the discourse of Black and female marginalisation within the shrinking labour market by specifically identifying its repressive race and gender relations. He emphasised that women were excluded from the mainstream of productive employment, but recognised that an educated black woman from an emerging respectable family might find employment as a stenographer clerk in the public service if she was willing to queue behind her historically privileged white and 'coloured' sisters. He tells us, furthermore, that 'the nursing profession, although it had not yet been designated as such, or elevated to that status, was attractive to many girls [of all races] who had completed primary school and would have done well in secondary school . . .'(Blackman 1995: 21). Nita Barrow, on account of her lower middle class status, was among this minority in 1935, two years before Clement Payne's intervention in the colony's politics.

The social circumstances of Barbadian – and indeed West Indian – workers were typical of those found throughout the British Empire one hundred years after the abolition of slavery. Constitutional reforms in the decades after the 1830s emancipation process did not open the franchise to workers in sufficient numbers for them to exercise any formal political authority. The electoral system was used by the planter-merchant elite to strengthen its leadership. When Nita Barrow entered the nursing service as a probationer in 1935, the majority of Blacks in Barbados were still excluded from the political polls. Even with the reduced property requirement, voters were still required to have a minimum annual income of £30, and few artisans or agricultural workers earned £25 per annum.

The island, in 1937, according to Raymond Mack, had been accustomed

> for a hundred years to a social structure composed of a white upper class of plantation and sugar factory owners, appointed high government officials, and top professionals. A colored middle class of lower professionals, shopkeepers, middle range government employees, and clerical and kindred workers; and a black lower class of craftsmen, peasant farmers, cane field hands, and other laborers.

The nursing service was not a high profession, but was considered sufficiently prestigious to confer social respectability upon the white women who dominated its ranks.

The educational achievements of Blacks in Barbados had exercised no significant effect on the general pattern of resource ownership and the broad parameters of social structures. The 1946 census showed that the island, unlike other colonies, had virtual universal literacy among adults; only 7.3 per cent of the island's population over the age of ten years were listed as illiterate, the lowest in the British West Indies. Yet, the colony, according to Mack, 'had the reputation among West Indians of being the most prejudice-ridden island'. That census listed only 15 per cent of the labour force as skilled and professional, and 85 per cent as poor, landless peasants and labourers.

With a population of 148,923 blacks and 9,839 whites, 'race was so closely associated with class position that they could usually be used as synonyms'. The significance of this social condition for Blacks entering the nursing profession, and Nita Barrow's initial experiences, were enormous. Francis Blackman noted that the problems experienced had nothing to do with commitment to study or performance of duty. Most of these difficulties, he stated, were associated with

> the attitudes on the part of the white Barbadian and English staff that any black person performing a service for a wage was, in effect, rendering servitude, a remnant of the slave and master relationship of a period less than one hundred years past. Injustice towards and humiliation of nurses and trainee nurses were openly practiced.

This first generation of black women were knocking on the door of a profession reserved for white women since the slavery period. Creole white women perceived that they had the most to lose and were not willing to retreat on the issue. Trained nurses imported from England, who held the positions of authority, tended to see black probationers as labourers rather than colleagues and successors.

The workers' rebellion of 1937, sought in part to redress the institutional racism and class prejudices of the kind that confronted Nita

Barrow's generation in their quest to acquire the qualification of nurse. The domination of the profession by English matrons was no different from that in other areas of public service. The contempt for black trainees, the closing of social ranks by local and English Whites and the general attempt at Black exclusion by the establishment typified the social culture that shaped other parts of colonial relations. The medical staff at the Barbados General Hospital, not surprisingly, was all white, non-resident and visiting. All levels of the medical profession, then, reflected and supported the discriminatory relations of the empire. The workers' confrontation with the empire on the streets of Bridgetown, and other West Indian towns and villages, with sticks and stones targeted this specific industrial culture as part of the general mosaic of racist colonial domination.

It was commonly understood, as a consequence, since Black candidates were not openly welcome in large numbers to medical professions, that working class communities would not be targeted for health care by public policy in Barbados. The vital indices at that time indicated the extent of public health neglect. Infant mortality rates were generally high in all colonies although gradually declining; Barbados in 1946 had the highest rate (147) and Trinidad the lowest (75). The general death rates ranged from 15 per thousand in Barbados to 12 per thousand in Trinidad and the Leewards; outside of British Guiana, Barbados also had one of the highest birth rates at 29 per thousand (United Kingdom 1950: 52).

While Barbados claimed a reputation for having the most developed political and judicial administration, mortality data showed it to be a hostile society for young black life. During the immediate post-war years, there was some amelioration of these conditions as shown by the following data for 1951, but the general picture remained structurally unchanged. Barbados continued to experience an infant mortality rate just under twice the level of the regional average. It was here that black women faced the greatest resistance to their entry into the nursing profession. Nita Barrow's survival and advancement, then, reflected her considerable determination and commitment to the process of radical social change.

Barbados' possession of one of the highest infant mortality rates in the sub-region, furthermore, stood as testimony of the deep poverty that characterised the lives of the labouring classes in the Bridgetown slums and rural villages. Government indifference, or helplessness, with respect to the proliferation of urban slums resulted in the creation of an environment within which poor families became accustomed to burying their infant victims at faster rates than their West Indian counterparts. Black women's determined entry into the public health business through the nursing service and the workers' revolt in 1937, therefore, were intricately bound by the intransigent colonial culture and the popular search for the kind of governance that promoted social care and held the public accountable.

The interconnection of Nita Barrow's private and public spheres helped to illuminate the crisis of a torn and tortured colony. Revolts spread through the colonies like a windswept cane fire – driving south from St Kitts into St Vincent, Trinidad, Barbados, Guiana before turning north like September hurricanes towards Jamaica in 1938. Arthur Lewis, the young, on-the-spot West Indian intellectual, argued that the working classes were determined to confront social and economic injustices in all forms and were expressing a blunt refusal to accept any further the suffocating, debilitating racist nature of colonial governance. In the decade after 1937, Nita Barrow's career in public health nursing also swept through the West Indian colonies and was symbolic of the intentions that informed the aggressive democratisation process released by the workers' revolution.

As was often the case in such circumstances, the British Empire struck back with the establishment and field deployment of a Royal Commission of Inquiry. The records of such discourses show that the more prestigious the commission, the greater the perceived threat to the empire. In this instance, the Barbados revolt signalled the depth of endemic, anti-imperial rebellion, but no one had clear reason to believe that the protest politics of these West Indian colonies could send such disturbing shivers down the spine of the global imperial structure. The revolts against slavery, one hundred years earlier, had located the islands at the centre of a global political and philosophical debate. Also, the post-slavery rebellions of peasants and landless labourers created the contexts within which Marcus Garvey effectively mobilised the black 'wretched of the Earth' in a pan-African struggle for freedom and justice. But it was unexpected that the entire archipelago of poverty and misery could find the spiritual and intellectual resolve to stand up all at once in defiance of colonial domination. The seemingly unrelenting economic depression of the capitalist industrial economies also generated its own worker agitation and cannot be discounted as a significant contributory factor to what was in fact an age of revolutionary nationalism within the colonised world.

The Royal Commission was a high-powered one. It included prominent politicians, distinguished economic advisors, labour union officials and was chaired by the respected Lord Moyne. It carried out an extensive investigation of social and economic conditions in the region during 1938-1939, it held public hearings, examined the records of colonial governments and sought to hear the many voices of West Indian communities. Its task was to evaluate the life experiences of colonial subjects and account for the causes of the workers' rebellion in order to formulate appropriate and feasible remedial recommendations for the imperial government.

A summary of the commission's report was published in February 1940. The full report was circulated in Barbados in 1945. Its recommendations were clear. The British Empire was in trouble, and the West Indian part of it could be saved in the short term only if major transformations were to take place in the social lives of the majority. The report noted that the social services in Barbados were quite inadequate for the needs of the population, and that none of the West Indian colonies could provide, from its own resources, the funds necessary to put these services on a proper footing and foster development in general. The main recommendation of the commission to meet this situation was the establishment of a West Indian Welfare Fund (WIWF) which was to be financed by an annual grant of £1,000,000 from the UK exchequer for a period of 20 years. In addition, it called for the creation of a special organisation under the charge of a comptroller who should be assisted by a number of expert advisors.

In Barbados, the commissioners stated that the imperial government would have no good reason to be critical of its recommendations. The social and material oppression of the labouring poor had already been detailed in the 1897 Royal Commission on the Sugar Industry. The special objectives of the welfare fund, then, would be to finance schemes for the general improvement of education, health services, slum clearance and housing, land settlement and social welfare facilities. The comptroller was required to keep the social problems of the West Indies constantly under review and to collaborate with the local governments in the preparation of long-term programmes of social reform. In addition, and with respect to the financial administration of 'development' grants for the empire as a whole, the British Parliament enacted the Colonial Development and Welfare Act (CDWA) in July 1940 which provided that the sum of £5,000,000 should be made available annually from UK funds for social and economic development in the empire for a period of ten years ending on March 31, 1951; with an additional £500,000 a year for the same period for research.

Claus Stolberg's argument that the CDWA of 1940 was conceived and designed only to 'touch up' the worst eyesores produced by the economic and social deficiencies of British colonialism in the West Indies is consistent with the assertions and thinking of West Indian political nationalists of the 1940s. Stolberg is also on firm ground with the statement that an important consideration behind the promotion of this British social welfare and public health policy response was an awareness of the ideological objection to European colonialism in the hemisphere that had long informed United States politics. Colonial Office officials and West Indian labour leaders were aware that £1,000,000 was woefully inadequate and that at least £10,000,000 annually was needed to develop any meaningful programme.

With respect to Barbados, it was evident that public relations successes rather than social and economic development were paramount on the agenda of the Colonial Office. Gerald Clauson, economic planner in the Colonial Office, admitted the political rather than development aspect of the 1940 legislation when he stated that there have been two motives behind this proposal; the one a desire to avert possible trouble in certain colonies, where disturbances are feared . . . the other a desire to impress this country and the world at large with our consciousness of our duties as a great Colonial Power.

In addition to these objectives, Clauson pointed to 'the need to woo neutral opinion by demonstrating a constructive colonial policy, and the need to prepare for postwar criticism of Britain's role as a colonial power'.

In Barbados, furthermore, the conceptual and financial limitations and drawbacks of the 1940 CDWA were fully exposed by labour leaders. The Colonial Office in 1945 responded with two significant legislative developments. The first was the passing of a new CDWA, which greatly increased the fund and provided for more flexibility in its administration. The new act made available a total sum of £120,000,000, not by annual vote, but over the period of ten years ending on March 31, 1956. The second significant development in 1945 was the decision of the secretary of state to inform each colony of the amount of assistance it could expect to receive for the ten-year period of the act. The British West Indies was to receive £15,000,000 for the ten years, in addition to the sums spent up to March 1946 under the 1940 act. Of the £2,500,000 spent under the 1940 act, £1,800,000 went to the West Indies, and £1,500,000 of this to Jamaica, the colony perceived as having the 'most serious unrest'.

In Barbados, the colonial government considered the colony favoured for 'development aid' under the new legislative arrangements. The per capita receipts in the colony under the 1940 act was 14 shillings compared with five pence for non-West Indian colonial subjects. The proximity of the islands to the United States and Canada was certainly a majority consideration here. Britain was in fact paying for its political embarrassment in the American sphere of geopolitical influence. It started by recognising that the general health and sanitary conditions of the region, thanks to worker protests, constituted an open wound that required considerable nursing, although with an inexpensive aid programme. Africa was virtually ignored and India was considered too far gone with respect to the politics of welfare reform pacification.

Table 4
Funds Available to West Indian Colonies Under the CDWA, 1945

Colony	Funds (£)
Barbados	800,000
British Guiana	2,500,000
British Honduras	600,000
Jamaica	6,500,000
Leeward Islands	1,200,000
Trinidad and Tobago	1,200,000
Windward Islands	1,850,000
West Indies General (Bahamas)	850,000
Total	15,500,000

Source: *Development and Welfare in the West Indies*, 1945-MI6, Colonial Office Report 1947

Table 5
Population Estimates for the West Indies (Thousands)

Colony	1896	1921	1936	1946
Jamaica	695	858	1,139	1,296
Trinidad and Tobago	248	367	448	558
British Guiana	279	298	333	376
Barbados	186	166	188	192
Windwards	146	162	210	252
Leewards	131	122	140	109
British Honduras	34	45	56	59
Total	1,719	2,018	2,514	2,842

Source: *Development and Welfare in the West Indies*, 1945-46, Colonial Office Report 1947, p. 55.

The immediate postwar comptroller for development and welfare in the West Indies, Sir John MacPherson, understood the magnitude of the reform process in Barbados. He stated explicitly that 'no permanent advance in the public health . . . colonies can be secured unless staff fully trained in preventative medicine' could be built up and secured. This staff, he noted, should work towards the establishment of a 'solid foundation of improved environmental hygiene – that is to say, improved domestic and commercial sanitation, improved water supplies and better housing'. The Development and Welfare Organisation was set up to achieve these objectives with greater focus on preventive – as opposed to clinical – medicine.

By 1946, Barbados was preparing to benefit from research funded in this way. Reports were submitted on a number of problems in the area of preventable diseases and special matters directly affecting public health, such as the containment of leprosy and tuberculosis, human nutrition and international quarantine procedures. The operations and work of the Yellow Fever Control Unit in British Guiana, the Malaria Research Units of British Guiana, Trinidad, Jamaica, the Windwards and Leewards, and the Caribbean Medical Centre for the Control of Venereal Diseases were hampered by the chronic shortage of trained nurses in the region. In 1942-1943 a scheme was put in place under the guidance of the London County Council hospitals to receive 72 West Indian nurses over a period of four years for four-year training courses. The cost was estimated at £226,250. The first 27 nurses were already in England when the war ended in 1945. MacPherson considered this initiative a mere beginning and reported the need for a considerably expanded programme.

The provision of training facilities for nurses was arranged by the appointment of sister tutors, and by sending selected nurses to the United Kingdom. Sister nurses were appointed between 1943 and 1945 in Barbados. The 27 nurses from Barbados, British Guiana, British Honduras, Dominica, Grenada, Montserrat, St Kitts, St Vincent and Trinidad assigned to London hospitals were expected to return home on completing their four-year programme and take up duties in public hospitals and rural clinics. In October 1946, a delegation from the United Kingdom consisting of persons nominated by the General Nursing Council and the Royal College of Nursing arrived in Barbados to examine the situation and to make recommendations with respect to the deployment of nurses graduating from the London Hospital programmes.

The nursing delegation was also expected to make recommendations with respect to the training of nurses in Barbados and other colonies. Reports of racism experienced daily by black nurses in England, in addition to the difficulties experienced by the London County Council in securing their placements in hospitals, resided at the core of a need for an urgent policy shift to train nurses at home. While Barbadian nurses were aware that their racial experiences in post-war England paralleled those of other blacks, direct responsibility of the Colonial Office for their professional training officially set them apart from their compatriots in the transport, manufacturing and auxiliary service sectors. The delegation completed its visits to all territories by April 1947 and submitted a report that covered all aspects of training and the principles that should be applied to raise the local standards of nursing in the various territories. In Barbados, modifications of the training curriculum were immediately introduced on the basis of their recommendations and new legislation relating to the organisation of the profession drafted.

A critical decision taken by the Colonial Office from the delegation's report was that the Royal College of Nursing should arrange a one-year course of training in ward sister duties for select senior nurses who had received their basic training in Barbados. This recommendation was supportive of the position set out by the Moyne Commission whose report stated:

> We are impressed by the fact that very few West Indian nurses hold senior positions in nursing services. We consider it a real grievance which should be remedied as soon as possible. The present training of nurses in small hospitals and their accommodation and conditions of service are . . . unsatisfactory. It would be far better to have a few good training centres in large hospitals with adequate residential quarters. Above all, a good type of sister tutorship should be appointed and a training syllabus of lectures and practical work suitable to the health conditions of these colonies should be carefully arranged at each centre. (Blackman 1995: 37)

Fifteen nurses from various territories were selected for this training course, the cost of which was borne by a Colonial Development and

Welfare Scheme. In addition, the Trinidad government sent six nurses at its own expense for the ward sisters course and two for a postgraduate course in district nursing. Three members of Queen Elizabeth's Colonial Nursing Service were sent for courses of training in hospital administration and health sister duties under the scheme.

The facilities for training and residency in Barbados were improved by the opening, in 1948, of a Maternity Training Hospital which was funded by a grant of £24,000 from the Development and Welfare Fund. It was also expected that these facilities would provide part of the staff of qualified nurses required for the University College Hospital under construction in Jamaica.

Meanwhile, the first group of nurses granted scholarships for training in general nursing and midwifery in the United Kingdom were completing their basic training. In some cases, nurses applied for permission to take post-diploma experience or additional courses of postgraduate instruction. In 1949, fifteen locally trained nurses who were selected for the postgraduate training in ward sister duties in the United Kingdom were reportedly 'acquitting themselves with credit'. During 1950, grants under the West Indies Training Scheme were given to seven nurses and two technicians for courses of instruction at the Caribbean Medical Centre in Trinidad in the techniques of treatment and control of venereal diseases. Within the context of these advances, the American-based Rockefeller Foundation, active in the field of West Indian public health care since 1943, expanded its programme to facilitate training on a West Indian basis for public health nurses and sanitary inspectors. The Public Health Training Station in Jamaica was supported in part by the Rockefeller Foundation.

Nita Barrow's professional benefit from these developments constitutes critical reference points. After completing five years of training in Barbados under the auspices of the Colonial Development and Welfare Project, she made use of Rockefeller funding to enter the University of Toronto School of Nursing in 1943 to pursue a one-year course in public health – the target area of specialisation by the Colonial Office. The expected result of this career path was that she would take up employment with the Colonial Development and Welfare Project. Instead, she accepted another year's Rockefeller funding to pursue further studies in public health, after which she travelled to Jamaica to participate in the Colonial Development and Welfare-funded public health nurse training programme organised by the West Indies School of Public Health. The position she occupied in the programme in 1945 was assistant instructress. The following year she was given responsibility for the training of public health nurses as well as for part of the training of public health inspectors. The school provided extensive training for public health nurses and sanitary inspectors up to 1951. During this period, grants under the West Indies Training Scheme were provided to enable ten nurses and eleven sanitary inspectors from various territories, other than Jamaica, to take the nine-month course given at the school. In addition, territories sent students, at the cost of local colony funds, for basic, and in some cases advanced, courses.

In March and April of 1951, the chief nursing officer of the Colonial Office, Florence Udell, OBE, visited Barbados to obtain firsthand information on the stage of development of the nursing and hospital services, the facilities for and standard of training in the region, the recruitment and staffing requirements, with particular reference to the placing of West Indian nurses who were receiving training in the United Kingdom under Development and Welfare scholarships. A conference on medical services was arranged in Barbados to coincide with Udell's visit to discuss general colonial nursing policy and its application to the West Indies. Of special concern was the objective of achieving recognition of West Indian qualifications by the General Nursing Council of England and Wales.

It was also agreed by conferees that officials of the General Nursing Council would make periodic inspections of West Indian training schools and that facilities for postgraduate training in the United Kingdom would be expanded. Furthermore, that there should be enactment of nurses' registration ordinances and creation of statutory nurses' councils and the formation of professional nurses' associations. The conference endorsed a recommendation that, when unification of the government medical services was projected, this should also include unification of nursing services. The proceedings and recommendations of the conference were circulated to governments and were recognised as a seminal departure for the progressive improvement of the status and standards of the nursing services in the region.

Conference recommendations were endorsed by the Barbados government, and one important development was that the nurses' training school of the University College Hospital would be organised on a basis from the outset to meet the requirements of the General Nursing Council. Grants for training in the United Kingdom were made subsequently from Development and Welfare funds only for special post-registration courses and those leading to the sister tutor's qualification on other teaching diplomas or certificates. During 1951 and 1952, several such grants were made under the West Indies Training Schemes and one was made for special instruction in the nursing aspects of the radium technique. Public health nursing accounted for the largest number of the new courses in 1952, with 22 out of 61. Some 60 per cent of these new courses were arranged

Table 6
Allocation of Grants, 1957

Territories	Number of New Course	Total Allocation
Barbados	3	1,603
British Guiana	8	2,037
British Honduras	5	1,415
Jamaica	7	3,706
Leewards	12	3,765
Trinidad and Tobago	6	2,357
Dominica	7	1,095
St Lucia	6	1,462
St Vincent	4	1,319
Grenada	3	639
Total	61	19,398

Source: *Development and Welfare in the West Indies*, 1952, Colonial Office Report 1953, p. 88.

for training in the West Indies, which was in line with colonial policy to conduct as many courses as possible in the region.

These efforts, however, were of a minimalist nature in comparison with the magnitude of the health care problem within Barbadian society. Stolberg's conclusion that the Colonial Development and Welfare acts, and the policy initiatives that emerged from them, were no more than 'symbolic gestures aimed at the world outside of the empire', and designed to have a 'pacing effect within the West Indies', provides an accurate framework of analysis. It was not a coincidence, he argues, that the West Indies, described by W.M. MacMillan in 1935 as 'on the whole ahead of Africa, where the medical services are so inadequately staffed', was chosen as the first region to receive the new programme's benefits. It was part of the wider strategy to 'pacify the United States' anti-colonial opinion and neutralise the growing interest of the USA in the region'.

The training and deployment of nurses and other public health officials as a result did very little to alleviate the root cause of the poverty and malnutrition that was endemic among the majority of Barbadians. Altogether, £1,273,061 was made available between 1946 and 1950 for medical, public health and sanitation projects from a total budget of £10,793,781. Twice as much went to projects in agriculture, and marginally more to programmes in (1) water supplies, drainage and irrigation (2) education and (3) transport and communication. The single greatest investment in agriculture and veterinary science reinforced the plantation bias of the economy and signalled commitment to agriculture and the planter elite as the principal local development agencies. There were no surprises in this regard. Colonialism was designed in Barbados to consolidate productive resources and the institutions of assets management in the hand of local and imperial white elites. The dependency of the landless poor, who constituted some 80 per cent of the population, upon seasonal employment on the depressed sugar industry, resided at the core of the subsistence crisis that typified black life.

Table 7

Funds made Available for Development and Welfare, 1946-1950 (£)

Colony	Public Health and Sanitation	Total for Colony	Expenditure as % of Total
Barbados	18,837	640,001	2.9
British Guiana	56,286	1,761,188	3.2
British Honduras	37,102	764,412	4.9
Jamaica	532,457	4,010,696	13.3
Cayman Islands	22,486	41,132	54.7
Turks and Caicos	1,815	55,216	3.3
Antigua	10,756	257,656	4.2
St Kitts-Nevis	47,752	133,004	35.9
Montserrat	15,752	54,766	28.5
Virgin Islands	8,390	465,974	1.8
Dominica	39,260	432,765	7.5
Grenada	19,002	279,855	6.8
St Lucia	45,387	646,587	7.0
St Vincent	39,151	262,412	14.9

Source: *Development and Welfare in the West Indies, 1950*, Colonial Office Report 1951, p. 10.

Table 8

Infant Mortality Rates in the West Indies, 1950 and 1952

Colony	1950	1952
St Lucia	104	-
British Honduras	120	-
Barbados	140	136
British Guiana	77	76.9
Leewards	78	-
Jamaica	-	81.2
Trinidad	-	78.2

Source: *Development and Welfare in the West Indies*, 1952, Colonial Office Report 1953, pp. 85-86.

The high infant mortality rate in Barbados was directly related to the degree of landlessness among the poor. The crisis of subsistence was greatest here where historically the greatest alienation of the workers from ownership of the land was most extreme. This relationship was recognised by officials administering the Colonial Development and Welfare Fund. Several attempts at funding land settlement policies were initiated, but all fell short of what would constitute a viable land reform programme. Colonial officials recognised that, as had long been the case, the infant mortality for Barbados was the highest.

The health problems of the Barbadian poor were aggravated by the fact that the colony was the most densely populated; the implications of the success of any land settlement scheme were negative from the outset. Demographic pressure on economic resources in Barbados continued to mount as reductions in infant mortality after the war accounted for noticeable increases in population. The region as a whole showed significant levels of natural increase. Between 1948 and 1952, the annual rate of increase was 2.4 per cent and it was projected that by 1970 the region's population, in the absence of significant emigration outlets, would double. Increasing levels of poverty were expected, given the inflexibility of resource ownership and usage patterns. Officials of the Colonial Development and Welfare Fund were not optimistic that their programmes would have any significant impact on the severe health care and infant mortality crises. In fact, the comptroller for development and welfare, Sir John MacPherson, noted in his report for 1945-1946, that 'in nutrition, the most important aspect of school health in the West Indies, it may be said that there is a little light in the sky but the dawn has not yet broken'.

Table 9
Population Density in the West Indies, 1948

Colony	Population/ Square Mile
Barbados	1,221
Windwards	326
Trinidad and Tobago	304
Jamaica	292
Leewards	258
British Honduras	7.5
British Guiana	4.5

Source: *Development and Welfare in the West Indies, 1947-1949*, Colonial Office Report 1950, p. 109.

From the outset, public health nurses emphasised that the unsanitary conditions of Barbadian slums were a principal contribution to ill-health and high mortality. Housing surveys conducted in the post-war years revealed the very high proportion of unhealthy living conditions in towns. Officials of the Development and Welfare project concluded that 'the standard of sanitation in urban housing is deplorably low. It consists often of a standpipe in the street shared by several families, and a bucket latrine, also frequently shared'.

Table 10
Annual Natural Increase of Population

Colony	1921–25	1951
Barbados	300	3,800
British Guiana	1,200	12,500
British Honduras	600	2,100
Jamaica	11,500	31,200
Leewards	600	2,600
Trinidad	4,300	16,000
Windwards	3,300	6,200
Total	21,800	74,400

Source: *Development and Welfare in the West Indies, 1952*, Colonial Office Report 1951, p. 86.

While it was recognised that drastic action was needed with respect to slum clearance and resettlement in order to remove or minimise the threat to public health, officials realised that the funding made available by Colonial Development and Welfare was woefully inadequate.

Under these conditions, Barbadian subjects of the British Empire had no reason to expect to live to a ripe old age. While life expectancy increased gradually in the years between the wars, Barbadians could not expect to reach their sixtieth birthday. Life in the colony, for most subjects, was short, malnourished and unhealthy. Public health nurses and other officials were sent forth into slum communities in the colony as emissaries of the empire with plasters for the small sores and bandages for the big ones.

Table 11
Life Expectancy in the West Indies (Years)

Colony	1920–22		1945–47	
	M	F	M	F
Jamaica	35.89	38.20	51.25	54.58
Trinidad and Tobago	37.59	40.11	52.98	56.03
British Guiana	33.5	35.8	49.32	52.05
Barbados	-	-	49.17	52.94
Leewards	-	-	49.53	54.76
British Honduras	-	-	44.99	48.97

Source: *Development and Welfare in the West Indies, 1949*, Colonial Office Report 1950, p. 57.

The government of the United States spoke about the health menace to the south, and implicated Britain as responsible for the ugly diseases and early deaths that resulted. The Barbadian working classes, in general, did not see the issue so clearly in this way. They knew that their material poverty, landlessness, and lack of political rights had more to do with the privileges of local elites than with the policies of imperial governments – although they knew of, and understood, the historical alliance between the two.

Yet, despite Britian's primary concern with the politics of the empire, advances were made with respect to the development of policy and public infrastructure to deal with the historically neglected issue of public health. The establishment of the Colonial Development and Welfare initiative, which called into being the extensive training of health care officials, represented a break from the tradition of the plantation, vestries and almshouses as agencies for dealing with public health. In this sense, public health policies and initiatives constituted the frontier on which the British sought to modernise, on the cheap, its extensive empire.

The open wounds of colonisation were there for all to see when the post-slavery dispensation took shape during the 1850s and 1860s. As is so often the case, these wounds of social neglect and negation had to erupt into open bloodshed before imperialists would act with any meaningful humanitarian concern. Progress, once again, was found in the aftermath of a path of material destruction and the social display of anger and hatred by the dispossessed and alienated.

The workers' revolt of 1937, then, opened new vistas for a new dialectical interaction between various segments of the colonised population. The improvement of public health care was welcomed by the working class people in so far as it is constituted the acquisition of badly needed skills. The differential availability of health care services across the social structure, however, reinforced their view that colonial professionalisation inevitably results in the setting of market rates way beyond their own financial parameters.

Nita Barrow understood and engaged in all of these moments and processes within which Barbadian public health care emerged and evolved. While in many ways she was a product of colonial policy with respect to the establishment of a democratic nursing culture, Nita Barrow had the special talent of turning the imperial sword into a native ploughshare by building social bridges that created powerful alliances for human liberation. Her imagination and ideological postures were never confined by the thinking and polity initiatives of the Colonial Office. She was a rebel who knew how to make the best of available resources in the search for strategic advances among the poor. The wounds that she nursed were these of her own people seeking release from colonial entrapment. She knew that black people's pathological condition was one that produced what Frantz Fanon described as 'pain all over'. In her attempts to alleviate this condition, Nita Barrow inflicted her own telling wounds on the colonial order, and offered to many throughout the colonised world the kind of nursing hand never envisaged by the Colonial Development and Welfare Project.

- *Five* -

Independence and Nationalism

Independence in Historical Perspective

*I*t is no longer contentious to argue that the principal socioeconomic relations of Caribbean societies – created, shaped and matured in the context of an iniquitous slave-based colonial culture – have been resistant to the formal procedures of liberal constitutional decolonisation. Scholars have shown that, within the dialectics of historical change and continuity, post-independent dispensations remain characterised by divisive colonial legacies which are still held forth as normative ideals.

In the indicative case of Barbados, importance should be attached to the political decision to appoint the last colonial governor as the first head of state (governor-general) of the 'independent' regime in 1966. Indeed, as Errol Barrow, the champion of the so-called 'parting of ways' event and first Prime Minister of Barbados, was fond of saying – 'the Lord giveth and the Lord taketh'. For some analysts, independence as a constitutional development was conceived precisely in such ambivalent terms and, therefore, lacked the political will necessary for propulsion away from the colonial scaffold.

It is within the context of this psycho-political inertia, compromise or refusal that Lawrence Fisher's book, *Colonial Madness: Mental Health in Barbadian Social Order*, fully exposes the fundamental contradiction that haunts the still maturing nationalist consciousness. For Fisher, the black community remains psychologically kidnapped by social relations, economic structures and ideologies that have their origins within the ancient plantation regime. The overt display and articulation of these still virulent forces within contemporary society represent, for many, nothing short of an open attack upon the relevance and legitimacy of the African derived mindscape, and symbolise the unashamed promotion and institutionalisation of minority eurocentricism. For many persons, including those not prepared to contribute to a discourse on race, power and politics, such a state of affairs raises certain questions about the social location of socioeconomic authority, and the more serious pathological concerns that surround the issues of national identity and personality.

Fisher's argument that long-term resource marginalisation, political impotence and dependency have impacted negatively on Blacks, points to Gordon Lewis' thesis that, in modern Barbados, more so than in any other independent West Indian state, the 'racial bullying and economic intimidation' of the black population has ensured that white power remains 'pretty much the order to the day'. This reality represents, at least as far as Lewis is concerned, a severe indictment of independence if perceived in transformative socioeconomic terms, hence his call for caution in associating it with the term 'progress'.

The politics of the post-independence order, however, should be located within a systematic periodisation of the struggle to dismantle, or render impotent, the structures and ideas that informed the colonial ethos. It can be argued, even if in general terms, that the primary sociopolitical agitation within the country in the last 300 years has been that waged by the oppressed black majority against the white and coloured property-owning elite for a 'moral' share of resource ownership, institutional participation, social honour and economic security. Consequently, the tripartite interrelation of white economic power, black political protest and social progress in the process of decolonisation can be used as a guide in the search for evidence supportive of the Lewis paradigm which posits that an alliance of white capital and black politics constituted the ideological basis of a problematic social contract in the post-independence period.

Table 12
Barbados Population by Race, 1970

Race	%
Blacks	91.0
Whites	4.0
Coloureds/Mixed	4.0
East Indian	0.4
Others	0.6

Source: *Population Census*, 1970

The intellectual coherence of such an argument can be strengthened by the admission of evidence presented by Hilbourne Watson, Trevor Marshall, Cecelia Karch, P.I. Gomes, George Belle, Don Marshall, Christine Barrow and others, which shows that whites in contemporary society, who constitute less than five per cent of the island's population, 'enjoy a life of privilege, ease, and comfort' based upon their dominant control of the corporate economy. For these scholars, the ownership and control of economic resources are so decisively related to the acquisition and use of sociopolitical power, that the economic hegemony of whites guarantees them the ability to gain a 'larger share of the decision-making process' and set for the country a 'development policy favourable to their interests.' This widespread perception is currently at the fore of the social consciousness of the post-independence generation. For this 'new breed', who should not have experienced colonialism first hand, there has been some remodelling of the ancient structure – more doors opened and ceilings raised. But the ideological and economic foundations remain clearly recognisable, and most rooms with a view to, and at, the top are still believed to be reserved for persons who cannot be visibly identified as having 'African blood flowing in their veins'.

A typology of civil rights struggles, then, can identify independence as a major act of democratic self-affirmation, the legitimisation of popular ideology and culture, and the consummation of phase two of the black struggle – the seizing of the State by the majority. The attainment of universal adult suffrage in 1950, sixteen years before independence, made possible the emergence of democratic government and the creation of the context and foundations for phase three of the struggle, the dismantlement of traditional forms of resource monopoly and the attainment of a democratic economic culture.

The ideology and actualisation of independence, therefore, with all its political rationalisations, cannot be separated from the general forces mobilised by, and through, the civil rights movement. Though as a historic event it ritualised the triumph of natives over imperialists, it also symbolised the formal political reduction of the local white elite and the institutionalisation of labour-based black political authority. But, as Raymond Mack observed, Whites soon realised that the 'only way' to 'protect their economic power' was to 'accommodate to black political power' within the context of popular democracy.

It was, however, a politically problematic and socially uncomfortable realisation and adjustment. Powerful elements within the white economic elite resisted independence with all the might they could muster and intimated that, in the event of their failure, an economic strike or withdrawal of enthusiasm could result. In general, the forces they mobilised against the movement were considerable but insufficient to deter the ruling Democratic Labour Party. Their political lobbies argued that independence would sever links with imperial authority, which were vital to the maintenance of their class and race dominance. In addition, their racist ideology was expressed, according to Ronald Mapp, a veteran black labour politician, in their generally discreet utterances that 'the coloured boys' could not 'run anything'.

A mixture of anti-black racism and perceptions of social and economic interest, therefore, accounted for the white elite's opposition to the independence process. This meant that, as a political and constitutional concept, nationhood was born within the context of racial fear and hostility. Many within the white community could not politically celebrate the event, and some wished it a short life, hoping that the country would plunge into the constitutional chaos that had engulfed

British Guiana in the previous decade. These developments, noted Karch, had serious implications for the country in the future and ensured that race was to remain 'a salient factor in Barbadian class relations'.

Table 13
Typology of the Civil Rights Struggle in Barbados

Phase 1   Social Rights (1627-1838)

Emancipation

Legal Rights   Social Rights   Political Rights (1838-1966)

Phase 2   Political Rights (1838-1966)

Political Franchise

Institutional Representation   Democratisation of Public Office

Phase 3   Economic Rights (1966-present)

Economic Enfranchisement

Access to Market Economy   Access to Corporate Management

Redistribution of Economic Resources   State Sponsored Affirmative Economic Action to Majority

Such developments, however, should not have surprised anyone familiar with the political history of the colony since the end of the nineteenth century. As the civil rights struggle intensified before and after the First World War, the white elite took measures to strengthen its control over economic resources. In spite of a history of internal strife and competition, planters and merchants recognised the implication of a growing black political movement which was designed to break, in the short-term, their political hegemony and ultimately loosen their control over the national economy. In 1917, elements within the traditional planter class (that still firmly controlled the colonial state) established Plantations Company Limited with the intention of increasing the size of capital funds available to the industry and enabling them to purchase and retain plantations, thus minimising the land engrossment tendency of the Bridgetown merchant houses. In addition, the company was designed to pilot the planters' entry into the commercial sector (thereby taking competition to the merchant class) and to capitalise on investment funds being accumulated in the non-sugar sectors.

In 1920, the merchant class, realising the effectiveness of the planters' corporate innovation, responded by forming their own large-scale firm, Barbados Shipping and Trading Company Limited. The presence of these two corporations signalled the origins of white corporate monopoly capitalism in Barbados and a further stage in the successful economic domination of the colony by a white elite.

The entrenchment of Westminster-style government in the post-independence period was perhaps inevitable given the refusal of the ruling Democratic Labour Party and the opposition Barbados Labour Party, to distance the island from the ideological and socioeconomic framework inherited during the colonial era. Independence within the confines of the imperial Commonwealth system was what the Democratic Labour Party government had proposed and attained in 1966, and the rejection of republicanism, in itself a popular measure, was also another obvious indicator of the limits which would be placed upon nationalist transformation thereafter.

With the planter-merchant's political party discredited and removed from the political arena, it was obvious that its members would seek protection for their vested economic interests within one or both of the dominant labour parties. Both parties had cultivated traditions of criticism of the oligarchical political attitudes and practices of the planter-merchant elite, but both had also sought to court its economic power and managerial expertise within their political strategies. For labour leaders, these positions were not considered contradictory. As a result, a conciliatory arrangement between white corporate power and black political administrations emerged as the dominant political equation of the post-independence period.

The Democratic Labour Party, which had grown up alongside the anti-colonial nationalist surge of cold-war years, while being supportive of liberation causes in Africa and Asia, for example, remained cautious on the question of white economic and racial domination in Barbados. Indeed, its all-black government in 1970 found it necessary to prevent Trinidadian-born, American black-power activist, Stokeley Carmichael, from addressing public audiences in Barbados during his short and well-policed visit on the pretence of government commitment to non-racial politics and the defence of white minority rights. The 1970 Public Order Act not only sought to suppress the black-power movement, but also to escalate police surveillance of known black-consciousness radicals. Nonetheless, the party won the 1971 general election with a handsome majority, including strong support from the grateful white community.

The leadership of the Barbados Labour Party, with its political image becoming increasingly associated with the interest of the corporate sector, remained skeptical, if not critical, of black radicalism. The economic crisis of the mid-1970s, which followed the escalation of oil prices, resulted in a premium being placed upon financial and managerial acumen within regional politics, rather than black economic empowerment. This context was effectively exploited by the Barbados Labour Party in the 1976 general election. Now led by Tom Adams, son of Sir Grantley Adams, the Barbados Labour Party, with an undoubtedly private-sector image, was able to defeat the Democratic Labour Party and restore the sagging confidence of the corporate elite within the country.

It remains difficult to assess the extent to which the independent State was constrained in terms of socioeconomic transformation without looking closely at the political ideology of Errol Barrow, popularly considered as the father of independence, even though the Congress Party under Crawford had carried independence as a major issue during the 1940s. Both Lewis and Belle have offered political judgements on the Democratic Labour Party Administration under Barrow's leadership between 1961 and 1976. For Lewis, it was the politics of modernisation and not social transformation while for Belle it was the politics of factionalism and populism. Lewis argues that Barrow sought less to integrate Blacks into the economy than to modernise Whites' control of it. For example, he stated that successive debates on and investigation into the sugar industry under the Barrow regime degenerated into questions about management and organisation, rather than ownership and control. Also, to questions of economic development, answers were sought not in black economic enfranchisement, but in tourism expansion, labour emigration and sugar subsidies. As such, the Independence issue in 1966 was not associated with ideologies of internal transformation.

In order to loosen the white commercial elite's hold over policy, Barrow's strategy was to modernise the economy away from sugar and the distributive trades by expanding tourism and manufacturing. These sectors, he suggested, would give government a sufficient revenue flow in order to reduce dependency on the merchant-planter alliance and, at the same time, give him sufficient elbow room to challenge archaic and regressive socioeconomic attitudes. He was successful in the diversification of the country's economic base, but did not achieve a corresponding weakening of the merchant-planter control over development policy. In fact, during the 1960s, the economic base of the white elite increased substantially, and by 1976 they were still strong enough to participate in the defeat of his party and the reinstatement of the Barbados Labour Party. According to Belle, the planter-merchant class continued to monopolise the best agricultural land, the sugar industry and dominate tourism and the distributive sector. Also, an examination of the centre of its economic power, the conglomerate Barbados Shipping and Trading Company Limited, simply confirms that this class had grown from strength to strength.

Unable to implement structural changes in the ownership of productive resources, Barrow resorted to a wide range of social policies designed to create the potential for long-term transformations. These included free secondary and university education, national insurance schemes, incentives to small black businesses and a comprehensive health policy. These policies, however, represented a retreat to Fabian socialism and the politics of gradual reform, both of which were considered respectable and unproblematic from the ideological viewpoint of the dominant class and race.

With these policy developments in mind, and the subsequent passing of anti-black protest legislation in the form of the May 1970 Public Order Act, Barrow's conservatism surfaced in a manner that struck at the very roots of the Independence concept. This pandering to undemocratic white entrepreneurs, repressing black activism and conceiving these policies to be in the interest of the country in the context of a dying colonisation, must surely be considered part of the basis of his defeat in 1976. Certainly, by that time his image as 'father of the nation' took a significant hammering, especially since the populace was referring to his apparent arrogance and double standards on the questions of race, class and power.

During the period 1976 to 1986, the swing to the right of the Barbados Labour Party, especially under the leadership of Tom Adams, led to the formidable entrenchment of white power in Barbados, while the Public Order Act continued to exist as a deterrent to black power hopefuls. The psychological profile of the Tom Adams' regime was certainly one which confronted the black masses with big capital and high finance. Fear of victimisation of black radicals was commonplace and the belief that government would use security forces against radical activists was widespread.

With the election in 1986, the black population defeated the Barbados Labour Party regime and returned Barrow to power in a 'silent revolutionary' fashion which restored his credibility as representing the nationalist conscience. For many, he was offered a second chance to carry out radical changes in the country. He was expected to crush the arrogant, manipulative offensive of the white business community. He was also expected to return Barbados' foreign policy to a more independent path. His death on June 1, 1987 meant that all these expectations were never fulfilled. Many people believed he had a plan to assert nationalist sovereignty in a more aggressive manner, as was the case between 1966 and 1976. Some, however, believed that he would take a populist position on domestic policies and be a vigorous radical on foreign issues – strategies which would fall short of a radical transformation of the country's socioeconomic structures.

The political articulation of the black civil rights movement since independence, however, came mainly from minority elements within both labour parties. They failed, however, to mobilise forces for meaningful democratisation of economic resource ownership. In spite of the alienation of the planter-merchant elite from political office, its political influence has increased considerably since 1966. During the 1986 general election, for example, a major argument levelled against the Barbados Labour Party government by Dr Don Blackman, a former cabinet minister who crossed the floor and joined the Democratic Labour Party, was that its leadership was manipulated by the corporate elite to such an extent that it had become a mercantile puppet administration.

If labour governments of the 1940s and 1950s seemed unprepared to confront planter interests, then since Independence they have been equally unprepared to tackle the manipulative might of the mercantile elite. As a result, a fundamental national division of labour, what for some amounts to a post-colonial political form of Hobbesian social contract, emerged in independent Barbados having, as its principal parties, Whites dominating the economy and Blacks dominating the state. Within this 'alliance for progress' were two assumptions, both buried deep in the culture of colonial racism. First, that since the Whites, with few exceptions, had opposed the rise of popular democracy and independence then they had in effect disqualified themselves for public service in the new governmental order. Whites, then, were either rejected as candidates by the labour parties or took the view that they had no moral authority in relation to the praxis of representative democracy. Second, Whites mobilised their ideological argument that Blacks had no propensity towards big business, and implemented policies to keep them out of the market economy. Blacks were effectively kept away from the centres of economic power in the private sector; they were rarely invited to sit as directors of corporate boards or to serve as managers.

Institutional anti-black sentiments in the private sector grew up alongside anti-white sentiments in the public sector and, by the 1980s, references to discrimination against Blacks in the corporate economy became the centre of popular social discourse. To some extent, the post-independence emergent black middle class, politically impotent in terms of its relation to white capital, capitulated in the face of its historical role as a transformative force. Unwilling to challenge the merchant aristocracy in the market place, it developed a dependency ideology and consciousness that compromised its position as the formal guardians of state power. According to Karch:

> The black middle class embraced the prevailing ideology system; many were proponents of Empire. The majority sought access to the system; they did not seek to destroy it. Status as a middle class and their dependency on the paternalism of the oligarchy, and the colonial system, blunted the nationalist revolutionary spirit of black middle income groups and go a long way in explaining the recent political history of the island. Individuals from this class, not the class as a class, became political leaders and spokesmen for the majority population. It was the massive unrest of the black working class which propelled them into the limelight. Where leadership emerged from the ranks of the working class, it was repressed.

The origins of their subordinate relation can be traced, in part, to the Grantley Adams refusal to challenge the plantocracy's monopoly of land during the post-rebellion decade when the nationalisation of the sugar industry and land reform policies appeared as policy objectives of the labour movement.

Resolving the Crisis

The crisis of the race relations in the marketplace relates, then, to the systematic political suppression of democratisation policies, and the deep-seated dependency of the conservative black professional middle class. Both these developments in turn are rooted in the structure of economic power and its attendant ideological package. Indeed, it is commonly articulated that the white elite, in spite of its opposition to the independence process, has emerged as its principal beneficiaries in social as well as economic terms.

The ownership pattern and the control mechanisms of major businesses are no guarded secrets. It is immediately obvious that the commanding heights of the locally owned corporate economy are controlled and manipulated by merchants and executives drawn from a white community. These persons constitute a commercial and financial (though not an industrial) elite which wields levels of power (social and political) far in excess of what their demographic proportion suggests. They control the large locally-owned corporations in all economic sectors; the largest local life insurance company; and the most prestigious accounting, auditing and financial service companies.

By virtue of sitting on the boards of these corporations and dominating their top management executive positions, these groups are placed in a position to direct the destiny, not only of the corporate sector, but of the overall national economy. After 1950, when adult suffrage was achieved, labour governments, elected mostly by Blacks and administered totally by Blacks, have found it necessary to pander to these 'interest groups', to the extent that these groups now perceive their interests and the national interests as one and the same. They constitute, furthermore, a silent and hidden force that successfully direct the political directorate to its own end.

Indeed, some analysts say that their policy since independence has been to kidnap the State and use it to discredit, alienate and remove potential and actual critics of their dominance. Over the years, critics of all kinds have been labelled as 'undesirables' and 'misfits' by the mass media which they influence directly through advertising power. The collective economic control of this elite is also expressed in terms of its ability to determine the number and nature of black executives who occupy high level managerial positions in local corporations.

Blacks admitted to the corporate boardrooms generally feel a deep sense of either gratitude or resentment; neither of which emotion is healthy in terms of building a market culture for national mobilisation and development. They are made to feel like outsiders since they all know where their ceiling is located; they all know on which doors they cannot knock. The odd Black who slips through the crack in the structure is either very good, and hence indispensable, or a beneficiary of white paternalism. Either way, they have no strong foundation on which to rest, and survive on the fragile goodwill of suspicious bosses. This state of affairs, though as yet not measured by the economists, is believed to be having its toll on the corporate economy in terms of low productivity. It has been said that an instinctive withdrawal of enthusiasm (and hence productivity at the management level) is a common response to the institutional racism they experience in corporate management. As in slavery, Whites see this as evidence of laziness and ineptitude. The *Economist* magazine (July 8, 1989) looked at the crisis condition of race relations in corporate Barbados and made the following observations:

> In a family firm, family members naturally get promoted, so young whites sometimes get promotion over experienced blacks. Work sometimes gets contracted out to a second cousin or a classmate from primary school; there, too, whites may sometimes give jobs to whites. There are plenty of black jockeys at the races these days, not many black owners. It is easy for blacks to feel powerless, and for whites to feel they are under siege in their own country. A tiff between a white manager and a black employee can be brooded on in private as a racial squabble. Some of the suspicions are real, some imaginary, some a bit of both. Given the history, perhaps the surprise is how little racial tension there is in Barbados today.

The refusal of successive governments to address corporate institutional racism has led to the open display of race ideologies within the economy that are clearly harmful from the point of view of national efficiency. Accordingly, Waldo Waldron-Ramsey wrote in 1989:

> There is a legend, of sort, that in Barbados only Euro-Barbadians or Caucasoid Barbadians can manage and run business enterprises here. That they are better at it than any other race. That they have had many years in the experience of management, and so, almost as a group, they are now, ipso facto, experts at business. On the other hand, people of African origin have no such tradition and acquired expertise to rely upon. That

Africans or people of the black race have other strengths and expertise as a people. But managing big business is not one of them. Our colonial education and experience have been so contrived and devised, that they lend a certain credence to that myth. And worst still, many of the African race in Barbados, would seem to have been seduced by this facile, weak, and unsubstantiated argument. There is no truth in it at all. But this had been part of the colonial plot to weaken the sinews of the majority in the colonial population, and to render the imperium infinitely more secure by augmenting the faith of that section of the population which could more readily identify with imperial masters.

Since the general election of 1986 in which the Democratic Labour Party was returned to office after ten years of opposition, with a crushing 24-3 defeat of the ruling Barbados Labour Party, the question of democratisation of economic resources and open market opportunities has hung in the air, lacking focus and organisational direction. Dr Don Blackman, the Democratic Labour Party MP for St Michael East, had waged an ideological war against the government of the Barbados Labour Party (of which he was a former minister) for its subservient relationship with the mercantile elite. He also made a tremendous impact upon popular consciousness with his speeches on black economic alienation.

Dr Blackman charged these commercial groups with the monopoly of corporate power. This allowed them to function as the real Cabinet of the country, with power to overturn decisions made at the highest levels by the people's Parliamentary representatives. In several talks, he referred to the merchants and money lenders as 'white shadows', a force not to be seen but always to be felt. These 'white shadows', Blackman argued, were the real government of Barbados since they had the power to manipulate the state machinery for their own interests and had forced government into accepting the view that the corporate interests and those of the nation were one and the same.

Against this background, discussions about the ownership of resources and the control of financial institutions developed; sometimes debates were serious, other times they were just reflective of the empty political emotionalism that party politics can encourage. In any event, the public was being encouraged to look at the way in which corporate power was undermining the fabric and spirit of democracy and to consider the significance of this development for social and race relations within the society.

The transfer of power from colony to self government, as Karch has noted, 'was not accompanied by a challenge to the control of the economy by a small, cohesive, white elite'. Though class relations and race relations were modified with black political administration since the 1950s, Karch noted, 'the basic division within the society continues to be a dichotomy between black and white'. Even in tourism, the plank of the post-independence economy, the leading instrument of modernisation according to state policy, where 'control is local, it is white.' In fact, according to Karch, 'it is the white section of the population that has benefitted from diversification in much the same manner that the transformation to the corporate plantation economy favoured them earlier in the century.' With these conclusions, Karch emphasised that 'the persistence of the racial factor in inequitable structures of ownership and control alerts us to the necessity of examining the importance of race in the maintenance of the economic order'.

Current debates about the relations between white economic power and black politics, which have now become endemic, suggest that the only way forward towards a non-racial democracy is to address the question of economic and ideological relations within the market economy. On this matter, the weight of history is great, but the late Professor Elsa Goveia warns us of the danger inherent in not honestly confronting historical legacies as a prerequisite for positive policy formulation:

> Ever since the time of emancipation we have been trying to combine opposite principles in our social system. But sooner or later we shall have to face the fact that we are courting defeat when we attempt to build a new heritage of freedom upon a structure of society which binds us all too closely to the old heritage of slavery. Liberty and equality are good consorts, for, though their claims sometimes conflict, they rest upon a common basis of ideas which makes them reconcilable. But a most profound

incompatibility necessarily results from the uneasy union which joins democracy with the accumulated remains of enslavement.

That Blacks need to attain their economic franchise through economic democratisation is undoubtedly a matter of national importance at this time. If there is an inevitability about this process then one might add that the correct position to take is to abandon the politics of economic democracy and allow history to take its course; this way the reconstruction of Blacks' economic culture, devastated in part by slavery and post-slavery conditions, would certainly be achieved. This position, however, illustrates a certain disregard for the forces and logic of history and an undeveloped understanding of institutional evolution.

If labour governments of the 1940s and 1950s seemed unprepared to confront planter interests, then since 1966 they seem to have been equally unprepared to tackle the manipulative might of the commercial elite. By 1970, the BS & T had expanded its operations into almost every sector of the economy to become the largest locally owned corporation in the island. The growth of the local corporate sector was directly related to the development of the economic integration of the Commonwealth Caribbean following the collapse of the federation. Barbados played an important leadership role in this process and took advantage of economic opportunities made available to it. The idea of a regional economic association was revived in the mid-1960s. At the initiative of Guyana (which had remained outside the West Indies Federation), articles of a Caribbean Free Trade Association (CARIFTA) were drawn up in 1963 and were accepted by Barbados and Antigua. The provisions of the agreement were largely modelled on those of the European Free Trade Association. All 12 Commonwealth Caribbean countries were able to agree on the formation of a free trade area, based largely on the text of the 1963 agreement, and CARIFTA came into existence in May 1968. At the same time, the Eastern Caribbean islands were developing closer forms of cooperation which culminated in the formation of the Eastern Caribbean Common Market in June 1968.

In October 1972, some of the CARIFTA member countries decided to form a Caribbean Community and Common Market (CARICOM). The community, which came into being on August 1, 1973, represented a deepening of regional integration and has achieved such objectives as the establishment of a common external tariff, a harmonised system of fiscal incentives for industry, double taxation agreements and the formation of a Caribbean Investment Corporation designed to channel equity funds to the less developed member countries. It initially comprised Jamaica, Trinidad and Tobago, Guyana and Barbados but by the end of July 1974, all the other CARIFTA members had acceded to the community agreement. Following independence, then, Barbados became increasingly immersed within the region's economy and polity and, in fact, began to perceive its interests in regional terms.

The expansion of the white controlled and owned local corporate sector, in addition to the steady growth in the number of foreign multinational companies in tourism, manufacturing, banking and finance, stimulated the development of a black professional middle class which constitutes perhaps the most noticeable social feature of the post-Independence era. The middle managers and clerical staff of these corporations were the material out of which the present cult of 'professional elitism' was created. These upwardly mobile groups filled part of the vast socioeconomic gulf which hitherto separated the white elite from the black labouring masses.

To a large extent, the emergence of the middle classes had to do with social processes released by the Democratic Labour Party government's free education policy in the early 1960s. For the first time in the island's history, society seemed fluid, and working-class families were able to produce individuals who could be found within all social groups. These social changes have been hailed by some as evidence of the basic egalitarian nature of the post-Independence social order, though the argument has also been made that the rise of the black professional elite was more the result of significant white emigration to places like Australia, South Africa, Canada and New Zealand, after the attainment of independence.

These developments in social structure had a significant impact upon the process of cultural institutionalisation that had been stimulated by constitutional independence. Certainly, radical elements within the black middle classes, under the influence of the pan-American black consciousness movement of the 1960s and 1970s, appeared to be socially rejecting some formal aspects of their European cultural heritage and began the movement for the redemption and validation of their Afro-Barbadian traditions. In this regard, they were merely proving what the working classes had long been expressing – that there is a dynamic, legitimate Afro-Barbadian culture. The rural villages and urban slums gave form to a vibrant social culture whose song, dance, art, theatre, drama and language derived from a root long driven underground by the repressive plantation world, but awaiting an intellectual environment for its revival.

It was Elombe Mottley, son of Ernest Mottley, the conservative black spokesman for the discredited planter-merchant political party, the Barbados National Party, who appeared in the vanguard of the Afro-Barbadian cultural renaissance which is undoubtedly a most dynamic feature of the country's social life. The formation and development of 'Yoruba House', an organisation dedicated to cultural understanding and revival, under Mottley's directorship, provided a forum for cultural activity which was symbolic of the Afro-Barbados which world-famous Barbadian artists – novelist George Lamming, poet Edward Kamau Brathwaite – and the brilliant multi-talented Frank Collymore – had long been writing about.

In 1978, Edward Brathwaite was invited by the Tom Adams government to conduct a survey of indigenous cultural activities and to draw up proposals for a national development plan for the cultural sector of the country. In his report, Brathwaite stated that despite individual efforts in various sections of the arts, it could not be said that Barbados had developed any significant institutional cultural infrastructure in the period prior to political independence. Elombe Mottley had been instrumental, along with Daphne Joseph-Hackett, in the establishment of the Barbados National Theatre Workshop and Anthony Hinckson, poet-playwright, had pioneered the formation of the Barbados Writers Workshop in 1969. Black Night, a grass roots forum of writers, poets and dramatists, also under Mottley's guidance, led the way in the early 1970s in the development of community/street art which drew upon the folk tradition. In June 1978, Mottley, along with the Ministry of Education and Culture, mounted an island-wide community and theatrical event, the traditional 'Crop-Over Festival'. It was a major achievement for the government of the Barbados Labour Party. There can be no doubt that this event, now an annual one, was the most remarkable folk-festival ever held in Barbados and, together with the National Independence Festival of Creative Arts which began in 1973, remains the beacon of the national cultural upsurge.

The institutionalisation of culture, since the mid-1970s, in the form of a proliferation of theatre workshops, dance and musical groups, professional artists, writers and folklorists all working within the Afro-dimension of social experience, attests to the extent to which the social culture of the country has been undergoing a transformation. Indeed, this sociocultural independence had been emphasised by Prime Minister Barrow since 1966. He had never articulated national independence in exclusively political or economic terms. For him, it had to be first and foremost an intellectual process whereby citizens should always, in his words, critically look at their 'mirror image of themselves'. His death on June 1, 1987 at the age of 67, was mourned by the nation with an unprecedented display of sorrow which expressed more than just the passing of a founding father of the State, but the tragic loss of its most popular nationalist leader of the modern era.

Since Independence, there have been profound social changes and cultural developments, though the dominant economic and political trends were clearly to be anticipated. The island's economy did perform satisfactorily during the crisis years of the 1970s and, unlike many of its neighbours, experienced no significant internal political turmoil. During these years, its role as a commercial centre for the Caribbean Economic Community increased in significance and, by 1980, it was undoubtedly the major centre for international finance in the Eastern Caribbean – a status it had held during the formative years of plantation slavery. The country has certainly lived up to the challenges of nationhood, and citizens pride themselves for being among those American nations with the highest material living standards and greatest democratic freedoms.

- *Six* -

Chattel House Blues:
Economic Enfranchisement
Movement Begins

*D*uring the 1980s there was much controversy in Barbados about the inability of large numbers of black people to make significant inroads into the economic environment as private entrepreneurs. Where there is broad consensus, however, is in recognition that the continuing disadvantaged economic position of the black majority with respect to resource ownership and control produces social attitudes that run counter to sectoral productivity demands, sociopolitical stability and transracial psychological cohesion.

Since the 1930s, when political mobilisation began for the entrenchment of institutional values necessary for the establishment and consolidation of a democratic ethos, politicians have sidelined the vexing question of white minority domination of the economy. Decades of political retreat from this question allowed for the deepening of traditional racist ideologies and institutions that should have no place in a modern popular democracy. Foremost in the ideological line-up are ideas that promote negative views about the market capabilities of Blacks.

Participants in the recent debate can be divided into two basic categories. These may be called the Culturalist School and the Structuralist School. Advocates of the Culturalist School argue that Blacks have no organic historical relation to a commercial culture and, as such, do not possess the required psychological propensities and values necessary for effective survival within market economics.

They also suggest that Blacks are not, in this regard, victims of colonisation, slavery or racism, and that their problems have to do with being members of a pre-capitalist, pre-market, communal civilisation. Blacks need, therefore, to be schooled over a long period of time, in the modernising culture of western market thinking.

Believers in the Structuralist School, on the other hand, argue that under slavery and post-slavery conditions, a systematic attempt was made, by means of legislation and social ideologies, to structurally exclude Blacks from participation in the market economy. Three centuries of economic exclusion from the institutions and facilities through which commercial life flowed meant that Blacks were socialised to perceive and approach the business environment as alien and hostile. According to this view, the economic environment, made up of markets, banks, insurance companies, trading chambers, et cetera was fashioned and managed by Whites to serve their ethnic community rather than the country at large.

The Structuralist School, furthermore, posits that the white minority acquired their economic advantage and hegemony under the most immoral and cruel conditions of slavery rather than through competitive market relations, and as such should be subject to historical redress and reparations.

The validation of these arguments requires an examination of the historical evidence, especially the data which relate to legislation as a means of favouring one section of the community over another. First of all, the evidence shows that both Blacks and Whites arrived in Barbados/the New World with cultural constructs that included long histories of familiarity with local and international trade, commercial agriculture, production-oriented technology and entrepreneurial values. During the early seventeenth century, when the English colonial project was established, West Africans could claim a longer record of international trade and commodity production than their fellow English settlers whom they outnumbered in Barbados in 1670. Soon after this juncture, however, white Barbados governments went about the task of suppressing, by means of legislation, the commercial culture of the black population.

Governments recognised that enslaved Blacks, on arrival in Barbados, would do what was natural to them; that is, set up markets to buy and sell goods, even within the restricted confines of plantation slavery. The first systematic discussion on black commerce in the House of Assembly took place in 1694. Two bills were brought before the House, both designed to penalise Blacks for practising commerce. After a decade of careful observation by the House, it was decided in 1708 that the time had come to act in the criminalisation of blacks' economic culture. The law was passed on January 6, 1708, the first of many in the eighteenth century. Entitled, 'An Act to Prohibit the Inhabitants of this island from Employing Negroes and other Slaves in Selling and Bartering', it attempted to tackle every aspect of Blacks' trade, both as a white-controlled enterprise and as an independent activity.

The preamble to the 1708 Act linked black trade to criminality and other anti-white activities with the following clauses:

> Whereas sundry [persons] do daily send their Negroes and other slaves to the several towns in this island . . . to sell and dispose of all sorts of Quickstock, corn fruit, and pulse, and other things . . . which they traffic among themselves, and buy, receive and dispose of all sorts of stolen good, be it enacted that: no person or persons whatsoever shall send or employ any negroe or negroes ... in selling, bartering, or disposing of any goods, wares, merchandize, stocks, poultry, corn fruit, roots, or other effects, or things whatsoever.

Provisions were made for the punishment of Whites who either purchased items from Blacks or employed them, as well as for Blacks themselves. Offending white persons found guilty could be fined, while 'all and every negro . . . who shall be found selling or bartering any of the before mentioned goods or commodities shall have and receive . . . one and twenty stripes on his or her bare back upon proof thereof made by any white person'.

Since some Whites, as a result of physical incapacity or illness, required trade with Blacks or needed Blacks to trade for them, provisions were made for this minority. It was in this regard that the white legislature sought to fully dehumanise Blacks in the market economy by associating them with the images of criminality. The 1708 law stated:

> . . . all such negroes . . . shall have at all times that he or she, or they are selling the same, a metaled collar locked about his or her or their necks or legs, with the name of his or her masters [engraved] thereon, and the name of the parish wherein they live, and also the name of the person who made such collar.

The law also provided that:

> The clerk of the market . . . is required to hire annually two able men . . . to apprehend any Negro or Negroes that come into the said town to sell, or dispose of any goods or commodities whatsoever without being licensed as aforesaid, either by having some white person with them, or a metal collar on his or her leg.

These clerks, as well as constables, were empowered:

> to diligently inspect the tipping houses, huckstering shops, markets, and all other suspected places within or near the said town, and in case they . . . shall find, or know of any white person or persons that shall trade, barter, or any ways deal with any negro or negroes, they shall proceed against such person as before in this Act is appointed, and in like manner against all negro or negroes.

The white community and elected representatives remained dissatisfied by the obvious ineffectual nature of these legislative provisions. Bridgetown continued to attract increasingly larger numbers of black traders from the countryside who, in addition to those resident in the town, appeared determined to ignore the laws restricting their business. During the two decades after the 1708 Law, reports reaching the Assembly confirmed the continued increase of black traders, once again forcing the Legislature into action. In 1733, a law entitled 'An Act for the Better Governing of Negroes, and the more Effectual Preventing of the inhabitants of this island, from employing their Negroes or other slaves in selling and bartering' was passed. This time it made specific references to the expansion in volume of goods, foodstuffs, and metals which Blacks traded in Bridgetown. It also specified the commodities in which Blacks could not trade under any circumstances.

The 1773 Law was more comprehensive than that of 1708. This was undoubtedly a result of the more extensive spread of black trade in the early eighteenth century and legislators' perception of it as a threat to white economic domination. The list of items which constables and market police were empowered to confiscate from Black traders included 'sugarcane, whole or in pieces, syrup, molasses, cotton, ginger, copper, pewter, brass, tin, corn and grain'. Particular concern was expressed for the welfare of marginal white traders and small planters who seemed unable to compete with black traders. In order to protect these persons, the 1733 Law provided that it should not be lawful for any Blacks to plant for use other than that of their masters:

> any cotton or ginger whatsoever, and that if any negro or other slave shall be found with any such, or exposing the same for sale, such cotton or ginger shall be deemed as stolen goods.

In addition, white persons who purchased such items from black traders were to be prosecuted at law as 'receivers of stolen goods'. This law was amended in 1749 with the insertion of a clause which made illegal the habit of Blacks 'assembling together at hucksters shops' to buy, sell or socialise.

The effects of these legislative provisions were never considered as satisfactory in the face of Blacks' persistent refusal to comply. The manager of Codrington Estate stated, in 1749, that nothing short of 'locking them up' could keep them away from markets, and such an action would probably result in riotous behaviour. In spite of the 1733 Act, and the 1749 amendment, Blacks continued to expand their participation in the internal market economy. The women, in particular, who were very active commercially, seemed most determined to ignore legislative provisions. The legislature, once again, came under political pressure from small white merchants claiming that black traders posed unfair competition and that the mobile nature of their businesses constituted a 'public nuisance on account of the noise and litter which surrounded them'.

The Assembly responded by appointing a committee to 'settle and bring in a Bill for putting a stop to the Traffic of Negroes'. The Bill became law on March 15, 1774, as 'An Art the better to prohibit Goods, Wares, and Merchandizes, and other things from being . . . sold, bartered, or disposed of (by) the traffic of Slaves, free mulattoes, and Negroes'. This law sought to diffuse almost half a century of accumulated anger in the white community generated from the spread of black business. This time, however, the emphasis of the legislature was not to do the impossible, that is, eradicate black commerce, but to confine it to petty levels, such as street vending; the objective being to ensure that slaves could not accumulate money by trade to purchase their freedom and that free Blacks could not participate in the property markets.

Provisions were made for the punishment of Blacks who sold, in addition to the already mentioned goods, butchers' meat, and for the prevention of selling 'on the Lord's Day', the only day that Blacks had free from plantation labour. It also made illegal blacks' business 'in or about any of the streets, alleys, passages or wharfs of any of the towns . . . or in or about any of the highways, broad-path and bays'. Blacks found guilty of those offences were to be imprisoned, put in the stocks by constables and have their goods confiscated. The Act, however, gave some measure of legitimacy to 'country' Blacks who were allowed to 'sell firewood and horsemeat' – items which posed no competition to white merchants and planters.

To those 'enterprising' Blacks, however, who played the market game by creating shortages and inflating prices, the legislators were particularly hostile:

> And whereas many injuries . . . do continually arise to the inhabitants . . . from the traffic of . . . negroes, who go on board vessels arriving here, and purchase from thence livestock to revend, and who also go a considerable

way out of the respective towns to meet such persons as bring in stock, fruit roots, and other produce, . . . and do buy up and engross the same, by which means the price of stock and provision are greatly advanced . . . , be it enacted . . . that no slave whatsoever shall either, on board of any vessel, on the land, buy up to revend, or engross, any live or dead stock . . . or any fruit, roots, vegetables or other produce.

Offending Blacks were liable to a penalty of 21 lashes on the bare back publicly laid on by the hangman or a constable. Since some offenders were likely to be women, the legislators provided that 'the punishment of slaves with child may, in all case, be respired'.

Sections of the white community remained dissatisfied and insisted upon renewed legislation for the eradication of black business. In 1779, the 1773 Act was amended by an 'Act to prohibit Goods, Wares and Merchandises and other things being carried from House to House or about the road and streets in this island, to be sold, bartered or disposed of ... from the traffic of Huckster Slaves, free mulattoes and negroes'. By this law, furthermore, the legislators intended that only free persons should be allowed to trade, thus removing most Blacks from the market economy. While severe physical penalties were established for Blacks under this law, poor whites and free mulattoes were required to obtain a trade licence which the treasurer was authorised to issue at a cost of £10 for one year, in addition to a fee of 25 shillings.

The 1779 Law was amended in 1784, providing a penalty of up to three months imprisonment for white persons convicted of buying 'cotton or ginger' from Blacks, illustrating the seriousness of the white legislature in removing the black economic threat. During the 1811 sitting of the Assembly, members received several reports which stated that 'Roebuck (a central Bridgetown street) was as much crowded as ever by country negroes selling their goods . . . .'

These traders, the report stated, were refusing to be physically confined. Roebuck Street was ideally placed and it attracted Blacks, in spite of stiff penalties attached to street vending. The Assembly was also informed that Blacks did not like fixed markets 'because the person about the markets set whatever price upon their commodities and the poor negroes are compelled to take that price . . . .' Freedom of movement, Blacks believed, was the most effective way of gaining control over prices. Bridgetown became a place of constant open hostility between Blacks and constables who policed commercial proceedings. Prisons were eventually fixed adjoining Bridgetown markets where 'disorderly' Black traders were imprisoned and flogged.

After 211 years of slavery, Barbadian Blacks entered the 'free period' as an economically pauperised, commercially disenfranchised people, lacking financial assistance or protection from the State and stripped naked by the virulent forces of supply and demand. From that time until now, generations of Blacks have launched a protracted struggle to obtain an equitable share of economic resources, participate equally in the market economy as owners and controllers of capital and entrench themselves within the economic environment as legitimate own-account agents in the accumulation process.

The struggle for economic enfranchisement, then, is as old as the presence of Blacks on the island, and is clearly endemic to the political process. This struggle has haunted the black and white political leadership from the beginning of the twentieth century when the political ideal of democracy was upheld. The democratic ethos called for the realisation of the principles of social equity and justice and equality within the legal and institutional environments. The long-standing economic disenfranchisement of Blacks by a white minority represented a contradiction to these principles, as well as a moral and ideological travesty. The political attempt to resolve this contradictory situation provided the motive force behind the 1937 Revolution.

Between 1955 and 1961, the newly formed Democratic Labour Party rising from the ashes of the Congress Party retreated from this tradition and sought less to integrate Blacks in the mainstream of the economy than to modernise white control of it.

Successive debate over the sugar industry, for example, degenerated into questions about management and organisation rather than ownership and control. Also, to questions of economic development, the Democratic Labour Party sought answers not in terms of black economic enfranchisement, but in tourism expansion, labour emigration, and sugar subsidies. Its electoral success in 1961, then, did not result in a return to Congress' 1940s policy of black economic enfranchisement.

Current debates about the relations between white economic power and black politics, therefore, have deep historic roots. That Blacks need to attain their economic franchise through economic democratisation is undoubtedly a matter of national importance at this time. Some have argued that there is an inevitability about this process and that the correct position to take is to abandon the politics of economic democracy and allow history to take its course; this way the reconstruction of Blacks' economic culture, devastated in part by slavery and post-slavery conditions, would be achieved. This position, however, illustrates a certain disregard for the forces and logic of history and an undeveloped understanding of institutional evolution.

The critical fact that should not be ignored is that all major structural democratic achievement that has been institutionalised in Barbados took place after serious social and political encounters, simply because of the time-honoured principle that privilege and power concede no ground without a major challenge. The Independence era, then, is yet to deliver, what for many citizens is the most significant civil rights achievement – the establishment of an economic culture in which patterns of ownership and control of productive resources are democratised. Perhaps historical lessons are rarely learned and structural change might be attained only after an event such as that in 1937 which delivered a wide range of political and constitutional advances.

Those who subscribe to the view that economic democracy is concerned simply with the redistribution of a fixed amount of wealth generating assets in favour of Blacks as part of a general economic redress against the historically privileged white property classes have shown no sensitivity to the democratic impulse. But they have been effective in keeping politicians on the defensive.

To avoid being charged with the adoption of Robin Hood tactics, political leaders suggest that, if the overall quantum of economic wealth is increased, the market would inevitably and eventually take care of an equitable redistribution. In this way, furthermore there would be no negative political implications and the democratic culture would not be further tainted by evidence of preferential racial treatment.

Only the economic mobilisation of the black community as commodity producers, systems innovators, corporate managers, investors and market creators – rather than mere political representatives and consumers – can provide the basis, at this particular historical juncture, for the establishment of the productivist ethos now urgently required. It is not an informed criticism that such a position is intellectually abstract and idealistic. On the contrary, it is based concretely on the empirical evidence available on the economic experiences of every developed market economy within the last 200 years. What this historical evidence indicates is that there is a fundamental misunderstanding and misconception of the relations between socioeconomic relations and structures and the attainment of economic growth.

Far too often, economists do not take note of historical forces in their assessments of the growth potential of communities. Their analyses, as a result, can be insufficiently time-specific or stage-oriented. They ought to consider three critical questions. First, what is the historically determined structural nature of the moment in which society functions? Second, are endemic historical forces tending towards the refashioning of structures and relations? Third, have existing structures and relations reached their maximum potential and are they largely responsible for diminishing returns and socioeconomic disequilibrium and dislocation? The answers to these questions point to the overriding conclusion that the dominant corporate community and corresponding asset-owning patterns are no longer capable of taking the country any further along the path of economic growth – either in isolation or in league with foreign entrepreneurial agents. As an economic elite, it has reached its maximum entrepreneurial, managerial and productive capacity, and is now in regression in both relative and absolute terms.

This regression is now threatening to take the entire country into an abyss characterised by anti-productivist values, market subservience, financial and monetary dependence – all reminiscent of the former colonial period in which it ruled unchallenged and without national responsibility. Only economic democratisation, the search for new economic agents and corporate vitality can advance the country in the medium and long term.

On the surface, it would seem that Barbados has the potential to hold its own within the rapidly transforming global economic order. The realisation of that potential, however, depends upon the attainment of economic democracy. Citizens need to acquire national attitudes in which a productivist impulse is endemic. The will to produce and reproduce value must be developed as a cultural response – fashioned by formal education and reinforced by social example. For historical reasons, only the white community has been properly placed to acquire this consciousness. Logically, then, only in an economic environment in which value creation is democratically feasible can this mentality be universally attained.

If the black community is not fully welcomed within the market institutions, but made to experience frustration, rejection and embarrassment, the vehicle of national economic mobilisation will be derailed. History seems to suggest that certain boats do not make return trips. First, we must start with the facts. Blacks in general are structurally excluded from the corporate institutional network and social culture. The truth is that access to the institutions, capital and knowledge that are necessary for value creation are denied the majority population in the course of everyday life.

This is irrational, irresponsible, anti-nationalist and inefficient. That is, it functions in ways contrary to national mobilisation. Three hundred Euro-Barbadian entrepreneurs could run Barbados' plantation economy in 1850; they cannot run the diversified economy today, nor at any time in the future. This massive legacy of black economic subjection has to be uprooted and removed. The role of the state is vital here – not only in terms of social persuasion, but for strategic economic legislation. Access to private sector directorates and senior management levels should be seen as functioning democratically. The base of corporate knowledge

– the ways and means of wealth generation – has to be widened and kept opened.

The more informed and skilled the nation's corporate agents, the greater the chances of creating a large pool of effective entrepreneurs. The reason being that top corporate positions constitute two important economic assets; one, an apprenticeship in value creation capability; two, a nursery for young entrepreneurial talent.

The logic of this argument should be fully obvious. Black businesses have a great chance of survival when owners and managers are critically positioned within the economic environment to access equity and information.

Few persons would disagree that there exists in Barbados today a significant pool of competent, knowledgeable black executives and managers. Even fewer persons would disagree that such persons are in general unwilling to cut loose from their salaried positions and transform themselves into own-account entrepreneurs with employment generating capacity.

The reason commonly given by such persons for their inertia is that the white controlled market economy is particularly hostile to Blacks and, therefore, their degree of risk-taking is much greater than their white counterparts. Since the organs of governments were taken over by Blacks 40 years ago, no systematic effort has been made to clean up the market environments by removing pollutants such as corporate racism, nepotism, inbreeding and insider close-shops – all of which have adversely affected the market performances of the black majority.

During this period, these non-market methods used for the marginalisation of Blacks have gained virulence because of the impotence and ideological confusion of the democratic state. The culture of manufacturing, promoted and developed by black entrepreneurs during the 1960s and 1970s, has been systematically starved of equity by a hostile money market controlled by whites and by the state's soft response with respect to the need for research and development in industrial growth. Meanwhile, the State and the equity markets continue to show support for the pillars of white corporate activity – in agriculture, tourism and distribution.

In no other sector of the economy have black people accumulated more skills and information necessary for growth than in agriculture. Yet, it is here that the degree of alienation, frustration and rejection continues to be evident at high levels. For over 300 years, the economic potential and ambition of Blacks have been frustrated in this sector as a result of white hegemonic ownership. Rural black folks remain to this day essentially a landless, resourceless, alienated people, squatting on lands to which they have an unquestionable moral right to own and use as the basis of long-term accumulation strategies.

That Barbados needs a sound development plan which is designed to place the rural black community in a central ownership relation to the agricultural enterprise should be clearly obvious by now. The use of sugar subsidies to prop up and maintain a fossilised eighteenth century racist rural civilisation under the guise of seeking productive efficiency has to be abandoned as constituting an inefficient use of scarce resources and a breeding ground for social discord. Rather, common sense suggests the adoption of a restructuring programme that seeks greater productivity and efficiency in resource use in a reorganisation of ownership patterns and structures.

At present, the government is legally and morally positioned to enfranchise the rural black population in its search for economic revitalisation in this sector. The much overrated tenantry legislation that seeks to entrench Blacks on the periphery of the dominant white rural enterprise is evidence of the abandonment of responsibility by the Black-managed State for rural folks. It smacks of the immediate post-slavery approaches by planters to secure black labour without challenging the dictates of the plantation as the primary emissary of European civilisation.

Sector by sector, we need to put our economy under the microscope and find antidotes for the viruses that are responsible for the high mortality of black enterprises. In tourism, on the equity markets, in manufacturing, agriculture and construction, Blacks have always expected the State to promote openness, fairness and justice. This is a prerequisite for the proliferation of entrepreneurs. Economic environments are not acts of God, but social constructs that can be adjusted, refashioned and honed to accommodate any social group targeted by macro-policy initiatives. Access to market institutions, corporate information and skills, affirmative action with respect to the land question and the promotion of value-creating education are the basic requirements of an economic democratic order.

- *Seven* -

Mutual Affair:
Struggle for Economic Democracy

$\mathscr{S}$ince independence, Barbados, like those states in other regional territories, has realised that political sovereignty could best be maintained by means of the acquisition of economic power. It also recognised that poverty was not inevitable; furthermore, the problem of poverty could not be left to the normal working of the local and international market. The history of the country, along with that of the economically developed nations, shows clearly that non-market methods were also critical in the development process.

What could be said of economically advanced countries could also be said of the agro-commercial elite in Barbados. It is an elite with deep roots within the slave system of the seventeenth to nineteenth centuries. Then, in association with Britian, it maintained a cruel and vicious regime of human exploitation that has done immeasurable damage to the collective consciousness of African people and their Creole progeny. Over time, this slave-owning elite transformed its relations to society, absorbed poorer whites and here and there a few non-whites, but at all times deepened and strengthened its opposition to black peoples' aspirations.

In the process of maintaining its economic hegemony, the elite used its control of the state, the church, and other civic organisations, again in association with the imperial support systems, in order to create an economic environment in which the black population was made to feel unacclimatised. When Blacks were bold enough to enter the marketplace as entrepreneurs, they were supposed to die as if by viral infection and natural law. Until recently, institutional racism, social apartheid and police systems were normal instruments used in the process of keeping Blacks in a predominatly labour relation to this elite. Some poor-white families were uplifted into the elite by means of marriage ties and other economic and social alliances. This dynamic process assisted the elite in making the argument that such persons entered their open-ended culture as a result of hard work and perseverance, characteristics not readily found among Blacks. In this context, the origins, development and current adjustments of the Barbados Mutual Life Assurance Society (BMLAS) can be discussed, showing the significance of its institutional history to the rise of national corporate capitalism and the corresponding race relations ethos.

During the mid-1980s black policyholders at the BMLAS launched a campaign against their exclusion. As the national debate intensified, the eyes of the financial world focussed on Barbados, long considered the leading centre of international finance in the Eastern Caribbean. The news flashed through London, New York, Toronto, Washington and Geneva. Shortly thereafter the *Jamaica Record*, a daily newspaper, picked up the discussions in Barbados and carried a number of very informative feature stories on black marginalisation in the Jamaican economy. These articles, written by the distinguished Professors Rex Nettleford and the late Carl Stone of the University of the West Indies, did not excite their readers to the same degree as the campaign in Barbados, mainly because black entrepreneurs and executives have made much greater headway in Jamaica than their Barbadian counterparts. In this regard, Jamaican society is considerably more open than Barbados, the reason being their different social and political histories.

The *Economist*, carried a report on Barbados in the July 8, 1989 edition. Entitled 'The browning of Barbados: racial conflict and frenetic social change', it laid bare some of the relevant features for readers:

> The small island's largest insurance company holds a meeting to elect two new directors and change its deed of settlement. No thrills there, one might think. But tempers run high, accusation meets counteraccusation, a great national issue takes shape. Two thousand policyholders besiege a hall

designed for a few hundred, the air-conditioning fails, amendments fly, the meeting is adjourned. Is the board trying to pull a fast one on the policyholders? The board is mostly white, the policyholders are mostly black. This may be a storm in a teacup at the start of the hurricane season. But the Barbados Mutual has total assets not all that much smaller than those of the nation's central bank. And if Caribbean teacups get too stormy, someone may get scalded.

The *Economist* had much more to say about the state of affairs in Barbados. The feature writer was frank about the matter and wrote clearly on what was seen as the harsh reality of the local circumstance:

After 23 years of independence, Barbadians are still trying to decide just who they are. Most are black, some white, a few descended from more recent Indian immigrants. The whites form about the same proportion of the population as do blacks in Britain, say 3%. They ran the place for most of its history. Although slavery ended more than 150 years ago, it is only in the past few decades that work for most blacks has meant something other than cutting cane in the hot sun.

The Barbados parliament is 350 years old this year, but for only a tenth of its history has the island enjoyed majority rule and universal suffrage. Forty years ago all its black members somehow got left off the guest list for a Government House reception; for a royal wedding there was whites-only housing in the capital; and it was near to impossible for the black Barbadian to get a job as a bank clerk or a jockey, let alone a manager or accountant. Lately the island has prospered. Working class people probably own a car and a well built house with indoor plumbing. Most politicians, senior civil servants and public sector managers are black. Lawyers, doctors, accountants and professionals may be any human colour. Nobody in his right mind wants to own a sugar plantation these days: property, retailing, building and tourism are where the money is now. The companies do have black senior managers (two sit on the board of the Barbados Mutual). But that does not stop them being perceived as white businesses.

Most 'big' Barbados companies would be prosperous family firms in Britain or America. In a family firm, family members naturally get promoted, so young whites sometimes get promotion over experienced blacks. Work sometimes get contracted out to a second cousin or classmate from primary school; there, too, whites may sometimes give jobs to whites.

One of the fascinating things about this report is that it would not have appeared in a local newspaper. Journalists have not yet been given the freedom to help their society to look fairly and squarely at itself and quite often the public can only read these rather frank and precise accounts of the national experience in the foreign press. Columnists, such as Waldron-Ramsey, are relied upon to perform this task. In one of his Sunday columns he noted:

> In the Mutual dispute, the proposal to put more Black directors on its Board, is seen as an attempt to diffuse the efficiency of The Mutual by inflicting inexperienced Blacks upon its arm of decision and policy-making. The truth is, there is nothing special about being a director of the Mutual or any joint-stock company. The Mutual has not been successful over the years, since 1840, especially because of the directors it has had. The truth is that The Mutual could not help but to be successful. Parliament and colonialism and its practices created a virile and safe environment within which the Mutual could thrive. The Mutual was created for the benefit of white people, in the first place. There has been no single director or group of them, who has been so outstandingly brilliant in anything on its Board, that can be held as the reason for the Mutual's success over the years. What Dr. Hilary Beckles has been doing is to expose and lay bare the de-mystification of the legend that, even after independence, Barbadians of the African race are not yet ready to assume the mantle of leadership in the domain of economic power of this country. He argues, safely and correctly, in my considered view, that Africans, or Afro-Barbadians, have been systematically kept out of the commanding heights of industry and commerce by a rigid and ancient colonial Euro-Barbadian complex, determined to retain industrial and commercial power at all costs. There can be no argument, but that there must be a distillation of that matrix of economic power. And the total argument must envisage a reassessment of the peaceful transformation of a colonial society, into a post-independence society positioned on the Benthamite principle of providing the greatest happiness for the greatest number.

Waldron-Ramsey touched upon the nerve centre of the national crisis, and his suggestion for advancement reflected clearly what those persons in the movement for 'change without chaos' had been articulating for some time; that is, democracy will be real only when access to the means of production and distribution is also democratised. Until such time, resistance to oligarchical domination will persist. These points have been made by persons who are aware that privilege and power concede no ground unless challenged by an organised force. This assumption lies at the heart of the national crisis which became known as 'The Mutual Affair'.

Throughout the crisis, pressure was brought to bear on those persons articulating the nature of change to theorise more precisely the situation. The question commonly asked was this: what is the ideological lineage of the concepts and actions? The answer to this question is most complex, unless it is assumed, as many commentators did, that a primitive analytical 'black-white' explanation was in action. Social theory, at its best, should emerge from a careful and historically informed reading of situations, and from this point of view the dialectical relations between class, culture and race in the context of economic and social development, must be placed at the centre of what was 'The Mutual Affair'.

It is true, as evident by the manner in which events developed, that the debate was essentially opening doors for the repressed, black corporate middle class. Historically, this group has been coerced into submission by the owners of capital, whose power over their career aspirations has remained substantial. These groups then, abandoned in the corporate world by the state they support, and lacking an organisational base of their own, or even a real foundation in the ownership of large scale productive capital (not money income), have been sitting in limbo waiting for a runner to start the race and pass them the baton.

The awakening of professional Blacks to an appreciation of their interest and historical destiny, therefore, was seen as a major objective. The debate was conducted in terms of the interest of the underprivileged, but analysts said that the campaign would be for the betterment of the professionals who had historically seized moments to project their aspirations. It is true that persons so defined who, hitherto, had been critical of concepts of economic change, had requested that the radicals recede and leave 'it' to them.

It seems clear, however, that such a conception of the popular action as seen in the Mutual Affair was rather limited and misleading. What was said all along, with increasing clarity, was that there is need to remove all the bottlenecks within the corporate world that prevent the rise of the best human resources. Institutional racism and racial 'inbreeding' have been identified as two forces operative in the private sector that prevented the optimum allocation of resources for institutional and national efficiency. In addition, these forces lead to the creation of hostile relations, not only in the workplace, but also in the wider society; such hostility is negative in that it is not conducive to resource productivity and social stability.

Ultimately, only economic action of the highest level of the state can advance the wider societal interest of marginalised social groups; and events such as the Mutual Affair will assist in creating the conditions for that eventuality. From this point of view, then, the Mutual Affair has certainly not been entirely an exercise in professional adventurism and careerism. Though such persons, in the short term, benefitted from the increased opportunities, the principles of democracy were advanced and, with the maturation of the concept of civil rights, the most alienated people will be better placed to clearly formulate their own agenda for further change.

The historical evidence shows clearly that the BMLAS had functioned for over 100 years as a leading financial bastion of racism against Blacks in Barbados. The circumstances surrounding its early development were characterised by the need to keep Blacks in the labour category as far as economic resources were concerned. Even during the mid-twentieth century, most Blacks in Barbados believed that the Mutual represented, perhaps more so than the imperial governor or even the statue of Lord Nelson at the top of Broad Street, the consolidation of white power in its ideological and economic dimensions. Blacks were forced to tiptoe into the Mutual; they could not expect to work there in any prestigious occupation. The Mutual was the symbol of white financial power and, hence, black marginalisation.

The corporate power of the Mutual is vested in the hands of the board of directors and senior officers who saw themselves as autonomous, in the sense that they did not view themselves as fully accountable to policyholders of all kinds. They hold substantial power, even though many of them do not own extensive property themselves. The team of largely white managers (a few non-white persons are admitted, but they have to be socially and politically loyal) had shaped the image of the Mutual at the level of the policyholder; and over the years had been unencouraging to black policyholders whose interests they are paid to represent. More often than not, these white managers were not formally educated for these positions, but landed their jobs as a result of family and other social connections within the white community.

These managerial whites had linked their own group interests to those of whites who own corporate wealth. Such wealth must not be confused with money income. The wealth of Barbados, measured in terms of marketable assets, such as land, buildings, machinery, raw materials, goods in process, stocks, bonds, animals, franchises, patent rights, copyrights and goodwill, resides mainly in the hands of whites, among whom are a few Jews and Indians. Though little is known about the detailed pattern of wealth distribution in Barbados, the general picture suggests that this thesis is essentially correct and that the BMLAS had been critical to the process of wealth accumulation in the white communities from the time of its establishment in 1840. In this sense, it had been instrumental in ensuring that, with the rise of the merchant corporations which they financed at the beginning of the twentieth century, a major distinction exists between wealth and income.

A close examination of the BMLAS illustrated the extent to which the white elite, by means of interlocking directorships and corporate financing, had long represented certain 'interest groups' at the expense of most policyholders. These interest groups, located mostly in the white community, were to be found in the merchant houses, finance houses and major local corporations within the country. The thrust of this situation had been to foster a building up of white power in the corporate sector. The socioeconomic nature of these developments was revealed in the way in which the finances of the Mutual, for example, were used, especially in the allocation of contracts that involve construction projects. Policyholders were kept ignorant and ill-informed while some directors and senior officers were privy to information, skills and connections obtained by virtue of being on the Mutual team. It is believed, furthermore, that cases involving conflict of interest based on access to 'inside information' were not far removed from the activities of some directors, though Barbados' company laws, unlike the USA's, do not see such business practices as undesirable.

Meanwhile, black policyholders, and some whites as well, were disturbed by the way their money was used to protect and expand these interest groups which, in turn, functioned in a manner hostile to their occupational and economic aspirations. The Mutual had therefore become closely interlocked with the major corporate entities, though the average policyholder, until the educational campaign launched by the Association of Concerned Policyholders, knew little about the investment interests it had across the economy. Indeed, because of the interlocking nature of the Mutual's board with those of other large corporations, it could not be termed an 'independent fiduciary'.

In a column published in the *Barbados Advocate* of Friday, September 30, 1988, Elombe Mottley, a popular cultural icon, got down to the core of the problem facing the democratic movement in Barbados and the Caribbean. After more than two decades of national independence, and after some 40 years of democratic political administration, he noted that the corporate affairs of the country were still essentially controlled by the white minority which had continued to place its ideology of ethnic solidarity and exclusiveness before the principle of democratic nationalism. According to Mottley:

> Because of inbreeding, The Mutual still fosters a management style and structure that allow blacks two token directors on the Board. The same concept applies to senior management positions. As a matter of fact, if I were to treat them like ink spots and pass a piece of blotting paper across

Bridgetown, a few persons would notice that the blotting paper was soiled. Inbreeding, not just nepotism.

The crisis at the BMLAS emerged when black policyholders began to express an interest in sitting on the Board of Directors in order to participate in the management of their capital which, hitherto, Whites believed they had a right to control, as if by nature and custom. The basic issue was clear: the white board members had seen the society as an avenue to their own corporate expansion and aggrandisement, and had used institutional power to marginalise black policyholders whose money they managed. For years blacks sat passively and watched. Here was a black Mutual Society, a 'socially white' board, daily saying to blacks, 'hand over your premiums and goodbye'.

For many policyholders, the crisis at their Mutual was more than a problem of the use of institutional power against them. It was a moral question. Indeed, during the campaign to have progressive and conscientious blacks elected to the board, Father Harcourt Blackett, a popular Roman Catholic priest, made his intervention on the basis that the tradition of excluding black policyholders was a moral issue. Others considered the crisis to be reflective of an unfortunate political division of labour within the post-Independence era, which established a compromise that allowed Blacks control of the state machinery and Whites control of the corporate sector. That compromise is now seen to be outdated, racist and crisis-ridden. The question which Mottley asked was the same as that asked across the country from late September 1988 to present. It is this:

> Am I therefore out of place to ask blacks, what should be their view with respect to their ownership of the Barbados Mutual Life Assurance Society? Should the ownership be subjected to in-breeding decisions (of whites) and policies of inbreeding? Should all policyholders have access to the same opportunity? For whom does the bell toll?

Mottley added that should blacks be allowed to represent their capital and their Society at all levels, the society would benefit. Such a development, he added, would be 'cross fertilization, not stagnation and inactive in-breeding'. This would allow 'opportunities for new ideas, greater growth and more rewarding harvest, less idiots and morons,' Mottley added.

From time to time, especially during the nineteenth century, policyholders of the BMLAS would accuse the board of not taking sufficient measures to inform them – the owners of the Society – of their rights in general, and about specific decisions that could fundamentally affect their interests. The board, under these circumstances, would be accused of placing the interests of certain 'special groups' above and beyond those of policyholders. This was especially so during the late nineteenth century when its investments in plantation lands were rapidly expanding.

During the 1890s, A.J. Pile, a director and a member of the Pile family that had amassed considerable plantation property on the island, some of it through direct involvement with the Mutual, was particularly concerned that the Mutual should not disclose information about the island's land market to all policyholders. Such information, solicited by the board through Pile, was kept away from other policyholders and used by directors, including Pile, to further their own land accumulation interests. The argument used by the board then was that such information, if made available to policyholders in general, would adversely affect the Society's particular speculative standing on the land market. This argument had long been used as a cover for the enhancement of the individual economic interest of directors and senior officers.

Because the Board of the BMLAS at the end of the nineteenth century was dominated by sugar planters and commodity merchants, it functioned as a clearing house for the family interests of directors, especially in relation to the land market. Directors made personal applications to the board for finance to obtain estates for their own use. Many directors used their influence on the board to amass estates and other forms of property. For example, at the end of the century, persons such as Mr Charles Cottle, Mr Gowdy and Thomas Gill assembled extensive properties by using the Society's finance while sitting on its board. The minute books of the Mutual show these developments quite clearly. On this point, Karch noted:

> While Charles Cottle was a Director of the Society, he was also Solicitor for many plantations which came before the Board, and he voted on measures affecting his interests when they were presented. Many other Directors of the Board owned or acquired plantations in this period. For example, Gowdy owned Cane Vale and Montrose, and was present when the question of lateness of payment came before the Board.

Moving from the late nineteenth to the late twentieth century, little had changed. Much of this 'insider trading' culture remained part of the normal function of the Society. Indeed, it would not be difficult to show how the board continued to be used as an institution for enhancing certain vested interests; some directors had even developed, over the decades, a perspective which suggested that they had a right of access to the benefits the Society could confer. Black policyholders, however, had not been placed in a position to so benefit, though the few black directors over the years had greatly enhanced their status and incomes in several ways. In this sense, the board represents the conjuncture of race and class in Barbados during the late twentieth century. It remained essentially an elite white instrument, and the few blacks admitted were accepted by virtue of their class association with the racial ideologies and interests of white groups.

In any case, the small policyholders who were not members of this privileged social and economic elite, had been kept ignorant of their rights and not briefed on how to use the facilities of the Society to increase their general interests. It is clear that, historically, the board had no intention of inviting the bulk of policyholders in on their guarded secrets. After all, it was clear that the Society had historically been a fatted calf on which 'interest groups', by means of being directors and senior officers, fed.

It was commonly alleged that, over the decades, the Mutual management had made no serious effort to inform policyholders, outside of the special clique that kept them afloat, of their basic rights within their Society. Most of these policyholders who are Afro-Barbadian did not know that they had a right to:

(a)   Attend the Annual General Meeting
(b)   Nominate directors to the board of the Society
(c)   Become elected directors of the Society

Since the Mutual management was dominated by Euro-Barbadians, and the vast majority of policyholders are Afro-Barbadians, it seemed reasonable to assume that the old colonial technique of keeping citizens ill-informed and ignorant in order to rule and manipulate them could not be far removed from the circumstances surrounding the functions of the board.

The vast majority of policyholders, who were black, had no idea about the investments of their Mutual, and did not understand, therefore, the meaning of the term 'All profits belong to the policyholders'. They were kept aware, however, of all new insurance packages offered by the Society, as this was one way to extract more revenues from them while keeping them out of the picture in relation to their rights.

This situation was a disturbing one, since the policyholder was frequently reminded that The Mutual 'is your Society'. What did this slogan mean for the average black policyholder? Everyone knew what it meant for corporate companies and the white elite community. To remedy this situation, and all other related illnesses, the Mutual was called upon to publish and circulate a newsletter or newspaper among policyholders on a monthly basis to inform them about the following:

(a)   management appointments and staff development;
(b)   investment patterns and ownership values;
(c)   trends within the industry, such as new insurance packages, medical requirements, technology and public relations/ marketing methods;
(d)   social and cultural outreach activities of the Society.

The Mutual and the 1937 Rebellion

During the 1920s, the democratic movement, organised around the energies of persons such as Dr Charles Duncan O'Neal, Clennell Wickman, Herbert Seale and the Garveyites, found that the BMLAS represented the central financial pivot of the racist planter-merchant alliances that stood in the way of popular democratic change. Indeed, the Mutual Building on Broad Street symbolised all that the democratic leaders objected to in Barbadian society. Blacks were not welcome at the Mutual, and all efforts were made to frustrate their willingness to become policyholders. Some blacks who managed to secure policies during the 1930s, for example, still talk about the mountains of discrimination they had to climb. They will also tell you that, when they walked into the Mutual building, white officers refused to attend to them until all the white clients had completed their business, even though they had arrived at the office before the whites.

Because the Mutual building on Broad Street symbolised economic and social apartheid in Barbados during the 1930s, it was not surprising that Clement Payne, the black liberator, had found it necessary to address matters relating to corporate finance. Payne's argument was that the business community had found the basis for ethnic solidarity in relation to the democratic movement. In one of his speeches he informed his working class audience: 'The Chamber of Commerce and Provision Dealers are all organised. Organise for the sake of your children.' Relating the need for a powerful black workers movement for his own campaign, he stated: 'I have come to the slums to organise you. I could have gone among the aristocrats, but they are deceitful. You have the ability and are able to judge things for yourself.' Payne then added: 'The white man's heaven is his V8 car, radio and four meals per day. You want the same!'

On July 26, 1937, the dastardly deportation of Clement Payne from Barbados to Trinidad by the government was followed by the congregation of workers at the Mutual building on Board Street. This move was to be expected. The Mutual was representative of all that they struggled against. The large, arguing crowd that surrounded the Mutual building, therefore, was acting in direct response to the perceived nature of power relations within the society at large. The objectives of the crowd in relation to the Mutual building were clear. They intended to burn it to the ground, including its occupants.

The building was placed under siege and employees were barricaded inside. Also locked in were the staff of Cable and Wireless Co. Ltd. They had put up 'heavy wooden shutters' to protect themselves against missiles coming from the crowd. The attempt to seize the Mutual building went on for at least three hours. Stones were thrown, windows broken, cars overturned and provisions made to consume it with fire; this was seen as one way to remove the scourge of racism from the face of the colony. The staff of the Mutual as well as that of Cable and Wireless could hear the crowd being urged to kill 'the blasted sons of white bitches'.

Shortly before noon, preparations were going forward to burn the Mutual building. Fire was alight and combustible materials were put in place. While these plans were being implemented, however, a squad of armed police came to the rescue of those employees within the building. Blank shots were fired at the Mutual arsonists and, 'by noon, detachments of police armed with rifles and fixed bayonets, smarting from the verbal abuse and physical bruises from stones and bricks the night before, were pursuing disorganised groups of rioters through the downtown areas'. Some of the 'Mutual arsonists' were killed in the pursuit and, according to Bonham Richardson, 'for the rest of the day an ominous silence hung over Bridgetown'. Once again, powerless black persons had lost their lives in a heroic attempt to remove the forces of oppression and domination from their social world. This time, at the height of their rebellion, they turned against the BMLAS which was perceived as representing these forces. That the BMLAS should find itself at the centre of black protest for justice and equality can only be illustrative of the terms and conditions under which it had functioned in the previous 97 years.

The Campaign for Economic Democracy

In 1987, the Bussa Committee was established. One of its main concerns was to bring a democratic ethos to bear upon the corporate system and the economic scene in general. The Bussa Committee had, at its core, a hardworking, dedicated team of persons from varying occupational and social backgrounds, but all with a clear grasp of this issue. Its task was to sensitise the community to economic matters and to assist it to become sophisticated in its responses to financial institutions. Fr Harcourt Blackett, the chairman of the committee, believed that social and race relations in Barbados could be improved and made acceptable to all only in the context of removing the obstacles to egalitarian, material use and control. For him, this was a fundamental question of social justice and human rights, both of which are above the realm of normal party politics and closer to the principles embedded in the Christian faith.

While accepting these points without difficulty, it also seemed that the long tradition of black economic powerlessness could not be addressed only in these terms. Serious and determined mass political mobilisation would be necessary to achieve any measure of democratic advancement. The history of Barbados, from the slavery period to the present, has illustrated this point, and the present conjuncture seems to conform to this general reading. For these reasons, the Bussa Committee coined the term 'economic democracy' and concluded, from an historical analysis of the civil rights movement, that the struggle for its attainment was going to be the hallmark of the next major epoch in our nationalist history. In this regard, the Bussa Committee was made up of patriots and nationalists who were determined to push the society along the path that historical forces had determined. For coining the term 'economic democracy', the committee was branded by sections of the media as radicals, communists and 'misfits'. But these statements had not deterred them; they saw themselves as falling within a tradition that had already gained some measure of support among well thinking persons, civil rights activists and humanists.

A number of discussions on the economy were held by the Bussa Committee. At one stage, it considered the establishment of an economic reform committee to investigate and disseminate information on the suppression of black entrepreneurs, institutional racism and the general ill-use of human resources in the corporate sector. It was obvious to most members that the human talents and energies in the country were not being used efficiently because of these bottlenecks and irrational obstacles within the market places.

These discussions intensified during the course of 1987 and early 1988. The call-in radio programmes, the print media, the street corners, the constituency political branches carried heated debates on the subject of black economic rights. One sensed, at all times, that the nation was waking up after a long slumber to recognise that the tradition of excluding the social majority from large-scale economic management and the ownership of productive capital was unacceptable. At times, however, the leaders seemed overwhelmed by awareness of the magnitude of the damage done to the economic culture of black people during the 211 years of chattel slavery, and the 100 years of neo-slavery. The corporate world, at times, seemed permanently out of reach for black people. At times, many persons believed, in relation to blacks and economic power, that the horse had already bolted. At other times, the same persons would insist on the need to keep up the struggle for the children and for the country.

Until May/June 1988, the Mutual had not entered into the debate in any specific sense. Statements and discussions were general. The committee spoke of the national economy and the institutional structure without focussing upon any one corporate entity. There was, however, the crisis which surrounded the government's decision to allocate a major road building contract to a black firm, Rayside Construction Company Limited. This decision resulted in the largest white construction firm on the island, C.O. Williams and Company Limited (which claimed to have made the lower tender) taking the government and the Minister of Works, Dr Don Blackman, to court with the charge that racial discrimination had entered the deliberations of the cabinet.

Dr Blackman, who possessed one of the finest intellects extant, and by far the most articulate political spokesperson of his generation, was very popular among the working classes and sections of the progressive middle classes. He suggested that, in the context of a post-colonial society, some measure of state-sponsored affirmative action was necessary in order to build the national economy and create the prerequisites for resource mobilisation and social stability. It seemed clear that, in order to bring competition to the construction industry and expand the number of viable firms within the industry, it was necessary to spread government expenditures (taxpayers' money) among a wider range of economic agents.

During the month of July 1988, discussions about black economic marginalisation in the corporate sector intensified. The number of persons making their contributions increased rapidly and call-in radio programmes were dominated by the theme. To some extent, the responses from the powerful mercantile elite, with its firm grip over the distributive sector, were rather disappointing. They cried out 'racism!' and claimed that there were certain elements within the society who were hell bent on advancing the interests of the black community at the expense of all whites. The inability of these merchants to grasp the finer details and intricacies of the arguments illustrated, to some extent, an unwillingness to embrace change.

As emotions ran high in July and the charge of racism was levelled against those who spoke in favour of more corporate democracy and greater opportunities for qualified black managerial executives, a breath of fresh air blew over the country with the contribution of Roman Catholic Bishop of Bridgetown, Anthony Dickson. Prior to his intervention, Bishop Dickson had been under pressure from some elements within and without the Catholic church to use his authority in order to 'gag' the outspoken priest, Fr Harcourt Blackett, who was based at the Church of Our Lady of the Universe in Black Rock, St Michael. Bishop Dickson obviously understood the relationship between the anti-democratic mobilisation of vested interests and the need for Christian social values to prevail. In a radio broadcast, which was published by the

Daily Nation on July 6, 1988, under the title 'Facing up to the Issues of Social Justice', Bishop Dickson made some rather incisive statements, some of which are extracted below:

Allegations of racism, discrimination, social and economic injustice, are once again topics for public and private debate. For some people the emergence of these topics are a cause of anxiety, fear, anger, and disgust. Some would hope that these issues would go away so that we can once again settle down to life as usual. But is it not our experience that ugly things swept under the carpet have a way of emerging when least expected? Is it not better to try in a systematic and positive way to face and work through these issues with a view of having a clearer and objective understanding of them and arriving at solutions which will be lasting and beneficial to all?

Social Justice
Moreover, although rightful differences exist between persons, the equal dignity of persons demands that a more humane and just condition of life be brought about. For excessive economic and social differences between the members of one human family or population groups cause scandal, and militate against social justice, equity, and the dignity of the human person. Human institutions, both private and public, must labour to minister to the dignity and purpose of human beings. At the same time let them put up a stubborn fight against any kind of slavery, whether social or political, and safeguard the basic rights of persons under every political system. (No. 29 The Church in the Modern World).

Aspiration to Equality and Participation
Though we may not wish to dwell on the past, but look to the future, the fact remains that a person's past has a great deal of influence upon him. So does the history of any race. The experiences of slavery, dispossession, inferiority and inadequacy have left deep psychological and emotional wars on the black peoples of the world, not excluding Barbados. These scars do not disappear just so. They do not go away by encouraging people to forget the past. One way of helping to heal these scars is to assist the black population in this country to fulfil their deep aspirations to equality and participation. These aspirations grow stronger, and their fulfillment more urgent, the more persons become better informed and better educated. These aspirations are legitimate since, within a country which

belongs to each one, all should be equal before the law, find equal admittance to economic, cultural, civic and social life and benefit from a fair sharing of the nation's resources.

Racism
Two obstacles to the fulfillment of the legitimate aspiration of the black community to equality and participation have been racism and an inadequate understanding of the right to private property. Racism [that] signifies that one race is superior to the other, often gives rise to bitterness and is the muse of division and hatred. The proponents of racism thought nothing of keeping the doors closed to the inferior race, thus preventing its participation in the economic, cultural, civic and social life of the nation. Racism is such [an] evil since it is contrary to the dignity of the human person, the essential equality of all persons, is an obstacle to human solidarity and an affront to the Creator.

In spite of Bishop Dickson's attempted elevation of the debate to a more vigorous moral and philosophical level, interventions from the white community were invariably focussing on the largely mythical subject of Blacks' racism against Whites. Some insisted that Blacks were mobilising themselves in order to dispossess Whites of their wealth and property. In spite of claims to the contrary, that what was wanted was equal opportunity, these claims persisted. By throwing the racism argument like a 'red herring across the trail', many Blacks came to identify with these sentiments.

Defenders of the elite white business community went all out to discredit the call for economic equality. Comparisons with Hitler's anti-Jewish (anti-black as well) insanity was also thrown in the ring in order to suggest that the ideas had bloodthirsty intentions. Claims were made that black radicals ultimately wanted to drive Whites off the island and steal their property.

In spite of such unconstructive statements, David Comissiong, a young, intelligent senator within the Democratic Labour Party, was impressed with the objectives of the movement and, in his weekly column in the *Sunday Sun* of July 10, 1988, argued firmly that Whites have a nationalist responsibility to help level racial imbalances within the corporate system. He argued this point clearly and placed it within the correct historical context. He wrote:

> On Tuesday, July 5, 1988, Bishop Anthony Dickson, the leader of the Roman Catholic Church in Barbados, delivered what must surely be one of the most profound and valuable public statements ever made in this country. In his statement, the Bishop displayed a deep Christian understanding of, and empathy with, the aspirations to full equality and participation on the part of the masses of black Barbadians. He also exhibited a clear vision of the just Christian society which must be our ultimate objective in Barbados, as well as a firm determination to face up to the unpleasant issues of race and injustice in a realistic and rational manner, and to put in place practical solutions. What makes the Bishop's statement all the more compelling and valuable, is the fact that Bishop Dickson is a white man. This is a very significant circumstance, which says to us that the task of creating a just and equal society in Barbados, is not the task of black people alone, but of their white brothers and sisters as well.

There was, however, one development in the media which was most significant. It was an encounter between corporate chief Philip Goddard of Goddard Enterprises Limited and the author.

Goddard and Commissiong met in the Voice of Barbados Studios as panellists on a programme moderated by David Ellis on the question of obstacles to Blacks in the corporate sector. Mr John Bellamy, president of the Chamber of Commerce, had already admitted that racism against Blacks has been a problem within the private sector, and that some members of his organisation were doing their best to reduce its impact. Mr Bobby Morris, Democratic Labour Party Member of Parliament, had taken up Mr Bellamy's statements and charged the private sector with harbouring ideologies not conducive to national economic development.

Against this background, Mr Richie Haynes, former Minister of Finance, speaking at a Highgate gathering, argued that the debate on the control and ownership of national resources carried too many racial overtones, and called upon responsible people to behave in a manner conducive to social harmony. The logic of Mr Haynes' argument was that persons on the Bussa Committee were responsible for the generation of race dialogue in the society, and that such dialogue was bad for the investment climate of the country.

Philip Goddard, on the programme, had defended the private sector by suggesting that its failure to enter into expansive manufacturing had little to do with mercantilist backwardness, but with the problems arising from small market size and access to adequate raw materials necessary for competitive production in many areas. I accepted the logic of some of his ideas, and after the programme he and I spoke for at least one hour in the car park on the need for serious discussion about our economy.

Richie Haynes' position on economic reform and black opportunity in Barbados was surprising. His attempt to locate the race question among the progressive elements within society, as opposed to among those protecting their traditional vested interests, took many off-guard. Dr Haynes was quoted in the *Advocate* of June 2, 1988, as follows:

> I urge those who believe that the answer to joblessness, poor housing, inadequate incomes, etc., is racial confrontation, to reflect on the damage which even a 10 to 15 percent decline in tourist expenditure will do to the Barbados economy.

This was read as more than a reformulation of the old scare tactic used in the attack on the democratic movement throughout Barbadian history. The logic is the same: each time black people stand up for their rights, they are typecast as destructive and subversive.

Not surprisingly, the Beckles-Goddard debate and the Haynes position were discussed by the media. The *Daily Nation*, in an editorial of July 14, 1988, attempted to concretise for the readers the villains of the peace. The editorial, entitled, 'None so Blind as those who Refuse to See', misrepresented the views of the Bussa Committee:

> More than 24 hours before UWI historian Dr. Hilary Beckles made certain allegations against Barbados' private sector, Dr. Richie Haynes was entering a plea for behavior by influential people which would not create social disharmony. Dr. Haynes, like most Barbadians, would be concerned

about certain statements pertaining to race; recently originating in Parliament and publicly welcomed. If Dr. Beckles was unaware of the advice given by the former Minister of Finance at Highgate last Sunday evening, he had no so such excuse regarding an equally emphatic opinion expressed earlier by business expert Mr. Philip Goddard.

The evils against which Dr. Haynes is warning are demonstrably injurious wherever racial conflict surfaces. Mr. Goddard's statements on the nature of private sector diversification can no less be substantiated through research by the lecturer – or anyone else. A clue to the historian's preoccupation may however be found in the interventionist theory. He blames Jamaica's economic woes during the 1970s on minority groups, not on the Manley regime. Dr. Beckles is just as certain that major commercial establishments like the Barbados Shipping and Trading, are too large for this island. Not a word, mind you, about over-staffed, expensive governments which sometimes legislates employees' salaries and arbitrarily plunder taxpayers' pockets to foot the bill.

Two weeks of intense debate continued. Mr. Haynes' new party, the National Democratic Party, began to attract the support of some big businesses, and in its infancy took an the image that was not populist. But both the opposition Barbados Labour Party and the ruling Democratic Labour Party had also enjoyed the support and blessing of the elite corporate interest groups. Senator Commissiong returned to the debate with a column entitled 'How the Whites kept Power' in the *Sunday Sun* of June 26, 1988, and the following night the author gave a public lecture on corporate power and economic growth in Barbados since 1945. By now, it was clear to all in Barbados that the country was groping its way forward to a position that would allow for deeper public engagement with democratic process.

- Eight -

Kamau's Journey:
From Bimshire to Barbados

*T*he socially self-defined white inhabitants of Barbados, some 15,000 of them in 1930, called their island home 'Little England'. They, in turn, effectively encouraged 'their' black inhabitants, almost 200,000 of them, to share the use of the word 'Bimshire' as a popular name for the island. It was an agreed upon nomenclature that reflected the colonial desire to promote the 'shire' identity in England's first far-flung island colony which was built upon the strikingly new idea of white supremacy and the institution of black chattel slavery.

Such anglophone representations of the society fashioned the ideological context within which Kamau Brathwaite grew to historical consciousness. The meanings of his inward and outward journeys, mind, land and sea voyages, constituted the vital, driving energy of a locally and globally fought struggle of detachments from the colonial scaffold of the shire. Collectively, they amount to an endemic war waged by a native son and his folk for X/Self respect, cultural freedom and spiritual reconstitution.

My perspective as a historian on this process of rediscovery, as intellectual unhinging and reconnection, differs from that of the literary critic in so far as it discriminates against literariness in favour of social history narrative. The argument is presented in a less critical fashion and asks fewer questions of an existential nature. In this regard, I begin by invoking the insights of Gordon Lewis into the Adamite 'Bimshire' of Brathwaite which serve to illuminate the site from which this 'war of respect' was conceived and fought.

Bimshire, Lewis tells us, was a world that meant what the 'white plantocratic' inhabitants wanted it to mean, no more and no less. They mimicked the culture of 'an English market town, Cheltenham, as it were', and revered a social world that gave way in 1914 throughout the United Kingdom. Determined to preserve the shire they dug in with the power of nostalgia and prepared to rule the folk forever. Other parts of the colonised world watched this 'reactionary conceit' in amazement. But one overarching result, Lewis tells us, was that in 1966, the year the colony crept into constitutional Independence, it remained 'difficult to speak of [it] except in mockingly derisory terms'.

The Bimshire of Brathwaite's birth, then, was more than the physical world of the plantation, and the merchant houses, churches, courts and political councils that served it. It was an 'inner place' where ideological discourses and cultural contestations for the soul were waged relentlessly as if all could be won or lost with the changed meaning of a word. And the 'words' were policed by official powers, since to 'speak' was to subvert the 'law and order' of the surface or to unearth the worlds beneath.

Barbadians from Bimshire, as a rule, could not speak freely; they whispered and spoke in tongues about things 'heard' but never 'seen'. There were no eye witnesses, only old news kept current as a pastime to entertain tourists in the day and children at dusk. Lewis, again, tells us that neither could the lords of the land 'write' about their home or themselves, except to tell of things that once mattered. He says:

> When, therefore, Barbadians do write about themselves it usually turns out to be, like Louis Lynch's *The Barbados Book*, an odd assortment of items, from historical details about the local churches, through a large section for the tourists, to an antiquarian nostalgia for the old folk ways and pastimes losing out. . . . Thus does the Barbadian climate of opinion live under the omnipresent shadow of a romanticized past. (Gordon Lewis, p. 227)

One of their enduring favourites, says David Lowenthal, relates to World War II when Barbados sent a telegram to England, saying 'Go on England, Barbados is behind you'. Hitler, on being informed of this message sent a signal to Barbados, saying, 'If you stay out, we will give you Trinidad'.

The rupture of this tradition of silence was nourished, in a way as a contradictory omen, by the womb that was *BIM (shire!)*, a discursive arts/literary journal for exiled and ignored Caribbean artists/writers. The magazine was edited by Frank Collymore who, within the colour vernacular, narrowly escaped whiteness. In the beginning, then, there was *BIM*, where Kamau and George Lamming, among others, were cuddled and cared for. Kamau, in flight to freedom from the police of the 'pure' plantation system, and knowing the evidence of things seen and felt, had *BIM* as a haven, a kind of maroon town. The tensions of this refusal to stay confined determined the dynamic and range of Kamau's military modalities, the trajectories of his voyages and journeys and the kinky texture of his thought.

To begin with, there was the dispossession of the people. Black Barbadians received what historians have described as the worst deal at the hands of the local elite and its imperial backers during the emancipation reforms and legislation of 1838 and after. In effect, they experienced a cold-blooded 'landless freedom' which ensured, a hundred years later, that Kamau would be natally trapped within a plantation sector that offered the lowest wages within the region.

The 'divorce of the people from the land' – no peasantry nor small farmer culture emerged here – guaranteed the 'economic and social subserviency of the black majority . . . to a degree unknown elsewhere', says Gordon Lewis. The 'stranglehold of the resident whites' created a 'cramped and introspective' mentality among the 'folk' who lived within their skin beneath the shadow of the plantation 'castle'. Little did they know, though the suspicion was always there, that Guy Fawkes was in the making.

The midday, middle passage sweat of the dispossessed and their silent struggles within Bimshire, fertilised the seed of all Kamau's work, starting with *BIM* in the early 1950s. At this time, he knew the personalities who postured as politicians of the poor; he watched them as they constituted themselves into an organisational process called the 'labour movement'. The local stirring of a workers' civil rights campaign, the discourse of black redemption, middle class self-mobilisation through the rhetoric of democracy and all such politics represented a formal, surface challenge to the makers of Bimshire. While, in effect, it widened the space for cultural discourse within civil society, the depth of an inner sense of black alienation, of subjection, the feeling of being kept prisoner, remained unattended.

Lewis has no time for the political challenge of this kind, but places his hope in the archaeology of the artist. He sums up the limits and the language of the political signifiers in this way: 'They fought for single causes rather than for a complete reconstruction of Barbadian life. In different ways, they opposed the oligarchy, but they had no clear idea of what they wanted to replace it with.' On this score there was disquiet; a quiet defeat that drowned out the drum by an orchestrated numbing of the African mind promoted by incessant afternoon chamber music that dominated the radio waves.

The Mandingo drum had been banned by the colonial government since 1688 when the slave-owners' legislature codified laws for the 'good governing of negro slaves'. Blacks took to the few remaining woods to beat the criminalised skin, but did so under the canopy of silence. This was how the young ones were schooled and scolded; 'hush ya mout fore ya get yaself and we in trouble'.

The orderliness of Kamau's youth was the sum of 200,000 black silences, private closures sealed in fear of life and death. The alternative was not evident, certainly not visible, and Kamau began by breaking the barrier with words, rhythmic sounds, using the drum and invoking the spirits that respond to it. In a short time his talking drum was being heard all over the land, including neighbouring lands, and across the triangle of the great crime.

Kamau's use of poetry and prose fiction as cultural media enabled him to declare 'unbanned' the Mandingo drum that had come to know only rippling sounds under gentle hands. The pulsating acoustic effect of his public performances brought back to a people the taste of a terrifying sound that had been foreign in formal places. The release of the hand had a hurrying effect upon the community that was seeking, especially after 1966, to imagine and invent new ways to live culturally as a constitutionally independent identity. No easy matter was it to come back from a de-historicised past with confidence, certainty and poise.

Suddenly, there was the sound of gushing young blood steaming within the symbolism of the liberated drum. But the experience of complete spiritual renewal, the ancestors had said, could only be attained with an untying of the tongue to disclaim the chains of history. In the beginning there was the 'word', and the word was in *BIM*, and it was war. But every word needed a home, a place of its own. Kamau's calling was to remove the surface of the killing fields, redefine the space and speak to the architecture of the rebirth. The rhythm of texts and sound were the digging tools and building blocks of the emerging folk on whose souls the enterprise was hinged.

Rooting his resistance in the spiritual world of the common people, the folk who fished, fetched and felled canes, was the core mission of Kamau's social philosophy. It transcended debates about the natures of literatures and the anxieties of the artist. Connectivity and commitment informed his moral aesthetic. His view was that the artist had a duty to bring in 'the voices of the people of the new nation making patterns of sound in hammer, engine, power saws, and the movement of earth and water'. This is what he said. This was what he did.

It was here in this well that Kamau chose to drop his bucket. Within the still tentative politics of the folk he devised a strategy to establish an enduring, authentic alliance that enabled him to live his own law that the artist should have a committed sense of social and moral values. How else could he have used the voice to verse the alienation of landlessness and give visibility to the culturally submerged?

Kamau offered a pedagogy of the rootless Barbadian as notes from the underground. Their response to endemic fluidity was the building technology of the 'chattel house', a stoneless castle that was sent packing from 'his' land when the plantation 'man' was mad. The ex-chattel would pull apart his wooden world and journey to a less angry estate in a humbled state. There were a million such rightless middle passages; the chattel house was the 'sign and symbol of their rejection by society'.

Chained to the shack that had no roots of its own, the folk could make no sound. Kamau rattled the gaggle, banged the walls and made noises that still haunt the plantation's peace, both day and night. He unleashed the spirits of Ta Mega, Negus and Ogun with sounds remembered at a Ghana gathering. But the villages here and there, across the triangle, could not house the echoes of his voice. The man of words from the woods had created a new context, the site where he fixed history and established the terms of resistance. The villager, then, was the folk, both modern and traditional who, like the sankofa bird, flies forward while looking back.

The sankofa, we know, is rooted in the Ghana that called upon Kamau to trace (back-back) the passage as part of the beginning of the inward voyage in search of 'rights'. The village of Bimshire was a place to begin the search for 'a sense of belonging'. The inner part of the journey was through a sunken well, deep beneath the living space, where secrets were buried and kept burnished by trickling sounds through limestone. Emerging, we recognised and claimed him with the restlessness he represented; the 'arrivant' who could never settle, reconstituted as the creole in eternal motion.

The middle passage for Kamau, then, was no healing place with wholesome hopes. It was too tearing an exploration of the flesh and the soul. It caused the former to absorb the terror of the lash until the blood ran cold, and the latter, to crack like a mirror, and reflect broken pieces of splintered dreams. Criss-crossing the passage, between island and continent, ocean and rivers, Kamau the creole claimed all the history that made his mould. Fully embracing the Atlantic shores he found his centre, however, in the primordial clouds of Sahara dust that arrives annually to cover and connect the submerged Africa of Bimshire.

He is a 'Barabajan', the son of a mother whose poem is that you cannot turn back because there is never a going back. 'Home', says Billie Holiday, is filled with pain, but for the Barabajan the homelessness of landlessness IS the 'pain'. But voyages and journeys of rediscovery can only begin at the new home. It is a place made by history and inhabited by the youngest ancestors. Bimshire, submerged Iboland, both occupied layers of the same space under the same sun. 'Islands and Exiles' and 'Mask' are the antithesis in the story of this rising son that penetrate like rays of steel the places beneath. Taking a stance, standing for Africa, the themes explored as spiritual liberation in 'The Making of the Drum', are the calls to arms associated with 'naming'.

The power to name a public place was never within the grasp of submerged Africa. The 'Edward' of birth that gave way to 'Kamau', like all the folk, was invisible in voicelessness. His focus on language and sound in search of the power to name things gave direction to the missile which he launched to breach the apartheid wall. Like Jamaica Kincaid's Antigua, the landscape and mindscape of Bimshire were named in celebration of the shire. 'Edward' was conceived in the language hegemony of the imperial monarchy. The wearing of the name, 'Kamau', given him by Ngugi Wa Thiong's grandmother in a kikuyu ceremony, was an Abeng that signalled the arrivant.

Jamaica Kincaid, speaking of Antigua, exposed the naming heresy that the shire had called into effect. She had this to say:

> In the Antigua that I knew, we lived on a street named after an English maritime criminal, Horatio Nelson, and all the other streets around us were named after some other English maritime criminals. There was Rodney Street, there was Hood Street, there was Hawkins Street, and there was Drake Street. Brathwaite's Bimshire, likewise, in 1813 had constructed as its proud centre piece a monument of Nelson, Lord Nelson if you please, an edifice offered in victorious support of Englishness, or at least the colonial version of it.
>
> But the acquisition of the capacity to name things in such contexts was a long and painful process of 'de-education' and resurgence. It was acquired only after a thousand voyages 'back back' to Africa where common folks discovered themselves buried beneath the bloody soils on which they stood. Scaling the walls of an imperial education required all the strengths of self and ancestral spirits; to rise was to laugh at, to mock, and to trample on the ideas that held the bricks of Bimshire together. Kincaid, speaking for Kamau said: 'We were taught the names of the Kings of England'. Edward was a King. She continued: In Antigua, the 24th May was a holiday – Queen Victoria's official birthday. We didn't say to ourselves, hasn't this extremely unappealing person been dead for years and years.

Kamau, furthermore, was schooled in the ideas of Rome and the values of Christian saints. There was nothing of importance and consequence in between. The name 'Tom' came to signify all there was to know about the black mind that absorbed and tried to live it all. A Tom, it was said, never raised his voice to the white man. Tom never said, hey I 'saw ya!'. The journey from Edward, around and beyond Tom, to Kamau was therefore a removal of the mask, a voyage through the middle, into the awaiting ancestral space.

On this voyage, Kamau has never allowed his feet to leave the ground. He remained planted, rooted realistically, even if elevated by cultural ritual. Behind the masks were the many fractured souls, broken, battered and bruised, some beyond healing. He understood how this reality was easily translated into a politics of treachery and divisiveness. The public murders of Michael Smith in Jamaica and Walter Rodney in Guyana came like flashes of flames that left ashes for the winds. There was always the dread of the oppressor's 'fire next time'. He was to receive a kind of stoning. In the Bimshire of his time, unlike before, there was no need for the flame: public stoning instead awaited all the pathfinders who rose from the underground.

Kamau used the metaphor of being a 'stranger in one's land' to illuminate the cycle of denial that accompanied the stoning. The voyages of discovery, the hearing of the drum, the basking in the healing feeling of the spirits and being a bloodied arrivant, speak to the silencing power of colonialism. How easy it was to be declared 'mad' by the empowered few above and sanctioned by the dispossessed many below. The villagers would shun you, and ask of you to be quiet in 'their' place. Their children are instructed not to hear you, and they would laugh with pointed fingers. The voyage, you soon discover, could so cruelly take the life it is meant to give.

The historian's eye had seen it all before. Kamau's navigation, then, benefited from the privileges of this knowledge and he returned 'alive', even if not 'well'. But Bimshire took its beating, and in a short time, the drum became louder as the folk stood taller. The Ogun became an icon for the few whose tongues were unleashed, enabling the 'Mighty Gabby' to sing 'Take down Nelson, Take down the Sea Dog'. The government has now agreed. Gradually, the people are remembering the places where the secrets were buried and the underground is slowly yielding truce from an ancient time.

The rediscovered voice, unearthed, now roams the sugar lands mingling with the water gods of the passage land and water connected by petals of blood. The spirits at the rising, called by Kamau's 'dread locked' invocation, no longer dwelled as pebbles in the sand but as poems in the land chanting down the stone walls of the 'high' church that blessed the deaths. Kamau wore his 'Tam' as a Muslim bore his 'Mat' – turned around a first step to send and receive the 'WORD'. Here, the limestone could not bear it all. The pocomania and kumina fell through, but the Ogun, the Vodun, the Obi remained – waiting for the call, the Spiritual Baptism, to trickle up to a dawn. Kamau, standing at the crossroads, tapped his feet, hummed and hissed, called and waited.

One response that came took the form of an echo. It was the announcement by Errol Barrow, a native 'sun', that told the villagers the time had come to 'no longer loiter on colonial premises'. The Union Jack came down on November 30, 1966. Gordon Rohlehr, who has followed Kamau closely, tells us that 'Independence', if a meaningful concept, 'must mean a new language, a redefinition of self and milieu'. It meant that Barbados had been pushed, torn and tortured to the junction. Kamau was standing there with Attibon Legba, the voodoo god of the crossroads. And he said, 'fill me with words/ and I will blind your god . . . Att/Att/Attibon!!!'.

But it was the midwife with the knife who had the final word on the new life. Raped, plundered and denied for 300 years, the womb had served as a tomb, and as the sugar men straddled the open legs of 1966 they found composure within their discomfort. Kamau looked around and saw that they too had a firm grip on the hand that guided the knife; the screaming cord they whispered was also a silencing rope. The new life received no slap; it breathed quietly and gazed through the bar of the crib that resembled the old world. Kamau remained at the crossroads, going nowhere, anchored to the limestone, calling again 'Att/Att/Attibon!!!'.

The refusal to fall, and the courage not to bend, did not blow with the common wind. Kamau says that those who did not stand were those who ran: 'My husband / if you cud see he / fragile, fraid o' e own shadow'. The Queen of England remained the 'mother', still the bosom of first resort. The landless remained in the castles of their skin, the only inns within. Nelson also stood his ground, demanding an Official Commission of Enquiry and a public referendum. Kamau, unashamed and stoned again, stands his ground undefeated: 'and I will dwell in the house of the merchants For NEVER.'

Brathwaite was right and precise. The strategy adopted by the planter-merchant houses, especially after 1966, was two-fold. First, to regroup and examine what role, if any, they could play in shaping and controlling the politics of the new nation. They chose to finance the new ruling labour parties, demand positions on the boards of statutory corporations and manipulate economic policy in such a manner as to convince government of the still effective political power of big business. They also impressed upon government that any discussion about 'development' should involve their members and more importantly, that the cultural and intellectual climate of the country should favour them if their economic cooperation was to be assured.

Black government developed no policy on land redistribution. The agenda of democracy did not include a discourse on ownership. The independent prime minister stressed the importance of government's partnership with the landed elite. There was no attempt at transforming race and managerial relations in the workplace; debates were confined to the need for black tellers in the commercial banks. No campaign was launched to address the redress of unequal resource ownership. This was a political betrayal of the arrivants – capitulation in the face of refashioned mercantile mastery.

Tourism was promoted as a major industrial sector during the first four years of the regime, and government revenues earned from this sector increased at a remarkable rate. A hotel construction boom assisted in stimulating the manufacturing sector that contributed to drift of the landless into the city. The planter too had come to town, completed his metamorphosis and emerged as a stronger force. Those who ruled did not govern and black government seemed in pursuit of the 'elusive pimpernel'.

The black community, though, appeared more confident in expressing its still stultified racial consciousness. In general, there was widespread feeling that society was posed for a push away from its colonial foundations and government had the potential, and support, to chart a new and independent path. But black politicians who had grown up under the Union Jack with Kamau (some of whom had walked with him during the anti-colonial nationalist surge of the post-war years in support of liberation causes in Africa and Asia) remained silent on the question of white economic and racial domination.

When the all-black government in 1970 found it necessary to prevent Trinidadian-born, American black power activist Kwame Toure (then Stokeley Carmichael) from addressing public audiences during his short and well-policed visit, the formal rationale was that the government was committed to non-racialist politics and the defence of white minority rights. A Public Order Act was passed that year which sought to suppress the black power movement and to escalate police surveillance of known black-consciousness radicals.

Unable or unwilling to implement structural changes in the ownership of productive land, government resorted to a wide range of social politics designed to create the potential for black redemption. These included free secondary and university education, national insurance schemes, incentives to small black businesses and a comprehensive health policy. These policies, however, were about the politics of capitulation of which Lewis spoke with disdain as the despicable seeking to be acceptable by the respectable.

Kamau was not silent on the persistence of institutional anti-black racism. He made reference to discrimination against blacks in the cultural economy that had been tugged to the centre of popular social discourse. He challenged the emergent black middle class to facilitate culture as a transforming force. It remained divided, unwilling to challenge the merchant in the market, it developed a dependency ideology and consciousness which compromised its social potential. According to Cecelia Karch:

> The black middle class embraced the prevailing ideological system; many were proponents of Empire. The majority sought access to the system; they did not seek to destroy it. Status as a middle class and their dependency on the paternalism of the oligarchy, and the colonial system, blunted the nationalist revolutionary spirit of black middle income groups and go a long way in explaining the recent political history of the island. Individuals from this class, not the class as a class, became political leaders and spokesmen for the majority population. It was the massive unrest of the black working class which propelled them into the limelight. Where leadership emerged from the ranks of the working class, it was repressed.

Deep-seated dependency and fear among the black professional class, then, intensified the stoning.

Other voices now liberated also poured scorn on the independent arrangement. Crippled behind the crib, the young nation did not burst forth with the rashness of its age. The energy of freedom contained, the promise unfulfilled, the Court of St James remained.

There are no longer any guarded secrets St John tells us. Ownership pattern and control mechanism now move like soldiers on parade. The commanding heights of the economy are the home of a minority white elite which wields levels of power far in excess of what its demographic proportion suggests.

Over time, a counter attack was launched. Critics of the new dispensation were labelled by its media sentinels as 'undesirables' and 'misfits'. Offers were made to a few who came on board as legitimisers in the market place. Academics became the new validating elite. But there was a sting in the tail. Some board room blacks feel a sense of both gratitude or resentment. They are made to feel as if they are outsiders since, by and large, they work for or are under the man with the land. They all know where their ceiling is located; they all know on which doors they cannot knock.

The impact of social creolisation upon the black community was profound. It meant that the African cosmology came under greater internal pressure as a result of the diminishing percentage of African recruits and external assault from the degradations of the white community. One effect was that Blacks learned to avoid severe penalties by not adhering too closely to it. But they responded in other ways. One was by taking underground those elements of culture which could survive without public display. These include aspects of religion and philosophic world views. Obeah, for example, survived underground in spite of legislation which outlawed its practice as a social ritual or religious construct.

In spite of intense anti-African pressures, enslaved creole Blacks were able to enhance and defend aspects of their ancestral heritage. The creative arts, religious social philosophical ontology, as well as language, survived as cultural institutions. There are several observer references to slavery on the island which show that the Blacks celebrated Crop Over with an expression of their artistic culture. In 1796, for example, Dr George Pinckard, a physician with the English military, described the festive performance of Africans during Crop Over. He wrote:

> They assemble in crowds, upon the open green, or in any square or corner of the town, and forming a ring in the centre of the throng, dance to the sound of their favourite African yell. Both music and dance are of a savage nature . . . ; their songs which are very simple,[are] harsh and wholly deficient in softness and melody.

Pinckard added:

> While one negro strikes the banjar, another shakes the rattle with great force of arm, and a third sitting across the body of the drum, as it lies lengthwise upon the ground, beats and kick the sheepskin at the end, in violent exertion with his hands and heels, and a fourth sitting upon the ground at the other end, behind the man with the drum, beats upon the wooden sides of it with two sticks. Together with the noisy sounds, numbers of the party of both sexes bawl forth their dear delightful sound with all possible force of lungs; . . . a spectator would require only a slight aid from fancy to transport him to the savage wilds of Africa.

Frederick Bayley, another Englishman, visited Barbados during the 1820s and stated how the enslaved Blacks, to the annoyance of Whites, would 'sit up during the greater part of the moonlight nights, chattering together, and telling nancy stories'. A nancy story, he said, 'is nothing more or less than a tale of ghost and goblins, which pass with the negroes by the appellation of Jumbies'.

In addition, Bayley wrote about their grand day of jubilee – Crop Over. During the Crop Over Festival, he notes, ' it was common to see the different African tribes forming each a distinct party, singing and dancing to the gumbay [an African drum], after the rude manner of their native Africa'. He added that the festival had now been made less African, with the fiddle and tambourine being used instead of the drum (which had been criminalised) while 'black and white', overseer and bookkeeper, mingled together in dance.

African culture, in becoming Afro-Barbadian, absorbed elements of Euro-creole ideas and practices. This was undoubtedly a circumstantial response to power inequality. But by virtue of its inner vitality in the survival quest, African culture remained the dominant popular form. There can be no doubt that Crop Over, now an annual event, is the most remarkable rediscovery of the Kamau project. Together with the National Independence Festival of Creative Arts which began in 1973, it has become the beacon of the post-national cultural upsurge.

The institutionalisation of African cultural identity since the mid-1970s, in the form of the Crop Over Festival, a proliferation of theatre workshops, dance and musical groups, professional artists, writers and storytellers, all working within the social experiences of the folk, attests to the extent to which Kamau's notes from the underground have refashioned the Bimshire of his birth and allowed a new Barbados to emerge. Kamau, then, has provided the main pathways for outer voyages and inward journeys.

At no juncture, however, did Kamau attempt to set aside the vitality or the importance of Eurocentric traditions. His use of the bass and the drum as the base line was not intended to eradicate or deny the melodies of Europe, but merely to mark a place of beginning, a home, from which his journeys departed. He provided, as a result, no dichotomised vision of culture but accepted the role of the dialectic in reading the creolising force of all histories. For him the Caribbean X/Self is best understood as a cultural melange in the tradition of all creole creation. On this score Derek Walcott joins him, the evidence of which is his *Omeros* (1990) that embraces the discursive vision of X/Self.

While the logic and intellectual force of X/Self are cast as everlasting subversions of imperialists' construction of what is the hegemonic 'West', Kamau accepts that Africa and Europe had been hinged together culturally by direct human interaction long before the crime of the Middle Passage. The militant assertion of Europe within the ancient relationship is read, however, as a betrayal of that engagement and a sin of an Oedipal nature. The West Indian, says the X/Self, denied none but seeks truths in moral and philosophical discourse. One compelling truth is that Europe, in enslaving the African, bit the hand that bore and fed it. The use of the Christian God as a wicked weapon in the armour of the pro-slavery military and technological assault placed the recast 'jet white' Christ at the disposal of slave traders, genocidal conquistadors and their financial and political sponsors. The recall of slavery by the European mind at a time of self-proclaimed 'enlightenment', globalised the cultural erasure that is racism. Racialised chattel bondage was their invention for the African; for the Asian, at a later date, it would be the bomb of Nagasaki and napalm of Vietnam.

The oppression of the colonial heritage, then, is not for Kamau an abstraction but a living condition. This perspective is in opposition to the reading of his work that denied him, as an artist, sociopolitical agency. No one from or in the Barbados underground, trapped in the prison of Bimshire, expected any political prescription for liberation from Kamau. But they followed his light with a hammer in hand. He showed us then how and where to dig; and he told us why. His message is a missile, powerful and 'smart'. THE VOYAGE TO THE PAST IS THE JOURNEY TO THE FUTURE. He is no 'playing' politician, but a self-confessed 'cultural gorilla', fighting for the 'alter Native'.

- *Nine* -

Crisis of Nationalism under Globalisation

i) Crisis of black intellectuals

*I*t is obvious to intellectual workers within academic institutions and the information industry that clearly defined roles have been assigned them within the nation-building process. Historical information, in particular, is now at a premium. There has been a proliferation of texts in which academics seek to identify and explain endemic historical forces that should be understood by persons responsible for social and economic planning. Intellectuals are therefore under pressure by the State and the citizenry to prove their relevance to a wide range of development concerns.

In all of this, intellectuals are forced to examine their own literary and verbal traditions and to carefully scrutinise the environment within which texts are generated. These environments are seen as places that can be socially and politically re-engineered in order to promote objectives relevant to research and development. They are encouraged, furthermore, to assess the extent to which specific educational institutions, and their supportive social value systems, are sufficiently focused to meet the grand objectives of social mobility, economic empowerment and political progress.

It requires no great insight to recognise that the central issue here concerns the role of the intellectual within the wider process of human development. If the focus is narrowed, however, and the discourse confined to the specifics of nation-building within the post-independence era, then the issue is even clearer. Assuming that the immediate post-independence generation can be considered a 'transitional type', then intellectuals are asked to examine the possible futures as likely destinies of society. Reading future trends is one way that Caribbean intellectuals can support the process of change. It is generally assumed that in Barbados there is consensus on the principal mission to dismantle what is left of the colonial scaffold. Reordering sociopolitical priorities and outlining important ideological issues in search of new life sources would follow logically. As the small nation launches itself into the global world as a self-directed entity, the responsibility of the intellectuals is the more considerable, and success or failure at each stage is usually placed at their door.

Let us begin with the essential vision of the Barbados nation-state; how to 'Think Globally and Act Locally'. Then, allow us to place this alongside the thinking of the ex-colonial powers that carved up and shared Caribbean places and spaces for the past 500 years. Imperialists in Europe had put in place a vision that said 'think globally and act globally'. Is it to be assumed that the Barbados predicament is a direct result of the ideological crisis of a decayed and discredited imperial vision? Is it to be assumed that Barbados at the beginning of the twenty-first century, cannot 'act' globally, and that its intellectual vision is constrained by its material limitation? The answer to both questions must take into consideration the nature and role of intellectual work within society, since such activity is invested with the task of proposing socially useful ideas and concepts that can transcend space and time.

Taking Barbados as a case study, some interesting observations can be made. It is assumed, of course, that the demographers are correct in stating that it is a black majority society; that the historians have not misled us in reporting that the legacies of 211 years of slavery are still alive and well, and sometimes arrogant in their postures and expectations. It is assumed, also, that a scientific analysis of the society can tell us important things about its social composition, relations, expectations and ideological attitudes.

These observations can be made with reference to the nature of the bonding, or lack of it, between society and its creative writers. It is necessary to explore these relationships because it is within the mechanism of such relations that important truths about society can be located. Literary signposts, such as Lamming's 'castle' of the skin, and his 'pleasures of exile', can guide us, so to speak, into the inner chambers of the social soul in order to discern how it feels about itself and the ways that this 'self' is (mis)represented.

One of the important facts about Barbados that leaps from literary and historical analysis is that the society is represented as possessing no ancestral identity transcendent of the 'colonial' era. In spite of the tremendous amount of professional archaeological research which has shown a vibrant and populous Amerindian civilisation dating some 2,000 years before the English encounter, the society's organised memory indicates no instinctive reference recall beyond 'the English coming'. Barbados, then, is represented within popular literature, educational programming and the social imagination as a 'total' product of the colonial mission of '1627 and all that' – 'discovery day', the English call it.

To some extent, educators are much to blame for the crisis with respect to ancestral memory. For sure, the colonial administration and its educational machinery had a major investment in this historical portrayal of the society. It suited their interests to indicate that the island's space was a massive 'void' seeking habitation and that their newly constructed society had no 'tradition' other than that which linked it to empire. But how do we explain the persistence of this refusal to recognise ancestry on the part of black educators before and after the 'parting of ways' in 1966 – the 'independence' moment?

The explanation, it seems, must begin with recognising that no intellectual movement dedicated to de-colonisation within the spheres of education, culture and psychic identity took control of the ideological process of 'representation'. This is not to say that such liberating 'minds' did not exist, or that their possessors did not labour long in defending the populace from the hegemonic powers of the colonial education system. It is merely to indicate that such persons did not constitute a 'movement' that was able to impose a new sensibility upon the society in terms of how it went about the business of organising its past for 'living'.

Certainly, many brave and honourable persons were active in this struggle, but more had capitulated in the face of sanctions imposed by the colonial state and had retreated into a mindless obedience that assured internal security and social honour. For the first generation of 'independence' children, then, 'history' began in 1627 when the colonising team 'handed' over the island to King James I of England – hence 'D-Day' and the Holetown (formerly Jamestown) Festival in which society now basks.

The maintenance of this state of affairs within the educational system meant that, for most Barbadians, their island's past begins abruptly in 1627. This understanding, in turn, is perfectly suited to the real task of the colonial educational system, which was to represent the island as having its memory linked to a 'total plantation' concept. And so, the story is told as follows: in the beginning there were the plantations, and then the plantations lost favour, but have survived, nonetheless, as a lasting testament to their aboriginal pedigree.

This powerful view, embracing all within its reach, was not systematically and aggressively challenged at the level of ideological representation and curriculum by counter-revolutionaries within the education business. As a result, it now remains an almost impossible task for the society to envision a time in which there will never be a plantation culture and all its social agents, such as white supremacy, planter-merchant privilege, empowered commission agents, transcending Anglican clergy and mysterious white goddesses enthroned or imprisoned in 'great houses'. I believe it was George Lamming who once said that black Barbadians' greatest nightmare would be if one day they woke up to find that planters and plantations were not there in order to assure them that, as a people they really 'exist'.

Herein lies the crisis of black intellectuals within the society. What have they done with respect to liberating society from this plantation 'cocoon' that incubates a mind of submissiveness to the legacy of the English mercantile model of socioeconomic exploitation? The fact that black society seems willing to settle with and, at best, negotiate a peace with an economically dominant white minority (two per cent of the demographic aggregate that controls over 75 per cent of the private productive capital) is very instructive. Any challenge to this equation of power constitutes a declaration of war, and history shows that such an existence is rarely ever considered attractive or desirable by the disenfranchised majority.

As late as the 1970s, working class black children, in town and country, still gathered marl for their parents to sprinkle around their chattel houses at Christmas – symbolic of the snow that plainly refused to fall down upon their cane fields. A white Christmas was psychically ideal, and how else could it be obtained in such sunny climes? Imported Christmas trees from Canada, decorated with cotton wool, was the next best thing and Santa Claus, the great white benefactor, though never sufficiently generous, was awaited as an act of theological redistribution. The neo-plantation world seemed more potent, and all this decades after the society had 'parted ways' with the motherland that had always seen her dark children as so many person-hours of cheap, servile and docile labour.

Barbadian children in 1966 were not told in school that President Dessalines, in declaring Haiti independent in 1804 and in renaming the French Colony of St Domingue, had restored its Arawakan name. 'Haiti', then, the ancestral name for the entire island, had reemerged as an act of memory reclamation, a moment of re-appropriation of the historical self – a struggle against the 'inner' plantation of identity, self-perception and social consciousness. At the corresponding moment of independence in Barbados, children debated at length whether the new nation-state should be called 'Barbadoes' or 'Barbados' (the Portuguese option) against the background of a call to officially recognise terms such as 'Little England' and 'Bimshire'.

It is necessary to return to Kamau Brathwaite's concept of the 'inner' plantation. Barbados was promoted within the literature of the Empire as early as the mid-seventeenth century as the 'first' and 'ideal' plantation. The model of sugar and slavery was perfected here, and exported to other parts of the West Indian complex. The weight of this historical fact, it is said, has pressed against the minds of inhabitants leaving psychological imprints upon which the winds of change have had a limited effect. The 'inner' plantation, it can be deduced from Brathwaite, has persisted and remains expressive, many have said, in areas such as self-identity (black and ugly), self-confidence (lazy blacks) and self-evaluation (po-great).

Many have intimated that the world of the 'inner' plantation is where intellectuals should dwell and do their lasting work. In Barbados, however, until very recently, only the performing artists and creative writers had sojourned there in numbers in an attempt to fulfil the mandate. It was a lonely world for these pathfinders who endured the intensity of hostile reaction from a system that felt its nerve centre being pricked with sharpened instruments. Operating at the core, as these persons were, allowed for no margin of error. The narrow confines of these armoured corridors were designed to tighten around the throats of offenders until such time as they chose the 'pleasures of exiles' from where the struggle could continue or be abandoned.

The social majority, Trevor Marshall has argued, rarely sees or feels the critical importance of these struggles as a matter of racial survival. Victimised and lacking the resources of autonomous existence, they often turn upon the messengers who they accuse of being 'aggravators' and 'self-representing'. The crisis of the relationship, then, becomes evident and has much to do with the universal perception that there is NO alternative.

But none of this should be surprising once we recognise that ancestral memory is linked so exclusively to the established world of '1627'. It would follow logically, then, that the political struggle of the majority against this world would not be placed in a prominent space within the organised memory. In fact, the tendency within society has been to negate and, when possible, deny the existence of these liberation struggles.

Let us examine two instances within the historical narrative: the 1816 war of General Bussa against slavery and the 1937 Clement Payne Revolution against the post-slavery plantation. For over 100 years, the 1816 war against slavery received no attention within the official political culture of the island. Black 'nationalist' politicians from the 1920s did not touch upon 1816 as a reference departure in the mobilisation of popular consciousness within the electoral culture. General Bussa, military commander, retreated into the 'folk' memory and had no 'official' identity. The event itself was not recognised within the school programmes for 'history' teaching. Yet, it was the single occasion on which over 10,000 black Barbadians rose up in an attempt to remove slavery and white supremacy practices and ideas from the space they inhabited.

How, it is necessary to know, does an action by a majority in search of justice become obliterated from active memory? Is this further evidence of the crisis of the intellectual? Certainly, the intellectual's task is to reaffirm the society's possession of survival energy and to indicate how life sources can be attained through the reorganisation of the popular will. Did historians contribute to the gathering of dust over events that constitute evidence of a people's search for progress and liberation? Was it their responsibility to keep before the popular mind memories and analyses of such an event in order to widen the social understanding of how and why social struggles can occur?

The answers to these questions must invoke the role of historians and political scientists within academic institutions. To be sure, a school of historical thought that can be considered 'Barbadian' is now developing. Many have agreed that Barbadian historians, unlike their counterparts elsewhere, were reluctant to enter the area of the popular struggle as this would certainly incur the wrath of the white supremacy system. Others have spoken of a retreat into the less turbulent waters of contemporary culture – a place where the forces of popular struggle do not call them into the frontlines.

There was a similar circumstance in relation to the 1937 revolution. Three social aspects of the memory of this mass uprising can be identified. First, there was the historic refusal by Parliamentary Barbadian politicians to identify with this event. For many, it was irrelevant to the questions that relate to the meaning of everyday life. Second, there was the matter of academic compliance with the establishment's representation of democratic achievement. Democracy, then, was not won, but bequeathed, and the peoples' struggles were denied and removed from memory. Third, an established tendency on the part of many in possession of a 'living memory' of that revolution to apologise for it and to indicate that it was a 'mistake' or an act of political vandalism, a 'riot', by rabble rousers and social misfits. For many, especially within the self-ascribed middle classes, the 1937 revolution conjured feelings of shame and guilt.

Few intellectuals, until very recently, have attempted to diffuse these social time bombs by indicating how walls can be turned into bridges in order to secure the passage of workers' actions into the halls of official recognition. Historical material was not assigned any healing powers and the worker's front seat within the narrative was skilfully altered by an aggressive act of reversal and interpretation. To date, there is no professional biography of Clement Payne and no published extensive analysis that seeks to explain the rise of modern democracy in terms of the grand refusal of workers in 1937. Happily, a younger generation of historians, Trevor Marshall, David Browne and Henderson Carter, are at work to redress this disgrace.

But the lack of an academic discursive practice in relation to the history of the popular struggle is indicative of the crisis of confidence between material workers and intellectual workers. When the 'Black Power' movement 'arrived', like a virus, on Barbadian shores during the late 1960s, its primary impact was cosmetic since it could not come to terms with restructuring the patterns of power – economic or political. Black power was cultural and white power was economic. Black was beautiful and white was powerful; brown people were perfectly balanced between both experiences and realities.

The painful result of all this was that when the Democratic Labour Party (DLP) government passed the Public Order Act in 1970, ostensibly to suppress black radicals, it consolidated a tradition of anti-intellectualism characterised by book banning and literary curfews. The seminal texts of the black Atlantic struggle were denied the people – the voices of Malcolm X, Angela Davis, Stokeley Carmichael and Eldridge Cleaver, for example, were criminalised while the racist texts of Kipling, Carlyle and other white supremacists occupied greater space within the nation's bookstores and public libraries. Yet, eminent academics did not launch a protest movement because of fear of government reprisals. The carpenter, then, had his tools confiscated but was required to build.

Within this context, the 'soul' of the young nation remained imprisoned by Eurocentric trappings and symbols expressed by the ownership patterns of the rolling greenery of plantation fields. To pay the piper was to call the tune – an act of power and a display of right. Those without assets were required to sing and dance and express merriment. But what about the 'souls of black folks'? During the 1980s, white American anthropologists were at work excavating the burial grounds of black folks' enslaved ancestors in the gullies and ravines of ancient sugar plantations.

Bones were boxed, skulls wrapped and mortuary goods carted away to university laboratories in the United States for 'scientific examinations'. For these re-arrested Africans, there was no spiritual ceremony, no promotion of a philosophical discourse, no theological reflection, no moral outrage, no 'nothing'. White ancestral remains resting in peace in the Anglican churchyards were secured by godly sentinels beyond the reach of such investigators. Real estate owners, shocked at such 'discoveries', rejoiced at having such a historical burden removed from their properties – and the quicker the better.

There was nothing on the statute books of the island within which such actions could be discussed. Since the seventeenth century, provisions had been made for the protection of the mortal remains of white folks – they had souls that legislators instinctively respected. No laws, however, were passed to guard the 'African'. But it wasn't very long that remains were 'dumped'. It was just 150 years ago – a grandparent's memory away. Thus, for many, they were still the 'living dead'. But why the disrespect and the treachery? Why did Barbadian intellectuals accept these things as 'normal'? Why did they 'absorb' such assaults upon the 'soul' of black folks?

It would help in this enquiry to return to the personality of the Barbadian 'colonial'. White Barbadians loaned to their black counterparts the idea that they were the 'best' colonials – 'go on England – Little England is behind'. Like the Whites, Blacks were the best in the region at cultural mimicry in all its forms; they defended the Empire as only people at 'the centre' knew how. They were royal loyalists and this meant the ultimate sacrifice of the soul upon the altar of imperial worship.

But these things were done in an 'Anancy' sort of way – mask and magic. Like the crab, we took everything underground and emerged occasionally in search of that which belonged to those on top. The African soul, then, Brathwaite tells us, became submerged – a circumstance that allowed black folks to bask in the glory of Anglo-Saxonism. While the native white soul, therefore, parades in sociological splendour, the black soul required archaeological signposts that said 'Dig Here!'. The former roams the landscape, free to explore with liberty, while the latter is tossed and turned beneath a foliage that drew upon its captured fertility but forever denies its contribution.

Such alienation, no doubt, indicated a fatal level of negation and dispossession. Driven underground by the potency of white power, the black soul now required surveyors and ethnographers to seek its location. Buried for so long, many now fear that it is perhaps lost or forgotten – rotten for lack of ventilation, the compost of a mercantile edifice that now disregards the functions and forces of African 'roots'.

Where are our anthropologists in all this? Where are those workers whose task it is to unearth and liberate the 'living'? For many decades, Lamming, Brathwaite and Tom Clarke refused to allow us to forget that this hidden, spiritual soul resides within us, and that only the re-engineering of specific intellectual environments can call it into active being. The internalisation of this struggle for the reclamation of self, then, is presented as an act of rediscovery of ancestry – a painful and turbulent journey against the tide of the inner plantation.

Everywhere within the places of popular discourse references were heard about the retreat of intellectuals from the edge of decision-making. The evidence used to support this view is the failure to launch an effective movement against these legacies of colonial culture. Some speak in terms of their promotion of a liberal education – the self-serving accumulation of certification – as opposed to the mobilisation of knowledge for social change and progress. The general conclusion that is frequently drawn is that intellectual bankruptcy characterises those who make a living in the knowledge industry, an indictment that far too often calls into question the relevance of the University of the West Indies.

Basic things, we are told, were not struggled for and achieved. For example, we are frequently reminded that colleges and schools do not offer our young the opportunity to study African history as a central part of their academic programme. Black children can take for certification at upper school level, for instance, European and American history but not African history. This is seen as evidence of some educational authorities maintaining conceptual hostility for African civilisation and the capitulation of black intellectuals within the context of the struggle for the legitimisation of things African. The fact that African history is presented to schools in little modules attached to a range of social studies concerns rather than as a distinct and discrete discipline is again taken as indicative of its subjection to things 'western'. Recently, a minister of education responded to this call with the statement that if the odd teacher wished to teach African history the government would not object. Again, official statements of this kind tell the full story.

A few historians, led by Trevor Marshall, and many artists, poets, novelists and musicians, however, are seen as consciously working toward the creation of an alternative vision which is consistent with the people's historical experience. The calypsonians, for example, have walked on the cutting edge of the popular experience while the academics, with few exceptions, have retreated into the safety of the western discourse.

ii) Owen Arthur's project: the Barbados Model

Barbados is faced, as a small but tough and determined nation, with a clear and present danger. The question is what will be its strategic response as it engages this third wave of globalisation. There are three things to be known upfront about this new version of global interaction:

1) that it is a contradictory process in that it both promises and threatens universal openness - yet its organising principle is the nation state based on virulent nationalism;

2) that it has no place for fractured and divided nations that lack agility and intellectually based knowledge power;

3)   that its politics is about strong nationalisms versus weak nationalisms, and that it promotes culture, more so than race, as the unit of measurement and inclusion in defining nationalism.

Within this context, Barbados is seeking to create a new political culture for the twenty-first century; one that has no room for sterile notions of unrestricted political tribalism which is more consistent with common sense and the realities of the globalised world. Academics are also seeking, as conceptualisers who are concerned for all the people, at home and in the Caribbean region, to do the best in these very turbulent, redefining, intellectually challenging and politically fluid, postmodern times.

Here in Barbados, in what is a constituency of the Caribbean nation, citizens find themselves under the leadership of a most turbulent, indefinable, determined, charismatic prime minister whose creative political imagination seems to transcend the narrow, confining, inelastic boundaries given him by tradition.

History is not a tomb in which society is mummified. History is filled, like the rainforest, with all of the solutions needed for survival. But it must be examined with liberationist objectives in mind. It can tell us how to escape, how to choose, how to imagine and how to act in earnest. There is no need for anyone to try reading the future. All that is required is an understanding of the past and present and a commitment to learn from them. The experiences of the past and the idealism of the future are not contradictory, and even if they are, it is wise to be a believer in the challenges posed by contradictions, as this is a sure way to generate energy and intellectual rigour.

Barbados has an ancient ghost to exorcise, not because it does not like the complexity of recognising multiple dimensions of existence, but because it is haunted day and night. This is not a reference to the kind of shadow politics that the English speak of, but to the local version, the existence of living shadows that have become obsolete, anachronistic and hostile to the new kind of life society is seeking to create. It is not possible to exorcise this oppressive spirit as individual activists, no matter how one may try. Persons who try are always publicly stoned and demonised in the process.

Progressive Barbadians need to build a movement, foster a new wave of social consciousness that will assault backward assumptions about wealth accumulation, ethnicity, power and social living. There are suggestions and each person should add them to those that have already been ventilated. They must be historicised in order to fashion what is increasingly being described as a unique Barbados development model. Such a notion is currently dominating the public media in Jamaica and has been ever since Prime Minister Arthur took the liberty of using his full Jamaicanness – legal, intellectual and domestic – in order to inform Finance Minister Dr Omar Davies that from time to time, in order to protect the advancement of civil society, you must put to rest a general in order to encourage the others.

Undoubtedly, many mistakes will be made in the attempt to give society a real example, long needed and overdue, of how to imagine and create an institutional environment for economic democracy within a political culture that is fractured and weakened by the backwardness of ethnic division, social mistrust and disrespect. It is important not to underestimate the potency of conservative values within leading sectors of the society. It is equally important to build alliances, inner links, across civil society, in order to move forward, not so much with the idea of black economic enfranchisement and economic democracy, but with the spirit of optimism and the magnitude of the general goodwill that exist within the society.

It was once said by the Rt Excellent Errol Barrow that a 'conservative' in postmodern Barbados is rather like a chicken whose head has been cut off; it may run about in a lively and noisy fashion, but the truth of the matter is that it is dead. He WAS wrong. Chickens have learnt to live without heads and that is why they are particularly dangerous. They have found others to breathe for them and to escort them safely across busy streets. They now live in a rather shadowy fashion, felt but not seen, like horses without names. But Barbadians, then and now, are seeking to identify with political and civic leadership they can trust because they believe that everything around them is brittle and that hard earned advances can be easily reversed. They see evidence of this in the region and their sensitivity is therefore based on rational thought. It is necessary, then, to redefine the struggle and to be clear about national identity and needs. If we do not do this, others will do it for us. It is a major intellectual task.

But it is difficult to be an academic activist in Barbados; one minute you are told to come off the hill and then the next you are told to go back and stay there. The 'conservative' elements of both political parties are most consistent with this perspective, and progressives have grown to feel like outcasts within both of them as a result. But that is how it is, and they must find comfort in the walls of the university which more than ever requires unequivocal support. It is an important university, it is on the people's side, and no alien force should be allowed to prevent it from serving their interests. It is also very important to speak about the conceptual pedigree, policy integrity and future meanings of 'the politics of inclusion'. It is necessary to do so while paying attention to the ideology of social reconciliation (with one eye fixed on the mandate given Sir Keith Hunte's National Reconciliation Committee) and the economics of private sector-led growth (with the other eye fixed on Sir Stanley Goddard), but with the full focus of the imagination riveted upon the prime minister's methodology and the strategic cultural visions of Minister Mia Mottley. The politics of inclusion is conceived within the grip of the economics of globalisation, but this point should be assessed critically.

As the recession in the world economy worsens, competition for the control and ownership of secure economic resources will undoubtedly intensify. This conflict will take place globally among nations, increasingly among blocs of nations with similar or crisis-free ideological relations, as well as between 'interest groups' within particular nations. The tendency towards the concentration of economic power in the hands of a few of these interest groups will also have significant consequences for the social and economic development of nations, particularly small nations that seek to build with democratic institutions and value systems.

Despite the usual hue and cry of party politics, the 1994 general election was about Barbadians finding a new centre, a new way of dealing with old problems. The refusal to accept currency devaluation and the discipline of belt tightening that followed illustrated the deep resolve of Barbadians to stand as a unified nation when faced with adversity. This is an enormous cultural asset that cannot be ignored in economic thinking about the future.

When internally scrutinised, and more importantly historicised, this statement says the following things:

1.　that Barbados, as a primordial site of sugar plantation colonialism and as the incubator of a model of slavery which it exported to the hemisphere, has a specific kind of cultural history that embraces all, and from which society now seeks both economic accumulation and socio-political liberation;

2.　that there is a strong democratic impulse imbedded deeply within the national consciousness, forged in the furnace of flight from colonial injustice, labour 'namelessnes';

3.　that there is a commitment to nationhood with a shared vision, despite ethnic diversities which have been politicised and which seem at times inhibiting and distracting;

4.　that there is a consensus on the minimum amount of commonality required to pursue the shared vision, and that the terrain on which the society can foreground this commonality for the purposes of nation-building is popular culture.

The consensus reached in the society thus far can be expressed in two broad areas:

1.　that economic growth and wealth creation are necessary for social integration, social stability, and that these ideals are interactive and dialectically related;

2.　that effective social integration, as an institutional reality in nation-building, can be predicated upon the premises of the common cultural heritage that was created and honed within the plantation vortex, and that this shared vision and common culture represents the principal asset in the search for economic growth with social justice.

But there is a major problem that will require the nation's collective wisdom, common sense and commitment. It is this: no matter how the dice are thrown, any successful stimulation of the Barbados economy will lead to a significant degree of further economic empowerment among the elite because this is the logical result of the pattern of wealth owning, entrepreneurial development and the continuing practice of institutional racism – all of which have been inherited and were not fractured or uprooted with the rise of the nation-state in 1966. The politics of inclusion must address this matter. Black economic marginalisation, unless addressed urgently with the full support of all stakeholders, will serve to subvert all the best efforts at nation-building.

There is simply no time to allow the notion of black, second-class economic citizenship to fester within the context of a globalising economy that is seen as a dream world for traditional entrepreneurs. It is also true that the cultural revolution taking place in society, stimulated by the young Mottleys (uncle and niece not father and grandfather – but that is another story), continues to give the majority of the community an important and precious space for building self-esteem and self confidence, keeping hope alive, projecting a clear vision of the future and for conceiving a grand, transforming reality of inclusion at all levels of the capital circuit.

Mr Arthur's project, then, it seems, is how best to ride these two horses in the same race so as to narrow, in the short term, the gap between first and second winners, and in the medium to long term, to create the context for a fair and even race that is neither rigged by privileged insider interests nor predetermined by the inequities of history. This must be the ultimate compelling vision for post-colonial society that possesses many of the required instruments with which to build a new and different future, including a growing desire, despite persistent racism, to move forward in a unified fashion.

It is always important in such discourses to mobilise the best of social theory in order to see ways with which to make the space prepared by history more elastic. Critical theory can assist with many practical efforts. For example:

(i)   how to understand and remove the legacies of institutional racism and sexism;

(ii) how to maintain the diversity of ethnic ancestry but manage its uniqueness to the collective benefit of the nation;

(iii) how to achieve social respect for all while debating civil rights without the violence of throwing mud or other missiles, or uttering profanities and always leave room for the kinds of creative solutions that enhance the sophistication of civil society. It was Adlai Stevenson in all his wisdom and simplicity who said, 'He who throws mud loses ground'.

The objective is learning how to 'talk smart' without the wastage of 'double-speak'. That is, how to discover and cherish the craft of knowing how to build civic trust, because the critical lesson of history is a very simple one – WITHOUT TRUST THERE CAN BE NO THRUST.

It is obvious that 'trust' for the 'thrust' can only be built in a lasting way upon the terrain of common cultural heritage, and that economic management is but one key instrument that can be used in the liberation of the human potential for material growth and social justice. It is necessary to build upon, and with the consensus of cultural heritage, and identify and promote those elements that represent energy sources for enhancing development options. In this way, it is possible to examine the Social Partners model, historicise its assumptions and potential and suggest strategies to go about the task of seeking to simultaneously achieve economic growth and social justice.

On October 6, 1999, an article by Lamberto Dini and James Wolfensohn, entitled 'Let's Start Taking the Benefits of Cultural Identity

Seriously', appeared in the *International Herald Tribune*. Since then, it has generated considerable debate among development theorists, particularly those who hail from the social science disciplines of economics and management. The authors tell us that:

> As we prepare to journey into the new millennium, with all its promise of new scientific and economic gains, we cannot afford to forget how culture and history can shape modern development. Fostering and protecting our cultural legacy is basic to improving the effectiveness of education, public health, the production of goods and services, and how we manage our cities. Culture lies at the very heart of efforts to reduce poverty. The self-awareness and pride that comes from cultural identity are an essential part of empowering communities to take charge of their own destinies.

While these truths might seem rather surprising to many today, they were understood and generally accepted in the past century before 'development' as a concept was invented. If you examine, for instance, the character of the first Industrial Revolution in Britain in the eighteenth and nineteenth centuries, you will find that the British were, and still are, known more for their 'culture' than their commodities. While 'Made in Sheffield' is no longer a household image in post modernity, 'Englishness' as an intellectual construct has risen in stature as an organising method. The last Industrial Revolution of modernity – that of the Japanese – was likewise built upon and driven by a cultural system that has distinguished these people in a way that their commodities can't because goods can be cloned to perfection but culture cannot.

It is desperately critical that Barbadians identify all those elements of cultural and historical self-perception that can help to refashion a postmodern identity that is consistent with the age of globalisation. The mandate is to generate new knowledge that can inform and empower a more developed national consciousness. What are the constituent elements of Barbadianness that can be isolated and promoted as forces of cohesion and a stimulant to fostering vital inner social bonds?

Again, the issue here is about a process that is a natural part of human development – the reinventing of self through historical re-readings and revisions. The reference here is not to crude, anti-intellectual distortions of historical evidence. Take the English again, for example. They have succeeded in projecting a self-representation to the world that they are possessed of a cultural propensity for tolerance, lawfulness and liberal reflexes despite the most barbaric history of imperialism, slavery, racism, military excess and the violent suppression of their working class (the Irish not included). The past ten years or so have witnessed the final collapse of the legitimacy of an earlier self-representation, that of Little England, because it was a dastardly imposition on a colonised people, and not rooted in any consensus. It served the interests of a few while it brutalised the psyche of the many.

Barbados, in the past 500 years, has given effect to a wide range of methods for eliminating and managing ethnic differences. It is important to distinguish between the processes of eliminating and managing ethnic differences. With respect to eliminating difference, Barbados had an early start. There is a history of genocide within its cultural development and all should be mindful of this. The first Europeans who trespassed on the island carried out genocidal pogroms with respect to the abundant native Carib-Arawak population. In the fourteenth century, this island was very densely populated, and by the end of the sixteenth century it was very 'densely empty' – laid bare by Spanish and Portuguese conquistadors searching for gold, slave labour and concubines. Since then, ironically, efforts have concentrated upon the more challenging task of managing ethnic difference.

The system of indentured servitude was used in the seventeenth century to keep the Irish poor excluded and dispossessed while the same system was used to facilitate the Scots, Welsh and English poor. Chattel slavery became the primary institution that was used to manage ethnic difference in the society for 211 years; thereafter, its legacy has continued to do a pretty good job for the descendants of the builders of that system. Managing ethnic difference within these oppressive contexts required the unrestricted use of state power to enforce race ideology and to create a system of apartheid in public governance, the market economy and in the spatial distribution of communities. Assimilation and integration policies were discouraged, and severe penalties awaited those who sought to promote such ideologies. All major institutions were racially segregated; these included schools and churches, as well as courts and political assemblies.

Intermarriage across ethnic boundaries was taboo, and Barbados, unlike all the other major regional communities, came into the twentieth century with a very small mixed-race population and a minimally diluted African gene pool. The social assimilation model, then, has not been a Barbadian favourite and has historically been excluded from any serious discourse about the social aspects of nation-building. The historic assault upon the ideology of social assimilation and integration meant that Barbados at Independence could not entertain the iconography nor vocabulary of 'the rainbow nation' or 'out of many one people' as the Trinidadians and Jamaicans have done.

'Pride and Industry' graphically represented an honest perspective that reflected both the mentalities of the poor but proud, hard-working black citizens, as well as rich, proud, hard-working white citizens. Pride and Industry, furthermore, carried a sub-text, a coded message, in much the same way 'the rainbow nation' and the 'out of many one people' rhetoric conceals a terrible truth about rampant racism against Blacks. The hidden message of Pride and Industry can be discovered in the way it suggests that being proud and hard-working can lead, in a way that is not mysterious, to both riches and poverty, depending on whether you merely worked on, or happened to own, the plantation on which everyone had sought to make a living.

The nation's founding father, the Rt Excellent Errol Barrow, is said to have expressed intolerance with his colleagues while discussing the hunger and bare-footedness among the working class with the assertion that everybody came from the plantations, and that the small difference between his experiences and theirs, insignificant and not worthy of mention, was that he came from a plantation which was owned by his parents.

The rejection of social assimilation models to change in Barbados led to two other approaches being tried, both of which have met with success for some, but mixed results for most. The first of these was the use of political engineering to manage ethnic difference. In order to reduce racial tension and conflict, a political assimilation model was developed – what has been described as 'catch-all political parties'. The objective of this approach was to break down the salience of ethnic cleavages by party membership and electoral integration. All political parties in independent Barbados adopted this model of political assimilation in order to promote political stability, economic development and social tolerance in civil society.

The second approach (in part a consequence of the former but effectively a rejection of the popular preference for a socially assimilating society) was the crude ethnic division of labour that came to underpin political and economic governance. The logic of this model was that the political use of power would reside with Afro-Barbadians, and the use of economic power would be retained by Euro-Barbadians. This was, and is, the basis of the post-Independence model of development that still fashions the contours of policy and serves to flavour the content of public discourse.

The model has been in moral crisis for some time but, nonetheless, in indirect and subtle ways it was responsible for both the defeat of the BLP in 1986 and the DLP in the last two electoral exercises. There is an opinion that the political process is trapped within this model that serves to subvert the sociocultural process of integration, and that only a genuine breakthrough can liberate this nation's human resources for the twenty-first century.

Those who rule and those who govern are said to exist separately, the State is possessed by one group, and productive capital by another, and so on. The perception might be more powerful than the truth and, as politics is as much about subjective perception as it is about objective reality, only end results can tell us effectively about the motions of the model. The bone in contention is of the proverbial fish kind that, having been lodged, now renders the society in a state of convulsion, seeking to purge itself of a cold past and a heated present. It is recognised that this ethnic division of labour is obsolete, regressive and subversive of the nation-building project. Some Euro-Barbadians have found their way back to Parliament and more Afro-Barbadians now represent private capital at all levels – though neither migration is as yet satisfactory in terms of numbers. The real crossing of the Rubicon has not yet taken place, though the time is right for the crossing and the path is clear.

Emerging from the background of this discredited and retreating model is the Social Partners model, which is similarly embedded within protocols of managerialism. Authorship might very well go to Mr Sandiford or Mr Trotman, but fear of return to the haunting past was the hand with which it was written. The precise nature of its origins aside, and in very much the same way that West Indies cricket came to global leadership with the unrelenting deployment of the pace quartet, Mr Arthur is seeking to propel Barbados with his four-prong social attack – the State as convenor, private sector, organised labour and civil society.

Speaking at the Mona Campus of the University of the West Indies on September 3, 1999, Arthur stated that the State 'must build new strategic alliances with the private sector, the non-governmental institutions, and all the institutions of civil society to create a new Caribbean, ordered in accordance with the precepts of a just and equitable and good society'. This constitutes the articulation of a strategy rather than a theory of development that is particularly suited to post-colonial societies. Its key aspect is that such societies can only progress in the globalised world if they minimise or abandon archaic, debilitating forms of contest and conflict (particularly racial ethnic strife) and build strong inner links, and alliances across civil society that can give real meaning to notions of shared visions and nationhood, through which the State can facilitate citizens in their quest for self-empowerment.

The Social Partners model has a radical dimension in the sense that it seeks to build within civil society such inner links that can sustain the persistence of effective economic planning human resource mobilisation and bring vital stability to macro-economic management. It is also radical in the sense that it seeks to transfer considerable power away from the executive of ruling political parties and share it with representative bodies of civic society. By this means, several objectives are reached:

1. ethnic groups can begin to forge and develop deep links for mutual support, and thus build upon new consensus 'centres' that represent public opinion. An important effect of this is the creation of new forms of high level ethnic interaction that can be the basis of building 'trust' for the 'thrust';

2. it can facilitate a breakdown in the ethnic divide between polity and economy, and fashion a new political economy for a stronger democratic base and a freer, more richly endowed, civil society;

3. it offers the potential for greater security to citizens who have long known that all the answers to development predicaments do not reside only with politicians, entrepreneurs, academics, labour leaders or other special interest groups or ethnicities within civil society, but rather that they all possess but a part of what is needed for effective planning.

The Social Partners model, furthermore, cannot be understood outside of the cultural history of the society that should be fore-grounded and used as cultural capital. There are a few examples of historical experiences that can now be seen as cultural propensities with considerable development potential. These are:

(i) Euro-Barbadians promoted a sense of the island as being at the 'centre' of a larger structure which called for a certain kind of conduct with respect to governance;

(ii) Euro-Barbadians developed a strong sense of identity with the island, and promoted a vision of nativity that sustains their economic commitment;

(iii) Afro-Barbadians saw their future in mass education, intellectualism, professionalism, political democracy, social harmony and human rights – all of which served to provide a mentality dedicated to stability, orderliness, fairness and neighbourliness;

(iv) Afro-Barbadians developed a strong commitment to civil society, sophisticated social interaction and public morality, that constitutes the finest type of human capital;

(v) both Afro-Barbadians and Euro-Barbadians, in addition to newer citizens from Asia, the Mediterranean, the Middle East and elsewhere, believe in the inherent goodness of national society, and are prepared to struggle for its advancement and prosperity.

The Social Partners model, however, has a long way to go before it can fulfil its enormous potential as a strategy for development through the building of vital inner links within civic society that can foster inter-racial cooperation, trust and responsibility. Importantly, it should be used, as Prime Minister Arthur has so graphically indicated, to bring closure to the promises made during the mid part of the twentieth century before new promises for the twenty-first century can be entertained. The promise to remove institutional racism from management in the private sector; to remove race discrimination in places such as private primary schools, entertainment centres, board rooms of corporations and the money market, must be effectively honoured.

The Social Partners must develop an internal operational review mechanism to monitor and address attitudes and practices that subvert civil society, and be intolerant of any such conduct emanating from its membership. In the same way, for example, that Sir John Stanley Goddard has been so critical of government over the decision to re-site the statue of Admiral Lord Nelson, he should be equally indignant, and publicly so, with the undemocratic white domination of the many corporate boards.

These are but examples of how the Social Partners can promote greater democracy in the public institutions of civic society as part of the process of building 'trust' for the 'thrust'. The Social Partners, then, must take power-sharing to its logical and ultimate conclusion. Broad Street must not be a place where white citizens accumulate and black citizens congregate. Neither must Heroes Square be a place where black politicians legislate and white entrepreneurs evacuate. They must take responsibility for the creation of an economic environment in which no one feels intimidated, because they alone can ensure that the politics of inclusion is translated into policies for economic democracy.

The centre of gravity within the Social Partners model should also revolve around how to revolutionise access to higher education for all. Barbadians have a cultural propensity to access knowledge because they received the rawest deal at emancipation, a landless freedom that drove them to rely upon education to escape the entrapment of the estates. This cultural propensity has given the society a significant advantage in terms of preparedness for the information age. Economic growth is so directly tied to access to higher education that society must find the resources to implement a policy of higher education for all within a restructured Barbados tertiary system that includes UWI articulated with all other institutions. This should be a principal project for the Social Partners. The 1993 World Bank Report on Higher Education shows that the Caribbean is at the bottom of the pile within the hemisphere in terms of access to higher education.

Since then, additional data have shown that the average in the hemisphere is now close to 45 per cent of the age cohort, with the USA standing at near 70 per cent and Latin America approaching 40 per cent. The anglophone Caribbean is less than 12 per cent, though Barbados leads the pack at about 25 per cent. This level must be taken up to at least 40 per cent in the next ten years if society intends to sustain development. This is a massive task, but it must be achieved if citizens wish to hold up their heads in the global village in the near future.

The Social Partners approach is the only mechanism that can deliver on this pressing national agenda. Furthermore, it is the most likely path to ethnic equality in Barbados because the knowledge power of Blacks in the global economy can be a self-liberating tool and an equalising force. Neither one of the political parties can produce such an environment by itself. Without an effective Social Partners model, Arthur's progressive and critical politics of inclusion can degenerate into the politics of illusion. Barbadian society cannot afford such damaging setbacks. The new and emerging political culture requires a greater elasticity, and the economic culture will require its many ethnicities.

The Social Partners model, finally, is the strategic mechanism that has the potential to produce a new ethnic sensibility as well as a plurality of possibilities that can set Barbados ablaze with energy. The danger, of course, is that the Social Partners must not be allowed to constitute themselves into a new governance elite which seeks to fossilise those elements of the past that are not needed for the future. They must not seek, by formal alliance, to hold back the growing momentum for a deeper democracy by determining agenda and policy for alliance-building in narrow, short-term ways. These are real dangers indeed, and the labour movement should always be mindful that modern democracy was nourished within its bosom, and that the lactation period is not fully complete. In other words, the Social Partners model carries the seeds for a liberating future, but it also carries the germ that can undo much of what has been achieved.

Barbados, then, is well poised to lead the way in illustrating how to create those vital inner links for the strengthening of civil society where the real responsibility for broad-based sustainable development rests. It has been prepared for this task by virtue of its peculiar cultural history which now seems, in a strange sort of way, more suited to the postmodern world. The State, as Prime Minister Arthur insists, must take the lead by reinventing itself in order to remain relevant and dynamic. But not only must the State reinvent itself, political parties too must find newer, more relevant identities or be abandoned as vehicles that can take us into the future. The reinvention of the BLP under Mr Arthur's leadership has given it a new relevance and authority from which the country now benefits. The other political party must do likewise if it wishes to continue as a noble instrument of development in the future. Postmodern mentalities are not committed to organisations that do not have a presence that is marked by high quality, high fidelity, pertinence and reliability.

- *Ten* -

Rethinking Nationhood:
The Caribbean Context

According to Lloyd Best there is no intellectually acceptable reason today why the Caribbean region should be poor. Academics three generations ago examined the circumstance of its persistent poverty from the perspective of several disciplines. They emerged with one fundamental conclusion; the power of the historical legacy is behind the Caribbean's impoverishment. This is no longer a valid point of departure. As a civilisation it should begin in earnest to take greater collective responsibility for its condition and destiny than it does at present. A tension persists within development discourse between history and economic policy. Greater clarity is required.

Academics have historicised the phenomenon of material poverty and social backwardness in the region in order to find trends and patterns of human conduct that act as constraints upon development efforts. They have also applied, though in a more tentative fashion, the tools of economics within their competence. In addition, through the cultural lens, they have searched the literary and artistic expressions of the people for evidence of a mature identity and sense of self worth.

But no matter how they twist and turn, dig and scratch, they surface with a compelling revelation. It is that Caribbean people are truly blessed and empowered with an abundance of resources and capabilities that are chronically underestimated and under-utilised. There has been a recent return to the conceptual writings of Sir Arthur Lewis on the potential of societies for sustainable development. This is not because of any sense of parochial nationalism. While nationalism has proven to be an important organising force in the post-colonial era, it is ultimately a reactionary ideology that breeds cultural prejudice and intolerance.

Sir Arthur's work is simply the most relevant and incisive available on the subject. He began with the intellectual processes that are internal to any civilisation. He saw the enormous potential of Caribbean civilisation, but insisted that it cure itself of the lack of self-confidence that was bred into the majority of the population under colonialism. For him, this has been the region's principal challenge. It is more a crisis of culture than the scarcity of cash and capital.

Caribbean people have had the kind of beginning and a type of preparation, that must be considered a fundamental asset with respect to modern development discourse. They should not lose sight of the evidence that shows the region as the mother of what is now celebrated globally as the West. It was here that the West was invented following that Columbus mission which transformed the world forever. It is here that the major civilisations of humanity met, even if violently, and produced the special, plural culture that is now universally known as the Caribbean brand; that continues to capture and exercise the imagination of all feeling and thinking people.

The West was never all about Europe, rather it was the interaction with Africa, Asia and the Americas (first in the Caribbean space) that produced a unique world view with a developmental mentality. It is a restless, anxious and turbulent kind of mind that insists upon effective production and rational approaches to problem solving. It insists, also, that there is considerable merit in the idea of progress and development as being an important human objective. The belief that poverty could be eradicated by means of large-scale production, that human freedom could be celebrated as a right and that freedom from fear could be attained by good governance became an early part of the regional reality.

These values led the majority of Caribbean people to fight against slavery, both of the chattel and indenture forms, and to end the colonial status at the first opportunity and with no regret among leaders. These are among the expressions of the fact that the Caribbean was the first global space of modernity. The features of international connectivity, particularly the perceptions that labour and capital could be obtained globally and that the entire world is an accessible market, were established cultural characteristics of the regional mind since the sixteenth century.

The seventeenth century sugar planter, for example, brought cash and capital from Europe, labour from Africa, Europe and Asia (once local supplies were exhausted), raw material and foodstuffs from North America and the places from which labour came, and sold globally through a sophisticated network of brokers and agents. This management culture expressed an extraordinary spirit of confidence and self-assertiveness. The majority of the population that fought for its freedom established another vital cultural asset within the civilisation – an unrelenting demand for justice and civil rights. Each ethnic group gave the Caribbean something much more important than the labour merely expected of them. They gave it a special gift; the wisdom represented in the spirits of worshipped ancestors and the irrepressible imaginations of their progeny.

These gifts were combined over time by the inevitability of human interactions. They multiplied and produced the grand Caribbean civilisation that is now offered to the world in return – in the quality of our cuisine, the artistic expressions of Sir Gary Sobers or Bob Marley, the democratic political impulse and systems now taken for granted. But the future will not be bright unless this sense of self-confidence and productivity found in the mentality of these Caribbean icons is democratised and settled everywhere as common sense.

Race in post-colonial Barbados

Barbados became the first race-based society of modernity in the sense that every aspect of society and economy was built completely on the principle of white supremacy. It was a unique experience. Globally, it was known by 1650 as the Barbados system.

The invention of the concept of 'race ' as a scientific 'fact' ascribed to nature and understood in terms of biology has to do with the rise of colonial society in Barbados and the Caribbean following European settlement in Africa during the early seventeenth century and the globalisation of the trans-Atlantic slave trade.

Today, this notion of race has been discredited. It is no longer considered a fact of science or nature but a social ideology constructed to serve purposes of societal division and political management. As Cornell West has said, race still matters, but is now on the run, driven out of respectable places, though it is by no means dead.

The Caribbean World can justly be considered as the social space within which modernity first developed matured concepts of race as the dominant and decisive principle for political governance, social organisation and economic ownership and management.

Following the advent of the Columbus mission to the Caribbean, an enterprise that brought Africans, Europeans, indigenes, and later Asians, together to create entirely new societies, concepts of race emerged as the superordinate factor that determined all social relations and cultural encounters in both colonial and imperial jurisdictions.

The advent of the English settler in Barbados in 1625 bred and reproduced cultural arrogance that translated into the invention of 'whiteness' as a social construct that underpinned and informed broad-based socio-economic ideas and policies. It is in this sense that it can be shown that the Barbados, especially, constituted a primordial site where the concepts of the West and of race were invented as popular organising tools that legally and ideologically framed the Atlantic world as a globally transforming force.

The subsequent growth of the ideologies of the West and race as virtual and visual realities, therefore, have a common history. They are linked by a unified ancestry that reached early maturity within the seminal moment of an imagined Caribbean discovery. In this way the Caribbean emerged, in an ironic way, as a kind of mother that gave birth and life to the modern belief that multiple ethnicities could be effectively identified, predetermined and fixed in hierarchical relations using laws, customs, arms and ideologies as markers and enforcers.

The Caribbean, then, was invented within the concept of New World discovery as the earliest mass experiment in modern multiracialism and it featured a network of new beginnings.

The framing of social structures and the texturing of cultural relations within the culture-colour prism established the Caribbean world as a model, a Weberian ideal type if you will, the first idyllic space within the imperial world as far as the coloniser was concerned. Whiteness was manufactured and packaged as the standard and benchmark; everything else was marginalised as the Other. Whiteness, as the determinant, was the centre that enabled this new world to be understood. The Caribbean, not West Africa nor the Mediterranean, not Asia nor the West European rim, was the laboratory of the modern race world order.

But in the Caribbean, the centre could not hold on account of the effectiveness of the contestations against whiteness and racism. Subversions of the social structure and the puncturing of its imagined support systems took place on multiple fronts: within the institutional systems of broad-based governance, through intense and intimate cultural engagements and as a result of the irresistible mixings of blood that re-engineered and re-faced society.

The majority of Caribbean people, furthermore, imagined and pursued a better world within the context of an Independence Experience that forged nations from colonies. In effect, the process required the tearing down of the walls of the world's first social apartheid systems. It also meant the laying of new foundations for a second, new world vision, one in which the principles of multiculturalism and multiracialism are entrenched within constitutions, social and cultural life, educational pedagogy, political imaginings and the arrangements of an open domesticity.

Nation, within the refashioned Caribbean world then, came to mean an assembly of multiple identities forging integrative social action around the idea that citizenship should not be fractured by the traditional markers of ethnicity and race. The Caribbean nation (struggled for and created by coalitions of ethnicities) sees its finest expressions within the deepening of these inner ethnic bonds and rejects, as a principal logic, discourses that promote division and disunity.

The Caribbean nation is framed as an umbrella of integrative identities that are locked into an ongoing debate about past injustices (understood as legacies of colonialism). Its effectiveness has to do with the way in which identity, particularly at the cultural level, locates ethnicity as a secondary reality. This is not to say that national identity does not mask perceptions of deep ethnic differences and divisions but rather that the notion of race has been destabilised by the biological and cultural evidence of creolisation. That is, notions of racial purity are easily disputed and set aside and ethnicity cannot fit effectively into usable phenotypic categories.

The ironic truth in Barbados and the wider Caribbean is that things are not what they seem, at least on the surface, and that the logic and patterns of history have created a popular understanding that an attempt to establish and politicise distinct race boundaries has the enormous task of confronting considerable biological diversity and cultural cohesion at the level of the formal structures and at the very concrete level of family and domesticity.

The Caribbean lessons, therefore, are many and recounting them should begin with the recognition that there is no place in post modernity that embraces such ethnic diversity within a shared cultural vision. In much the same way that the region was constructed under early colonialism as a model of racial division and conflict, the post-colonial strategy of harnessing diversity for collective energy can stand as a monument to a torn and tortured world now coming to terms with the value of this vision.

Everywhere, the logic of globalisation as a contradictory process is promoting the assertion of difference as the counterpoint to the fear of homogenisation. The notion of cultural difference is taking the form of ethnic identity and is calling for a realignment of the 'ethnic' with the 'national'. Nationalism, once understood as a cultural collective, is breaking down into ethnic units that are arrogant in their claim for exclusive space.

The Caribbean world stands against this destructive trend in its insistence upon unity in diversity. For this reason alone it should be taken as an ideal state of existence for post modern humanity and celebrated as one of the greatest achievements of the post-colonial world.

Contradictory Forces

The meeting of the OECD in Barbados in 2001 said much of what there is to understand about the globalisation and its contested political reality. But there is much more that must be made explicit. One of the inescapable features of all realities is the necessity to invent new words and to redesign language in order to establish new meanings and knowledge. Globalisation as a concept, furthermore, has become an important part of popular and technical discourse.

On the surface, it seems a perfectly simple word that invites no major contest over its meaning. Closer investigation reveals, however, that it occupies centre stage in the desire to understand and manage recent seminal developments. In the Caribbean, the word takes on special significance. Historians, especially, are very keen to establish that the process began in the aftermath of Columbus' mission to our islands in 1492. Columbus, we know, may not have been the first traveller to cross the Atlantic, but he certainly was the first to return alive and to tell the tale.

In so doing, the admiral linked the economies and societies of the old and new worlds forever, initiated the largest human migration in known history and inaugurated the reality of shrinking intercontinental dimensions to village proportions. Since then, the spaces known as the Americas, Europe, Asia, Africa, and the islands in between, have been physically domesticated and networked by multiple forms of communications technologies. The first global village, then, was the entire Caribbean world that emerged as the crossroads where Africa and Europe, and later Asia, met the Americas under the umbrella of the plantation that was an early example of a global economic institution.

The sugar planter, of course, was seen back then as the prototype of the global entrepreneur, and his mastery of the world market established the Caribbean as the place with a viable, even if morally tarnished, development model. He had no role models to emulate. Before him, there were the pirates and the buccaneers, global in their own right but very illegal in their offshore sector. They were a criminal element without doubt, but should be credited nonetheless with laying the infrastructure of the globalised modern Caribbean economy. The sugar planter, then, was a pioneer. He took on the world for 200 years and won. During this time, he had no peer as a global leader.

Think of it. He imported his labour from Europe and later Africa and Asia after he had used up local supplies or was denied access to it on his slavery terms. The importation of over five million workers from Africa into the Caribbean was no easy task. It required massive global organisation and mobilisation in addition to a fair measure of universal wickedness. He imported his food and building supplies from North America after he had destroyed, or rendered unsustainable, what was locally available. He produced a crop that was totally exported, mostly to Europe where his economic fortunes were linked through a mesh of finance houses and commission agents.

When he wanted a wife, or an education, he looked first to England and considered the local darlings of a lesser quality. He was, therefore, not only financially and economically globalised, but socially as well. Everywhere in the networked world during the eighteenth century, Caribbean sugar was available. Where there was none, it was desired and plans were put in place to secure access. The Caribbean was at the centre of globalisation, and most of the world understood this process as the natural order of things. Indeed, the entire Caribbean was considered designed and driven by these international forces.

But slave owners were not the only ones to put in place a globalised reality, fashioned in their own image. The enslaved Africans of Haiti became the first workers anywhere in the modern world to obtain political power and establish an independent, sovereign nation with a constitution that spoke to the liberation of all Africans. In the process, Haitians established the Caribbean as the first place to create a political system based on the democratic principles of universal citizenship, freedom for all and equality of all before the law. The rest of the world followed two centuries later, acknowledging such principles of governance.

No one, then, inside or outside of the OECD, has a deeper knowledge of and experience with respect to the transforming realities of globalisation. We were there at the beginning, gave it life and shape and continue to carry it within our veins. Furthermore, the Caribbean should be seen as the natural place to hold major hearings on the subject and it should be held up as an example of how best to avoid making horrid, unjust and unacceptable mistakes. Both slavery and colonialism were first expressions. The firm line taken at the OECD meeting, and the apology were in good order. The next step is to hold the line steady as we go.

Caribbean Institutions

The post-colonial Caribbean continues to struggle with its historical legacies in redefining its new identity with a vibrant and relevant nationalism. This difficulty, it is known all too well, will generate contention for some time, torn and tortured as societies are by changing engagements with a dynamic outer world.

Inevitably, some societies will be constrained by their definition of what reality is and will opt for pragmatic or rationalist positions on topical issues such as the importance of the Caribbean Court and the significance of the Imperial Crown. The location of these two institutions within the imagination of these societies will tell us a great deal about their potential for change and future viability.

Other societies will feel a pressing impulse demanding a departure from the scaffold of an ancient colonialism and a desire to fulfil the mandate of the independence promised by the founding fathers. Sovereignty is more about a state of mind than the mind of the State, and can either be fulfilled or betrayed but never compromised.

But definitions of reality will always represent the core of contests. Within our Caribbean world there is still a mixture of constitutional arrangements. Alongside the nation-states there remain a number of colonial systems, departments of imperial states and other structures that reflect various types of adjustments. The sovereign nation-states of the English speaking sub-region came into being during the mid-twentieth century's second phase of nation-building, preceded by Haiti, the Dominican Republic and Cuba, for example, that had blazed the trail with independence politics during the nineteenth century.

Stage three is now here, and the evidence of fragmentation, uncertainty and doubt is dictating the modalities being used as vehicles in which to travel. Again, notions of the hard reality are informing the discourse. The idea that there are no material benefits to be derived (the so-called price of bread thesis), doubt about our ability to effectively self-govern (the hanging court thesis), and our capacity to invent division when and where there is none (what God has put together let no man put asunder thesis) now constitute a recipe for inertia and conservatism in a circumstance that calls for strategic advances.

One of these hard realities, however, which is conveniently treated as a theory of the overzealous, is that if these societies do not hang together they will hang separately. Globalisation must be understood as a contradictory process, a double-edged sword, so to speak, that presents an open face on the one hand and a closed, made-up mind on the other. The banana bacchanal is the classic case that represents the two-faced nature of the globalising process.

But more critical for the region is that it must understand that the organising units and political principle of globalisation are the nation-state and nationalism respectively. Yes, there is a reality of openness and equal access, but the overriding reality is strong nations versus weak nations, or put simply, viable nationalisms versus untenable nationalisms. The only logical and viable strategic response to our predicament is the construction of a relevant and potent nationalism, and this has to be a new Caribbean nationalism that is underpinned by Caribbean institutions and constitutions that locate all power and authority within the citizenry.

The way to effectively plan for the future of sugar and tourism industries is no different from how we go about the discourse on the Caribbean Court of Appeal and the Monarchy. A unified Caribbean response is the only kind that is logical and meaningful. Those sections of the Caribbean sugar and tourism interests that identify with a Caribbean vision must develop political and market positions that reflect an indivisible Caribbean strategic response. There is no other way if Caribbean states and nationalism are to deliver a future with honour and dignity for citizens.

The entire mesh of debates on all of these issues are expressions of the painful unfolding of our historic desire to show, first to self and then to the world, that there is indeed a genuine and legitimate Caribbean civilisation that is worthy of recognition and respect. There remain unrelenting forces, internal and external, which insist that the region is about calypso, cricketers, banana republics, beach bums and habitation for leisure seekers in a fool's paradise.

It is also difficult to take bold decisions if the masses of people have not been schooled to discern the facts from the fiction. That is, the political directorate cannot be blowing cold on some issues and running hot on others that are all facets of the same general predicament. All of the issues that relate to how a viable and relevant Caribbean nationalism is to be refashioned are to be debated in relation to each other, not necessarily simultaneously, but coherently. Sadly, there is a growing feeling that things are being handled as independent bits and pieces with the result that there is doubt as to whether we are grasping the full picture.

Redefining the Nation

In December 2000, I was presented with an opportunity to make an impact on many young lives. The challenge was to say something relevant, durable and transforming while delivering the graduation address at the Sir Arthur Lewis Community College in St Lucia, an academy much respected and cared for. I fell short, failed maybe, but continued to reflect on the wider concerns and predicaments of young West Indians.

I chose to engage the graduands in a discourse with respect to their understanding of nationhood, citizenship and the objectives of development. There was no doubt in my mind that I was speaking from a position of advantage because the subject seems much clearer to my generation than to theirs. At no stage did I presume that the political projects of my generation would be readily embraced by them, or even understood in the same ways.

Permission was sought to set out the terms and meanings of nation-building for my generation. For the sake of establishing a formal chronology, we agreed that they were rooted in the specific circumstances of 1966, the year in which I entered secondary school. It was a time when the public space was filled with statements of epic proportions, Old Testament in tone and texture, such as, 'we now have a country', 'we must walk and don't look back', and 'the time has come to cease loitering on colonial premises'.

There was public consensus on the meanings of these edicts around which my generation framed its references and structured its thoughts. We had it easy, maybe too much so, because the script was written and, like the Moses manual, it only had to be embraced and followed, or so it seemed. We were given a structure, an infrastructure in fact, and all we had to do was get on with the job of building the nation by being disciplined citizens.

It was all very romantic. The politics of dispossession and ownership made for family quarrels between the majority from the peasantry and the few from the plantations. We were all equal now, or so it was written. The majority had no history of ownership to speak of. But now they had a country, the State, if not the land. Sadly, it was agreed to leave the politics of ownership of resources as an exercise for subsequent generations.

Learning to differentiate between ownership and dispossession within the nation was a challenge for us. No matter how we looked at it, the splintering and fracturing of citizenship as imagined and desired was the effect. As Richard Pryor said of post Martin Luther King American political culture, those who possessed shouted 'Just Us' and those dispossessed cried 'Justice'. Only the discerning could hear the divided sounds of the nation.

Without warning, I popped the big question – What is the mandate of your generation? It was not meant to terrorise but to frame the discourse and capture the imagination. Frantz Fanon, the iconic West Indian political philosopher, had asked this question of young Algerians on the eve of their national liberation. He stated, furthermore, 'each generation has a mandate which can either be fulfilled or betrayed, but never compromised'. The question seemed relevant. A generation born within the post-Independence dispensation was leaving the academy. How are they to deal with the clear and present dangers before them, and set out the terms of their own imagined idealism? If, for my generation, the buzzword was integration, for them it is globalisation. The former sought to transform from within, the latter to restructure from without. Either way, change is the operative concept.

The version of globalisation they are called upon to negotiate is threatening to destroy their very societies and render the nation they inherited non-sustainable. Though the contest is conducted in terms of the banana industry being non-competitive, a primary effect is to question and decide upon the role and fate of their small island nation. Whereas an earlier generation was engaged in the task of building the nation, these youths are called upon to defend it by all means necessary. Already they feel the force of globalisation as a contradictory process. It promises openness and a level playing field, but seeks at the same time to dispossess them of markets and of their nationhood and citizenship. They understand its politics in terms of strong versus weak nations, and see clearly that might rather than right is the rule.

Their condition calls for a strategic response that is logical and possible in terms of a rethink of the internal and external use of energies. A policy of mass higher education is desperately required. Deepening Caribbean integration to diversify productive activity and redefine citizenship is a must. The mandate of the youth, then, it seems, is to consolidate and redefine the nation and citizenship in more relevant ways.

Nationhood-Phase 2

There are two facts of Caribbean history that are irresistible and inescapable and that carry legacies that must be dealt with effectively, creatively and squarely within the four walls of common sense. The first of these is that we have not yet found the formula to fully utilise the enormous cultural potential and magnificence embodied in the ethnic and racial plurality of all our societies.

The second is that people of African ancestry were positioned, by virtue of their struggle, to remove slavery from the infant civilisation and to uproot the enduring injustices it bred, to lead the opposition to colonialism and therefore to head the first nation-states that emerged from the rubble. The political geometry of this contested past and tortured present should tell us that a fair amount of division, suspicion and opposition was built into the process that ultimately produced the independent states that followed the Federation's fall from grace. Much of this has origins within the weak bonds of race and ethnicity that is in fact the strength of the region.

In all the societies where Blacks led the independence discourse, other ethnic and racial groups generally withheld their enthusiasm and at times opposed the agenda. This was the case in Barbados as it was in Jamaica, Trinidad and Tobago and Guyana. As such black politicians and significant sections of the citizenry came to believe that they had a first and special lien upon the State, and were entitled to be the primary possessors of its power.

These and similar values and attitudes characterised the first stage of nation-building which, for the sake of time management, may be identified with the period including the federation process of the 1950s, the onset of structural adjustment and privatisation in the 1980s and the embrace of globalisation during the following decade. The region is now clearly located in the second phase of the nation-building, and a new political geometry is required to inform and guild the exercise.

First of all the region must take stock of where it is, what it has achieved, where it has fallen short, which bridges must be built, which fences require mending, and so on. Then it must recognise the need for a compelling vision that will enable it to identify progressive from backward political postures and policies. Finally, it must modernise its political morality in order to make it relevant to younger generations who are at the centre of all that is to be done for the future.

There are two fictions about the present that must be transformed into facts about the future. The first of these is that, while inter-ethnic contest for equality and justice is a necessary part of the deepening of democracy, the economic justice discourse, for example, ill-informed, uncontrolled, and reckless racial political conflict are likely to have the effect of throwing out the baby with the bath water. Secondly, stage two of the nation-building project, perhaps more so than stage one, will require all ethnic hands on deck and, unless this is achieved effectively, our nation-states, like our cricket team, will enter a spiralling decline and disintegration. The specific effects and general consequences of such a calamity require neither elaboration nor description.

For these reasons, the region should be very disturbed by the politics of ethnic conflict in the southern region. Blacks must remember that when they effectively monopolised the state during stage one of nation-building it can hardly be said that they passed the test for designing a culture of inclusion, least of all power-sharing. At the same time, newly empowered Indians may wish to reflect deeply on the politics of catch-up, monopoly and exclusion.

The intellectual and political challenge facing them in the consolidation of the nation in leaders of stage two may be even more formidable than the task Blacks had before them in establishing the nation in stage two. Eric Williams' cynical theorem of defeat and despair, 'what God has put asunder let no man put together', needs to be put in its proper place in the 'don't list' of the new political geometry.

The uncompromising equality of citizenship within civil society clearly has to be the cement that will hold the enlarged structure together. Many errors were made in stage one of the process and these must be acknowledged, accounted for and set aside within the context of statements of regret. The way to salvation must begin on the path of reconciliation. There is no other way.

While the vision of stage two was effectively captured with the rhetoric of stage one – 'rainbow nation', as in Trinidad and Tobago and 'out of many one people' as in Jamaica – the moment is ripe for the bringing of actions and thoughts together as bedfellows. It is only in this way that the Caribbean will demonstrate its credibility and sustainability as a viable and vibrant civilisation.

Republicanism

The monarchists in the region who have no difficulty in pledging loyalty to the Imperial Crown may very well be standing on sound historical ground. After all, was it not the Duke of York, the king's own blood, who in 1672 was the founding president of the Royal African Company which was mandated by the Crown to supply annually some 3000-4000 enslaved Africans to Barbados at rates of between 16-18 pounds sterling each?

Since then, West Indians seemed to have had many wonderful opportunities to articulate their loyalty to the Crown. Some of the stories reveal, with great humour, the depth of sentiment built up around this history. One such story was related by an English friend. It was an account of the Barbadian emigrant who arrived in England on the eve of the coronation of Queen Elizabeth II. Recruited to serve on the London Transport Board as a conductor, the Bajan arrived in the 'mother country' to witness the grand celebrations and festivities that marked the historic moment.

He had grown up, to use Austin Clarke's phrase, quite 'stupid under the Union Jack', and was therefore unable to imagine any state of being other than the colonial. In all innocence, he wrote home to his mother: 'Dear mum, arrived safely at Waterloo, but guess what? Would you believe that they are celebrating the coronation here, as well!'

Shortly before that declaration of surprise, there was the case in World War II when the governor of the colony encouraged Churchill's army against the Nazis with a telegram which urged: 'Go on Mother land, Little England is behind you'. This communication, it is said, so intimidated Hitler's high command, that an SS officer was instructed to reply to Bridgetown with the proposal that if the Barbadians kept out of the war, the Third Reich would give them Tobago as a pay-off.

But none of this is as significant as the account that relates to a member of the planter-merchant political group, the hurriedly strung together lobby which campaigned in London against Barrow's Independence plan. The lobbyist, it is said, impressed upon the Colonial Office that the reason they were opposed to Independence and nationhood was simply: 'The black boys can't run things and the place would fall apart before the cock crows thrice.'

But this is all very recent stuff. Barbadians have been trying to deal with imperial power, formal and informal, from the very beginning of England's colonial claim to the island since 1625. At the outset two earls of the royal court fought over the ownership of it. The king intervened, we have been told, and stated that he had given the colony as a legitimate gift to his 'intimate' friend, Peter Hay, the First Earl of Carlisle. When the bishops challenged the king's right to give away an island of the realm to his suitors, the king, we are told again, responded, 'The church began with its Peter and so Barbados will with mine'.

There is a connection between this event and the decision of the Barbados political elite in 1650/51 to reject imperial rule, and to tell the head of state, Oliver Cromwell, to go to hell. They declared Independence from the Commonwealth, became a republic in spirit and opened up free trade with all and sundry because this political stance served the best interests of the sugar sector. The English quickly forgave us, but to this day the Americans have not. As far as they are concerned we were 'yellow' and could be much further ahead if we had any spunk. I refer to the request by the Americans during their War of Independence against England that Barbados should join them in driving the English monarchy out of the New World.

The sugar sector, once again, that controlled policy and Parliamentary politics, debated the offer at length. It finally agreed, under the influence of Speaker of the House, John Beckles, not to join the Americans. But, as a gesture of moral support, voted public money to assist in the finance of the republican cause.

Black Barbadians in history danced to a different political drum. When the enslaved Barbadians planned a rebellion in 1675 to overthrow the slave owner government, the objective was to name Cuffee, their leader, the 'King of Barbados'. That is, an African-style monarchy. During the 'War of General Bussa' in 1816, evidence suggests that the Haitian model of rejecting an imperial head of state was a greater motivating force.

To suggest, then, that the debate over republican status will not influence the price of bread and is therefore not relevant to national politics is a version of cornbeef politics that is cavalier about the complex intellectual process through which citizenship, identity and nationhood were forged. The spirit and form of all nations, history shows, first have to be imagined, then debated, before they can be effectively rooted within a constitution.

The Bajan model and Jamaica

Since Prime Minister Arthur spoke on the Mona Campus in 1999 and hinted to his Jamaican government colleagues that financial discipline requires the symbolic 'execution of a General in order to encourage the rest', radio talk shows have been on to something called the 'Bajan model' of development. There is no longer talk of the Singapore model. Barbados is the topic. And the subject is the nature of national discipline. Here, there is deep frustration with the negative outcomes of development efforts. The lack of discipline at all levels is considered the prime cause. The desire is to know more about the Barbados method.

When I was invited as a 'new' Jamaican by the Trade Union Institute to deliver the Inaugural Michael Manley Memorial Lecture, my hands seemed tied. Professor Trevor Munroe suggested that I tackle the subject, as it had surfaced as an important issue in regional development discourse. I love Jamaica and readily agreed. I dealt in a comparative way with 'mentalities', institutions, relationships and policies in the two societies. These were historicised by focusing on the colonial system and heritage; how they were managed at Independence and efforts to embrace them within nation-building.

Manley was keenly interested in understanding how the past impacted differently upon the present of the two societies. Independent Barbados, he said, welcomed many aspects of its colonial heritage as home-grown, enabling assets, while Jamaica considered them all irredeemable liabilities. He respected the logic implicit in the Barbadian approach and saw its opportunities. History, it seemed, had made Jamaica less flexible. In the 1970s, Jamaica emerged as a leading site of ideological resistance to the unsympathetic West and debated the idea of 'opting out', as if this were possible. Barbados rooted its policy in bilateral friendships and selective engagements. An error was made in the reading of history. The modern Caribbean is located at the ideological centre of the West, even though in economic terms it is marginalised in the south of this West.

Formal opposition to private sector production, Christian social morality and electoral democracy were therefore likely to contradict the objectives of national development. Barbadians may have read this point very closely. The two responses, furthermore, were rooted in historical readings. The masses of Jamaicans fought slavery and colonialism relentlessly and paid a very dear price. The Barbadians, working within a less supportive geographical environment and situated at a sub-centre of the Empire, discovered at an early stage how to be more strategic and therefore less persistent with armed struggle as a democratising modality.

For Jamaicans today, the traditional elites that dominate them must be fought because the social justice denied them at Emancipation and at Independence is a more important objective of development than the economic growth promised. Barbadian workers, on the other hand, continue to show restraint in order to enjoy the benefits of economic growth, but have not lost sight of the desire for social justice and equity. In effect, then, the difference between the two societies is one of degree rather than kind.

At Emancipation in Jamaica, large numbers of Blacks secured land. Their Barbadian counterparts received a landless freedom. The former produced a class of independent small farmers, while the latter continued as wage labourers and located tenants. Ironically, land resources may have served to inhibit the Jamaican drive towards education as the key to enfranchisement. Black farmers were not supported adequately by the State and rural society bred widespread working class illiteracy and a deep distrust of the formal, national institutions.

The landless Barbadian masses cultivated a deep obsession with education as the only way up from poverty and out of despair. The middle class that emerged has remained reasonably sensitive to its roots, and supports a public policy of effective mass access to education. The Jamaican professional middle class now ponders the extent to which it has done its best for the country. Those in the ruined financial sector, especially, of whom Prime Minister Arthur spoke, tried but failed to consolidate the nation they inherited in 1962. Attachment to the display of material excess and the values of social arrogance and elitism has become a benchmark that serves to weaken the bonds of citizenship.

The Patterson government pursued a Social Partnership policy in order to stabilise the financial sector, but found that the leadership of sections of organised labour could not break free of the culture of party politics in which the winners take all. The private sector seemed willing to settle with labour in the economy, but bitter class and race conflict in the society took precedence.

But Jamaica remains a traditional Christian society that yearns for social peace. A minority of violent young men, victims of an inadequate formal education sector, rips daily at its core values and sensibilities. Among the poor, there is an anger that speaks to hardened hearts born of persistent poverty and disrespect. Meanwhile, richer classes are poor on social care for the needy. A home in Miami is the blinker they wear, and therein resides the crisis of the nation.

Role of Public Intellectuals

The Caribbean case may be quite different, but there needs to be more discussion about it, particularly within the context of the University of the West Indies. Since the publication in 1983 of Benedict Anderson's influential text, 'Imagined Communities', it has been the norm to argue that, with the collapse of colonial dispensations and the global rise from the ruins of nation-states, public intellectuals have been silenced into the new role of the expert consultant.

Lloyd Best may very well be a little harsh while lamenting the absence of an insightful Caribbean intellectualism to conclude that the regional academy has become home to a value-free 'validating elite'. A few critics have spoken of the death of the Caribbean intellectual tradition, and others have noted its subordination to the dominant bureaucratic mind and the corporate culture.

There is general agreement, though, that considerable unease exists within the intellectual community as a consequence of the region settling into an acceptance of the 'one from ten equals nothing' approach to politics. The expectation that intellectuals will validate this mathematics, and do so within the context of virulent globalisation that has no time or place for weak forms of nationalism, constitutes a call for their self-mutilation.

The conceptual framework of the predicament is readily discernible. The only rational or strategic response the region can have to the globalisation process is to reformulate and re-engineer our many nation-states into a vibrant regional formation that thinks and acts as a coherent force. With the gradual frustration of the 'Time For Action' manifesto, a spirit of pessimism has prevailed. The result is that the current political landscape of the region seems inconsistent with all of what we should know about ourselves and the world beyond.

But here is where we should begin. Public intellectuals, in general, are at their most effective and credible when able to speak to or on behalf of a community, real or reasonably imagined. Furthermore, they need to know or feel that the community they invent or represent is credible, viable, unified and singular. They seek to remove fractures and division and promote the idea of the 'whole'. The issue of their representativeness, then, is at the centre of all they do.

The Caribbean intellectuals are no longer clear on many of these matters. They have not been able to find a consistent and creative role in the post national phase of the nation-building project. The view that their energies were burnt in the struggle for nationhood, or that they feel marginalised in the evolved nation-state, is also fashionable but woefully insufficient as an explanatory framework for understanding this crisis. Neither is it acceptable to suggest that the political retreat from federalism and the descent into compromising 'Caricomism' has denied them a creative, imaginative space.

It is far more valuable, in terms of understanding how to go about the process of producing a relevant development discourse, to show how the idea of 'community' in the region can no longer be imagined as a singular, unified object to which intellectuals can relate in traditional ways. Take the situation in the USA, as an example. From Marcus Garvey through to Martin Luther King, Malcolm X and Jesse Jackson, black intellectuals spoke of, for and to the 'people', also known as the 'community', as an imagined unit that could be represented by them.

Then came the Anita Hill-Clarence Thomas spectacle that confirmed the existence of many black communities with diverse ideological needs and pointed out that 'national culture' rather than ethnicity was the principal organising unit as far as identity was concerned. The result is that the 'splintered community' is now represented by voices ranging from Condeleeza Rice to Louis Farrakhan.

The Caribbean circumstance is similar in many important ways. The younger generation of thinkers have not been able to rise above the residual ideas of their elders, who in turn continue to show insufficient commitment to fostering youthful creativity by asserting at all times the primacy of experience over intellect. The result is the creation of the 'don't trap' that enhances the will to abandon critical thought in favour of joining the validation elite.

The hey-day of the Caribbean intellectual may very well have been in the successful forging and framing of the nation-state from the potpourri of our history. But the nation can no longer be imagined today as it was yesterday, hence Prime Minister Arthur's politics of inclusion and Brian Lara's torn and tortured exclusion. Lara, as a nineties child, is in need of a new post nationalist framework to use his bat as much as the Windward Islands must find a post-preferential trading culture to sell their bananas.

C.L.R. James would have theorised the Lara lesson and offered it as a sign of our times. The Caribbean nation is now a global fact with remittances from North America and Europe keeping the wolf away from many States. There are no old and new enemies, only competitors and common cultures. The post nationalist public intellectual, then, will rise, but to be relevant must break free of the 1960s discourse and imagine 2050 as if it were now.

APPENDIX I

Summary of Speeches delivered by Rex V. Ulric Grant, at Golden Square, Bridgetown, July 22–24, 1937 as recorded by Raymond Hurley, Lance Corporal of the Police Force, Criminal Intelligence Department.

The subject tonight is about an injustice which was done to Payne. It is a shame and a disgrace to see the injustice which was done . . . The administration of justice today was done in a fraudish, highhanded way. Before Payne entered the Court he was convicted. Payne [was] only trying to educate his people politically, and the capitalistic element has started war against him. They have everything for themselves and are yet trying to exploit the poor masses. If we do not unite we will be found wanting. The Magistrate fined Payne £10 for nothing. Barbados is the wors[t] place in the world. It is run on a slave basis. In other places you can read and smoke. Barbados' jail was only for Negroes. Let us fight for . . . [our and our children's] . . . rights . . . . We are mistreated. Let us seek our rights. I fear no man on earth, and as long as I have breath in my body I will expose the wrongdoing in this Island. Our Constabulary consists of all black men, and all of them are to take orders from one man. If any policeman commits an offence he is fined from five to twenty shillings, . . . [and] . . . his poor family [is left] to starve for a month. Is it fair? Colonel Dickens and Puckering will fine a policeman or warder twenty shillings and . . . not care how their families get by, and yet some of the policemen are here now taking notes of all that is said and done. A change is needed soon too. Things in Barbados . . . [are] . . . disgusting. Governor Young needs more power. The white man has no human feelings for the poor Negroes, and if unrest starts in Barbados the capitalistic element will be responsible for it. We will have to fight for what we want but not with sticks . . . [unless] . . . we have to. (The crowd cheered defendant here.)

If we don't fight we will get nowhere for it is a shame and disgrace to know that slavery . . . still exist[s] in Barbados. Organisation is essential to any people, so let us . . . [cooperate] . . . and get into formation. Marcus Garvey organised four hundred million people. The capitalistic element is doing their best to get Payne off Barbados. Payne and I will die for you. Let us get together and march to Government House and put our [demands] before the Governor. Our MCP's ha[ve] left us to die. The capitalist preys on anyone who tries to uplift the masses. In British Guiana, coolies get one shilling a day whether they work or not. They also get other privileges, but in Barbados our children pick pond grass for nothing. Today, fifteen or sixteen policemen keep us from hearing Payne's case. I say it, the sooner we get organised the better for the community. One of these days the capitalist will wake up to find things in a drastic way. The decision in Payne's case had me inflamed. Fancy a Judge fining a man £10 for nothing! I [would] rather die by the sword than by famine. We must fight . . . these people. In the United States of America people only suffer for want of luxury but not food. In Harlem the people do not buy from any store which does not employ black men and women and you can only do these things when you are organised. We are being educated and in the near future will demand rights. Dig in[to] your pockets and assist in paying this fine and let us tell the powers-that-be that their time will come sooner or later.

Payne and myself want all you hungry and unemployed people to march to Government House tomorrow morning in search of recognition. The decision today was a ridiculous one, and apart from the injustice done . . . let us demand recognition. Let us also assist Mr. Payne to pay the fine. We will pay now, but when the time comes for the others to pay they may have to jump in the sea. (The crowd again cheered him.)

APPENDIX II

MY POLITICAL MEMOIRS OF BARBADOS

By

Clement O. Payne

Introduction

This book [was] published after accepting the many invitations and requests of my friends and interested fellow-citizens who [were] anxious to know from me, my recent political activities in Barbados [which led] to the unpleasant disturbances of that Island.

It is only a brief Autobiography of my social, literary, and political life in Trinidad, giving the full account of my political activities in Barbados, which is alleged in some quarters as [being] responsible for the 'Barbados Riot'.

In this book I give, without prejudice, a full explanation to my readers, the true facts of my four months experience which incidentally led to my deportation.

I therefore trust that my sincere efforts of presenting my brief Memoirs to you will be satisfactory.

At the age of sixteen, six months after I had completed my Elementary training at Barbados I became very interested in the politics of that country.

I held many prominent positions as a junior clerk in some of the recognised offices there during which I spent most of my spare time in reading and observing as much as possible: as a mean[s] of improving my knowledge on West Indian affairs I thought I would do some travelling and I elected to migrate to Trinidad, which . . . presented . . . a larger and therefore more appropriate field for my ambition.

On my arrival [in] that country, I found myself a stranger amongst strange people and in equally strange places. My stay was very short. I could not . . . really understand the people nor appreciate their doings.

In spite of this, however, there was still something about the people and the Island which held me in its bosom. What that something was I never attempted even to find out; but to my . . . surprise I found myself back in Trinidad [t]hree [y]ears after my first trial visit. The place seemed to me very prosperous on this occasion and I therefore decided to settle down as a Cleaner and Dyer.

It was not long before I became known to a number of persons, some of whom remain my dearest friends up to this day. Moving then in a circle of young ambitious men and women I quickly realised the time when I would get into my own. This was no vain belief nor idle thought, for just about this time I was attracted by the activities of the Universal Negro Improvement Association, where I was privileged to make my first public appearance . . . . I addressed a composite audience of about three hundred persons.

Fired with the zeal of my youth and being encouraged by the success I gained at this function, I thought that I would develop myself into a public speaker and as a result, I became a member of one of the leading Clubs in the Island, namely 'The Thistle Literary and Debating Club', [t]o which, I can readily attribute my successes as a Politician, and my failures if any.

I then embarked [on] larger fields of political activities; I was one of the organizers of the first Trade Union[s] established in Trinidad, namely 'The Trinidad and Tobago National Trade Union Centre', at that time functioning at Crystal Hall Henry Street . . . . [A]fter . . . [it became defunct] . . ., I [sought] other channels of activities by associating myself with a number of persons in organizing the 'African National Congress', which was affiliated to a similar body in British West Africa. Among other institution of public interest in which I was most active were, the 'WEST INDIAN YOUTH LEAGUE', the Easton Literary and Dramatic Club [and] the 'Thespian Dramatic Club'. I was also a member of the Eastern section of the Trinidad Workingmen[s] Association, now [the] Trinidad Labour [P]arty, and there I organized the first political Debating Club in the Island and was elected President. I may also mention [the part I played in] some of the political Elections and social services . . . to Government Institutions. I played an active part in the historical triangle Battle in the Western Ward for the seat on the Municipal Council which was won by Miss Jeffers. I also assisted on many occasions to return Mr. Patrick Jones [to] the said Council. In the social field, I Associated myself with the Salvation Army by giving Annual entertainments to the inmates of the Government Prisons. The last public dut[y] I performed before leaving for Barbados, was to assist in re-organizing some of the defunct division[s] of the Universal Negro Improvement Association . . . . [B]efore I . . . proceed to tell you of my thrilling experiences in Barbados, I would like to tell my readers that among the various Association and Clubs already mentioned, I held High Offices.

On March 26th, 1937, a bright Good Friday's sunlight welcomed me once more to the Island [which] I was always taught to love and have never ceased loving. It was Barbados. I found it a different country in many respects than it was after ten long years of my absence: of course this observation was made at a single glance of the Commercial Houses and many other places of business enterprise [et cetera]. After a short holidaying with my family and old friends, I then began to explore Barbados from every angle that was possible. It is necessary that my readers . . . know that, as one who ha[s] always advocated the economic wants and the political needs of the working masses of the West Indies, I would first find out the conditions of the working class. That I soon found out and the next step was to know whether there was a Working Class organization. After getting good information I soon discovered that the 'Barbados political organization'. a newly organized body, was the only Association in existence which . . . represent[ed] the entire working-classes of the Island. This information was interesting to me and I kept inquiring as to the whereabouts of the officers . . . . [I]t was not long before I was introduced to the Secretary who showed his greatest delight in meeting me, and after discussing political affairs he invited me to give an address at a meeting which was to be held . . . a few days from then. That I readily consented to, and a few nights after I made my first public appearance in Barbados. Not only was the audience satisfied, but from the many speakers, I gathered that the impression I created was a favourable one, with the result that I was asked by the officers to give all possible assistance I could to the organization during my stay in the Island. I then promised to do all I [could] for the organization in the interest of the working class STRUGGLE. I attended all General Meetings and addressed the workers on matters that needed their immediate attention, and soon discovered that the organization was in dire need of a 'Programme' . . . . [H]aving learnt that they ha[d] been functioning for nearly six months, I called upon the officers to carefully consider the advisability of preparing for the organization a practical workable 'programme'. This they agreed to an[d] my assistance was invited . . . . I consented [to this] and it was arranged for us to meet in Conference to prepare for the organization a suitable 'PROGRAMME'.

I regret to state here that the conference never took place, for what reason I cannot say, but I still continued my usual visits to the Meeting Hall and addressed the members. Winning their confidence and sincerity a dissatisfaction arose among them which in my opinion was due to the mismanagement of the Committee. [A]t this time they look[ed] . . . to me to intercede into their grievance and straighten out matters. Privately I was interviewed by many of them [who were] seeking my advice. I listened carefully to their appeals and without offering any opinion on the matter, I forthwith interviewed every member of the Committee and discussed the dissatisfaction of the members in regards to the working of the organization.

At this juncture, I very much regret to state that the impressions given me by them never led me to believe that the internal working of the organization and the political interest of the working Masses which they are supposed to be representing was a matter that seriously entertained their minds. I should let my readers know that the Committee referred to, was comprised of men of the Legal and Medical Teaching professions and also of the Mercantile Department. [T]herefore, after giving the whole matter my utmost consideration I arrived at one definite conclusion, and that was to organize the working people of Barbados: this I went about with my best zeal and interest and I got the help and support of a good many eager workers who were only too willing to see that the masses receive[d] a proper political education . . . . [F]rom amongst them I selected the most capable speakers with the required ability and begun my big Campaign of ORGANIZING. I started a series of Mass Meetings with the one objective aforestated, and here began the Romance of my political career in Barbados.

At these meetings the police took their usual course of being present and took notes of what was said from my platform. [C]onsequently, from my first meeting I was strictly under Police observation each moment of the day and night until things became [i]ntolerable. I then made protest to the Chief of Constabulary and the matter was to be investigated. I however continued my task of organizing, but to the dislike of the Police Authorities who were quite willing to enter into controversy with me but I repeat here what I often repeated there – THEY SHALL NOT.

My meetings as well as my name suddenly began to get popular among all classes and colour[s]. Public opinion was expressed in various ways and places, with the exception of the Press; the reasons for this I will explain to my readers later on. My venture at this time was making rapid progress. [O]ur followers led us to believe that they had accepted the philosophy of our teachings and were ready to make the objects of these meetings bear fruit. It must be clearly understood that at no time did I ever attack the Government on any legislative measures which affected the people, nor did I interfere with any of the grievances that had existed between the Government and the people. Had I done this it would have been a very unwise course of action knowing the one objective I had in view and the position I held at the time. I had enforced a policy that was always adopted at my meetings, part of it was against class or race hatred, libelling of Government, abuses of Government Officials, and the creating of hostile feelings between employers and employees. [T]his policy caused the police on many occasions to be thoroughly disappointed in many of their planned interruptions and arrests, but soon after they seemed to be[come] . . . [so] interested in the meetings, that interviews with some of the speakers were asked for; some of the Government officials sent to me stating their reasons, but others like the Inspector-General did not . . . . [B]ut I went and saw them all and heard what they had to say. The Government at that time was trying to play its trump-card on me but my slogan was as before – THEY SHALL NOT.

I continued my meetings with my usual policy to gain my objective and by that time had gained such wide popularity, not only in the City of Bridgetown, but also in the country districts. Among those who were quite willing to support my efforts were people of outstanding ability.

At this stage of my campaign, . . . the news from Trinidad [came] concerning the LABOUR RIOT which was received in Barbados like a bolt from the blue. Everyone was then interested and it was expected that I also would have been. [W]hile awaiting further news of the affairs, I carefully considered the views given by those who were supporting my Campaign. [T]hen after further news was had we met at a Campaign meeting and it was decided that we [would] speak to the people on the Trinidad labour unrest, and a big Mass Meeting was staged on this subject. It should be understood that public sentiment would be aroused, particularly among the working people, and the people looked to me, as a labourite to give mine. This meeting was a record one in the History of the Island. It . . . [may] . . . interest . . . my readers to know that the Police did all that was possible, and I may also say impossible, to prevent this particular meeting from taking place. [B]ut realising the delicacy of the subject I instructed my speakers [of] the manner in which such a subject should be handled and also reminded them of the surrounding difficulties. This Meeting was a bumper success amidst conservative threats and propaganda.

I [would] like to make plain . . . the fact that the one motive of this meeting was to allow the working classes of Barbados to know fully the conditions of their fellow-workers in Trinidad, and . . .[to make known] . . . my opinion on the causes of the Strike which led to the Riot. I claimed this authority, because I had left Trinidad just three months ago knowing all about the Labour grievances that had existed.

'The Barbados Advocate', the only daily newspaper in the Island and highly conservative in its policy . . . [very accurately published news on] . . . the Trinidad Labour Riot. It would be astonishing to many of my readers that during this time a 'strike' took place in Barbados' leading Foundry when some of the Engineers walked out. This Strike I considered to be important because those who had refused to work were the most skilful Mechanics employed. At my next meeting I severely criticised the attitude of the 'Advocate' for assuming the HUSH-HUSH policy of suppressing the publication of this strike when the truth about it was rampant all around Bridgetown. The other newspapers of the Island assumed the same attitude of remaining silent which I considered to be deceiving [to] the public. I [would] like my readers to know that the proceedings of Meetings organized by the workers never received publication by the Press. This is no strange news because it is known that Barbados is Governed by the highest system of Plantocracy. However, my meetings were carried on as usual and by that time the people were serious about organizing themselves. I then thought that the time was ripe to locate a Hall to start my real big efforts. [W]e then met at a Committee Meeting and after a careful review of the situation we agreed that the workers had received all that was necessary to enable them to be organized. [A]t the very next meeting a resolution was passed to the effect . . . . [A] vast crowd attended [that meeting] and my next step was to prepare for the workers a suitable 'Programme' . . . . I immediately set to work and in a short time had everything in readiness for the Grand Opening Night when I [was to] have presented to Political Barbados a new organization to be known as the 'Barbados Progressive Workingmen Association'. But at this time the Police were very active, trying hard to stall the progress of that great venture . . . by exercising every effort possible. I must admit that they ha[d] succeeded in preventing the working men and women of the Island from seeing the Birth of a new Political organization but how, I shall now tell you.

One day as I stepped out from attending a Committee Meeting into a certain street I found myself surrounded by five Detectives. [O]ne presented me with two Summonses to appear forthwith before the City Magistrate to answer to the following charges: That I wilfully made a false statement to the Harbour Authorities with regards to my place of Birth on my arrival in Barbados, secondly [for] landing in the Colony improperly. Under those conditions, I immediately consulted a Legal Counsel and appeared in Court. I pleaded not guilty and through my Counsel I got an adjournment, but at the resumption I was not in a position to . . . retain . . . a Counsel. [T]herefore I conducted my own defence, and after a lengthy hearing the Magistrate found me guilty and ordered me to pay a fine of Ten Pounds forthwith or the alternative of three months imprisonment. I appealed against this decision and left the Court House.

At this stage, I got the sincere support of the working classes both morally and financially, and the vast host of them, employed and unemployed, faithfully pledged . . . to give me all the support and assistance that was humbly possible to aid me out of . . . [the] . . . troubles . . . carefully planned and prepared by the Government. It must not be forgotten that a good many of these people knew me for years as a kid. [T]hey knew my family, they knew my friends, they knew me as a Barbadian; they also knew me as one capable of organizing them. [T]hey could not have seen their leader (who, night after night, told them things which came to them like a blessing from heaven) dealt with in a manner that was strange to British Constitution and British justice: so their loyalty and affection towards me was exhibited as never . . . before in the history of political Barbados. This was to the surpris[e] [and] displeasure of the Police and the Plantocracy of the Island. I called a meeting the night after my 'case' and without any printed advertisement I found myself facing an audience of about two thousand or more interested workers and citizens, wild with enthusiasm.

[Prior] to this meeting, the Police had placed a boycott on my printed advertisement. [T]herefore I was refused by many of the leading Printeries . . . [and so was not able to have] . . . Hand Bills and other Advertising work done that would have given my meetings better publicity. [However], my philosophical teachings to the masses was so [widely] distributed in Town and Country districts that the boycotted efforts of the Police proved a failure. This meeting, which was my very last in the Island, . . . was a historical one from many angles. People from nearly every station in life attended, which was . . . significan[t] in the Island of Barbados, judging from the environment where it was kept. It must be understood that among this vast assembly not less than seventy five per cent were real working men and women. It was at this meeting [that] I saw the perfection of love and loyalty genuinely exhibited; it was here [that] I saw the prelude to a gigantic workingmen Association; and it was here [that] I discovered the sincere support of honest leadership. The police formed a well represent[ed] percentage of this assembly and [had] expected many acts of violence to have taken place, but the people understood too well my teachings . . . [and they did not forget] one of my many slogans – 'Non-Violence'. It was at this Meeting [that] I spoke of my dissatisfaction arising from my conviction at the Magistrate Court and also of the ulterior motive of the Government towards me.

I had finally discovered that the Government had a beautiful trump-card to use and that was the card of expulsion. This, they tried for several weeks back, but a clue could not . . . [be] . . . found. Knowing Barbados as I do, and knowing also the old proverb, 'from Caesar to Caesar', I decided to go to Government House next morning . . . [to] . . . see whether I could get his Excellency the Governor to give me an audience with him so that my whole case could be presented. I also invited my members to accompany me on my way. I considered such an invitation to be reasonable and . . . justifiable because I was a public man, in public life, and had the Masses logically interested in me, and I in them. I knew the influence I had over them. I knew that they [would] always obey me .

. . [and] they accepted my invitation unanimously. [A]fter I saw the willingness of the people, I made it perfectly understood and called upon the police to take special notes and to witnesses to the following conditions that would make my advance to His Excellency the Governor. [The conditions were] that no one should be armed with any kind of weapons such as knives, sticks, bottles, fire-arms, or any missiles that may lead to destruction; That in case of any arrest made by the police, no resistance must be given and that all instructions given by me on the morning of my advance to Government House be strictly obeyed. I further warned the people not be seen that day with even a match stick or a feather. I seriously advised them not to leave their work and form part of the 'march'. I then proceeded with other matters that were of vital interest to the people. [T]his Meeting lasted for hours and terminated with the pleasure and satisfaction of the great crowd that [was] present. This convinced me that the course I had chosen in the name of honour and justice was warranted because there were no opposing element.

The morning opened nicely with splendid sunshine [shining] on the very spot which had been selected for the gathering. The people assembled at the appointed time and I addressed them on matters relating to the 'march'. I emphasized . . . the point of 'non-violence' and gave strict orders to dispe[n]se with all weapons if any person was so armed at eight o'clock. I led the March with an approximate number of three Hundred workers and citizens. [D]uring our march we s[a]ng Hymns and popular Anthems composed . . . [out of] . . . loyalty to the British Empire and in about thirty minutes we reached our destination. We stopped within fifty yards of Government House and after giving my last orders to the assembly I then advance[d] alone to the entrance where there [was] a big armed Company of Military Stalwarts eagerly awaiting my approach. I was met by the Deputy Inspector General of police who politely inquired where I was going. I told him that I was desirous of seeking an interview with His Excellency . . . [H]e arrested me and put me into the hands of a constable and [I] was taken to the guard-house at the Governor's gate. About five minutes after, thirteen others were also arrested. We were then taken before the Magistrate and charged [with] refusing to . . .

[disassemble] . . . when told [to do] so by the Police. We pleaded not guilty to the charge and were remanded until late in the day, a bail of Fifty pounds was given me while the others were given a Twenty-five pounds surety. We were recalled later and the charge against me was withdrawn. [T]o my great surprise I was served with an order of expulsion from the Island which was signed by His Excellency the Governor. I was reluctant in taking the order on the grounds of having an Appeal case pending, but on the advice of my lawyer who was retained by the people to defend me, I took it. I had confidence in him because he is the people's lawyer and the most outstanding Barrister-politician in the Island of Barbados — Mr. G.H. Adams. I was then taken into custody and kept there awaiting my deportation. While in prison, I received a Summons informing me of my appeal which . . . [was soon to] . . . take place. My lawyer, on visiting me, . . . [assured me] . . . that he was confident of winning my appeal case. During this time I was receiving the financial support from nearly the entire working class community. On Monday morning, 26th July, 1937, I was taken before the Appeal Court and won my case without my counsel addressing the Court. The news flashed through the City like lightening and was heartily received by the thousands of interested workers and citizens. I was then hurriedly carried away through a private gate back to prison. Having won my appeal, it was expected by the populace and as well as myself that the Expulsion orders against me would be cancelled, but the Government insisted in carrying out its intentions irrespective of failing to secure a conviction against me. I may mention here that during my short stay in prison awaiting deportation, my meetings were ably conducted by my assistants who were doing all that could be done to . . . [prevent] . . . my deportation.

At about three o'clock in the afternoon, my lawyer came to me in prison and told me that, after trying hard to secure my release, [he had] failed [but that] he was going to make a last minute petition to His Excellency the Governor. [This petition, he] brought . . . for me to sign, which I did, and in about four hours time I received an answer stating that His Excellency had refused to entertain my petition. I was then put into a car carefully guarded by Detectives and was then taken through a private passage leading to the Harbour, . . .[and] . . . placed aboard a ship bound for Trinidad. Around nine o'clock . . . [that] . . . night, whilst behind locked bars, I was allowed to speak to my family and just a few of my sincere members who had much difficult[y] in trying to see me. [F]rom . . . [them] . . . I learnt that a crowd of well wishers, friends, and citizens, thousands in . . . number, were lined up on the pier and other places of sight, anxiously awaiting my arrival to say goodbye. After a short discussion and shedding of tears, my final goodbye was said . . . – Remember to keep the lights always burning, continue to hold mass meetings, Organize, Educate, Agitate, but do not violate. With these words I retired to my cabin with a feeling that hardly could be expressed, but with a heart and memory which [could] never forget the love, gratitude, and the high esteem given me by the working men and women of Barbados. In a little while the ship [s]teamed out of the harbour, and I left Barbados as I met it; enjoying peace, order and law, but greatly improved Socially, Morally, and Politically.

Bibliography

OFFICIAL DOCUMENTS AND REPORTS

A Report from the Select Committee of the House of Assembly appointed to inquire into the Origins, Cause, and Progress of the late Insurrection (Barbados, 1818).

A Report of a Committee of the Council of Barbados, appointed to inquire into the Actual Condition of the Slaves in this Island (Barbados, 1822).

Annual Report on the Organisation and Administration of the Barbados Police Force, 1937.

Barbados Blue Book Statistics, 1900–1945.

Barbados Chamber of Commerce, Produce Books, 1930–46.

British Colonial Office Reports, Vols: 321/12; 317/6; 319/8.

Caribbean Labour Congress: Official Report on Conference, Barbados, 1945.

Deane Commission of Enquiry into the Disturbances in Barbados, 1937.

Documents Relative to the Barbados Disturbances, 1937; CO 28/321, f.12.

Enclosures in Confidential Dispatches, January 10, 1938, CO 28/321, f.1.

Henry Lofty. Report on the Census of Barbados, 1911–1921.

Local Forces Report to Governor, 1937. Government House Papers, 4/110. Barbados Archives.

Police Situational Reports 1937. GH 4/112; 4/109; 4/110 Files.

Proceedings of West Indian Sugar Commission (Bridgetown, 1929).

Proceedings of the West Indian Sugar Commission (Sir Henry Norman, Chairman) 1930.

Rankine, J.D. A Ten Year Development Plan for Barbados, 1945–56 (Barbados, 1956).

Report and Evidence of West India Royal Commission, 1897.

Report of the Acting Chief Medical Officer, 1929.

Report of the Committee appointed to consider and report on the question of nutrition in Barbados (Bridgetown, 1938).

Report of Select Committee of the House of Commons on West India Colonies, 1842.

Report of the West India Royal Commission (Moyne Report, 1945).

Report of the West Indian Sugar Commission (London, HMO, 1930).

Report on Census of Barbados, 1881–1891 (Bridgetown, 1899).

Report on the Elementary Education for the year 1899 (Bridgetown, 1899).

Sampson, H.C. Report on the Development of Agriculture in the Leeward and Windward Islands and Barbados, London, 1927.

Sedition Charge of Ulric Grant. Colonial Office Papers, 321/112 microfilm.

Sugar Industry Agricultural Bank. Minute Books, 1929–50.

The Governor's Address at the Opening of the Legislative Session, 1935–1936.

The Police Act, 1908, Sections 20–48.

Voters' Registers, 1920–1935.

BOOKS

Alleyne, Warren. *Historic Bridgetown*. Bridgetown: Barbados National Trust, 1978.

Anderson, Benedict. *Imagined Communities: Reflections on the Origins and Spread of Nationalism*. 1983. Reprint. London and New York: Verso, 1991.

Anon. *Addresses to His Excellency Edward John Eyre, Esq., 1865, 1866*. Kingston: DeCordova & Co., 1866.

Anon. *Jamaica: Its State and Prospects*. London, 1867.

Anon. *Memoirs of the First Settlement of the Island of Barbados*. Bridgetown, 1741.

Aptheker, Herbert. *American Negro Slave Revolts*. 1943. Reprint. 50th Anniversary Edition. New York: Monthly Review Press, 1993.

Ashcroft, Bill, et.al., eds. *The Post Colonial Studies Reader*. Routeledge: London, 1995.

Augier, Fitzroy, et. al. *The Making of the West Indies*. London: Longmans, 1960.

_____ & S. Gordon. *Sources of West Indian History*. London: Longmans, 1962.

Bakan, Abigail B. *Ideology and Class Conflict in Jamaica: The Politics of Rebellion*. Montreal and Kingston: McGill-Queen's University Press, 1990.

Banbury, Rev. T. *Jamaica Superstitions; Or, the Obeah Book: A Complete Treatise on the Absurdities Believed in By the People of the Island*. Kingston: Mortimer De Souza, 1895.

Barton, G.T. *The Prehistory of Barbados*. Barbados: Advocate News, 1953.

Bayley, Frederick. *Four Years Residence in the West Indies*. London: 1830.

Beachy, R.W. *The British West Indian Sugar Industry in the Late Nineteenth Century*. Westport: Negro University Press, 1978.

Beckles, Hilary. *Black Rebellion in Barbados: The Struggle Against Slavery, 1627–1838*. Bridgetown: Antilles, 1984.

_____ and Verene Shepherd, eds. *Caribbean Freedom Economy and Slavery from Emancipation to the Present*, Kingston: Ian Randle Publishers, 1993.

Beckles, H. McD. *A History of Barbados: From Amerindian Settlement to Nation State*. Cambridge: 1989.

_____. *Corporate Power in Barbados: The Mutual Affair; Economic Injustice in a Political Democracy* Bridgetown, 1989.

Beckles, W.A. *The Barbados Disturbances: 1937*. Bridgetown: Advocate News, 1973.

Bell, Howard H., ed. *Black Separatism and the Caribbean*. Ann Arbor: University of Michigan, 1970.

Bigelow, John. *Jamaica in 1850 Or the Effects of Sixteen Years of Freedom on a Slave Colony*. 1851. Reprint. Including Appendix A: 'A visit to the Emperor of Haiti'. Westport, CT: Negro Universities Press, 1970.

Bird, Mark B. *The Black Man; Or Haytian Independence*. New York, 1869.

Blackburn, Robin. *The Overthrow of Colonial Slavery, 1776–1848*. London: Verso, 1988.

Blackett, R.J.M. *Building an Antislavery Wall: Black Americans in the Atlantic Abolitionist Movement, 1830–1860*. Baton Rouge and London: Louisiana State University Press, 1983.

Blackman, Francis. *Dame Nita: Caribbean Woman, World Citizen*. Ian Randle Publishers: Kingston, 1995.

Brathwaite, Edward Kamau. *Barbajan Poems: 1492–1992*. NY: Savacou North, 1994.

_____. *Middle Passages*. Newcastle: Bloodaxe Books, 1992.

_____. *X / Self*. Oxford: Oxford University Press, 1987.

_____. *Contradictory Omens*. Mona: Savacou, 1985.

_____. *The History of the Voice*. New Beacon Books: London, 1984.

_____. *Sun Poem*. Oxford: Oxford University Press, 1982.

_____. *Mother Poem*. Oxford: Oxford University Press, 1977.

_____. *The Arrivants: A New World Trilogy*. Oxford: Oxford University Press, 1973.

Bridenbaugh, Carl & Roberta. *No Peace Beyond the Line: The English in the Caribbean, 1624–1690*. Oxford: Oxford University Press, 1972.

Bryan, Patrick. *The Haitian Revolution and its Effects*. Kingston and Exeter, NH: Heinemann, 1984.

Burton, Richard D.E. *Afro-Creole: Power, Opposition and Play in the Caribbean*. Ithaca and London: Connell University Press, 1997.

Campbell, Peter. *The Church in Barbados in the Seventeenth Century*. Bridgetown: Barbados Museum, 1982.

Chevannes, Barry. *Rastafari: Roots and Ideology*. Syracuse, NY: Syracuse University Press, 1994.

Clarke, Charles. *The Constitutional Crisis of 1876 in Barbados*. Bridgetown, 1896.

Cooper, Carolyn. *Noises in the Blood: Orality, Gender, and the 'Vulgar' Body of Jamaican Popular Culture*. Durham: Duke University Press, 1995.

Craton, Michael. *Testing the Chains: Resistance to Slavery in the British West Indies*, Ithaca: Cornell University Press, 1982.

_____. *Sinews of Empire: A Short History of British Slavery*. London: Doubleday, 1974.

Curtin, Philip. *The Atlantic Slave Trade: A Census*. Madison: University of Wisconsin Press, 1969.

_____. *Two Jamaicas: The Role of Ideas in a Tropical Colony, 1830–1865*. 1975. Reprint. Cambridge, MA: Harvard University Press, 1995.

_____. *The Rise and Fall of the Plantation Complex: Essays in Atlantic History*. Cambridge: Cambridge University Press, 1990.

Davis, Darnell. *Cavaliers and Roundheads of Barbados, 1650–1652*. Georgetown, 1887.

Davis, Kortright. *Cross and Crown in Barbados*. Frankfurt, 1983.

Dickson, William. *Letters on Slavery*. London, 1789.

_____. *Mitigation of Slavery*. London, 1814.

Drescher, Seymour. *Econocide: British Slavery in the Era of Abolition*. Pittsburgh: Pittsburgh University Press, 1977.

Du Bois, W.E.B. *Black Reconstruction in America, 1860–1880*. 1935. Reprint. New York: Atheneum, 1992.

Dunn, Richard. *Sugar and Slaves: The Rise of the Planter Class in the English West Indies, 1624–1713*. Chapel Hill: University of North Carolina Press, 1972.

Dupuy, Alex. *Haiti in the World Economy: Class, Race and Underdevelopment since 1700*. Boulder, CO: Westview Press, 1989.

Edghill, J.Y. *About Barbados*. London, 1890.

Eltis, David. *Economic Growth and the Ending of the Transatlantic Slave Trade*. New York: Oxford University Press, 1987.

Fick, Carolyn E. *The Making of Haiti: The Saint Domingue Revolution from Below*. Knoxville: University of Tennessee Press, 1990.

Fisher, Lawrence. *Colonial Madness: Mental Health in Barbadian Social Order*. New Brunswick: Rutgers University Press, 1985.

Foner, Eric. *Nothing But Freedom: Emancipation and Its Legacy*. Baton Rouge: Louisiana State University Press, 1983.

Frere, George. *A Short History of Barbados*. London, 1768.

Galenson, David. *Traders, Planters, and Slaves*. Cambridge: Cambridge University Press, 1986.

Gaspar, David B. and David P. Geggus. *A Turbulent Time: The French Revolution and the Greater Caribbean*. Bloomington and Indianapolis: Indiana University Press, 1997.

Geggus, David P. *Slavery, War and Revolution: The British Occupation of Saint Domingue, 1793–1798*. Oxford: Clarendon Press, 1982a.

Genovese, Eugene. *From Rebellion Revolution: Afro-American Slave Revolts in the Making of the New World*. 1979. Reprint. New York: Vintage, 1981.

Gilroy, Paul. There Ain't No Black in the Union Jack: The Cultural Politics of Race and Nation. Chicago: University of Chicago Press, 1991.

_____. *The Black Atlantic: Modernity and Double Consciousness*. 1993. Reprint. Cambridge: Harvard University Press, 1995.

Goodridge, Sehon. *Facing the Challenge of Emancipation: A Study of the Ministry of William Hart Coleridge, First Bishop of Barbados, 1824–1842*. Bridgetown: Antilles, 1981.

Goveia, Elsa. *Slave Society in the British Leeward Islands*. New Haven: Yale University Press, 1965.

_____. *The West Indian Slave Laws of the Eighteenth Century*. Barbados: Caribbean University Press, 1970.

Greenfield, Sidney. *English Rustics in Black Slain*. New Haven: Yale University Press, 1966.

Habermas, Jurgen. *The Structural Transformation of the Public Sphere*. 1989. Reprint. Cambridge, MA: MIT Press, 1992.

Hall, Catherine. *White, Male and Middle Class: Explorations in Feminism and History*. Cambridge: Policy Press, 1992.

Hall, Douglas. *Free Jamaica, 1838–1865: An Economic History*. New Haven: Yale University Press, 1959.

Hamilton, Bruce. *Barbados and the Confederation Question, 1871–1885*. London: William Kidd, 1956.

Handler, Jerome & Frederick Lange. *Plantation Slavery in Barbados: An Archaeological and Historical Investigation*. London: Harvard University Press, 1978.

Handler, Jerome. *The Unappropriated People: Freedmen in the Slave Society of Barbados*. Baltimore: Johns Hopkins University Press, 1974.

Harlow, Vincent. *A History of Barbados, 1625–1685*. Oxford: Oxford University Press, 1926.

Helg, Aline. *Our Rightful Share: The Afro-Cuban Struggle for Equality, 1886–1912*. Chapel Hill and London: University of North Carolina Press, 1995.

Heuman, Gad. *Between Black and White: Race, Politics and the Free Coloreds in Jamaica, 1792–1865*. Westport, CT: Greenwood, 1981.

_____ *'The Killing Time': The Morant Bay Rebellion in Jamaica*. London: Macmillan, 1994.

Hewitt, J.M. *Ten Years of Constitutional Development in Barbados*. Bridgetown: Advocate News, 1954.

Higman, Barry. *Slave Populations of the British Caribbean, 1807–1834*. Baltimore: Johns Hopkins University Press, 1984.

Hoyos, F.A. *Barbados. A History from the Amerindians to Independence*. London: Macmillan, 1978.

Hoyos, F.A. *Grantley Adams and the Social Revolution*. London: MacMillan, 1974.

Hughes, Griffith. *The Natural History of Barbados*. London, 1750.

'Jamaica Baptist Edward John Eyr.... In Reference to the Letter Addressed by Dr. Underhill to the Rt. Hon'ble Mr. Cardwell, Secretary of State for the Colonies'. Montego Bay: County Union Office, June 5, 1865.

Jamaica Committee, Facts and Documents re alleged rebellion in Jamaica and the Measure of Repression; including Notes of the trial of Mr. Gordon, *Jamaica Papers*, no. 1. London: The Jamaica Committee, 1866.

James, Winston. *Holding Aloft the Banner of Ethopia: Caribbean Radicalism in Early Twentieth-Century America*. London and New York: Verso, 1998.

Kincaid, Jamaica. *In a Small Place*. London: Virago, 1988.

Kelley, Robin D.G. *Race Rebels: Culture, Politics and the Black Working Class*. New York: The Free Press, 1996.

Knight, Franklin. *The Caribbean: The Genesis of a Fragmented Nationalism*. N.Y.: Oxford University Press, 1978.

Lamming, George. *In the Castle of my Skin*. London: Michael Joseph., 1953.

Levy, Claude. *Emancipation, Sugar, and Federalism: Barbados and the West Indies, 1833–1876*. Gainesville: University of Florida Press, 1980.

Lewis, Arthur. *Labour in the West Indies*. London: Fabian Society, 1938.

_____. *The Agony of the Eight*. Bridgetown: Fabian Society, 1965.

Lewis, Gordon. *The Growth of the Modern West Indies*. London: MacGibbon and Kee, 1968.

Ligon, Richard. *A True and Exact History of the Island of Barbados*. London, 1657.

Lowenthal, David. *West Indian Societies*. N.Y.: Oxford University Press, 1972.

Mack, Raymond. *Race, Class and Power in Barbados*. Cambridge, Massachusetts: Schenkman, 1967.

Mallon, Florencia. *The Defense of Community in Peru's Central Highlands: Peasant Struggle and Capitalist Transition, 1860–1940*. Princeton: Princeton University Press, 1983.

_____. *Peasant and Nation: The Making of Postcolonial Mexico and Peru*. Berkeley and Los Angeles: University of California Press, 1995.

Mark, Francis. *The History of the Barbados Workers' Union*. Barbados: Barbados Workers Union, 1966.

Marshall, Woodville, ed. *The Colthurst Journal*. N.Y.: KTO Press, 1977.

Martin, Tony. *Race First: The Ideological and Organizational Struggles of Marcus Garvey and the Universal Negro Improvement Association*. Westport, C.T. and London: Greenwood Press, 1976.

McCusker, John & Russell Menard. *The Economy of British America: 1607–1789*. Chapel Hill: University of North Carolina Press, 1985.

McGlynn, Frank and Seymour Drescher, eds. *The Meaning of Freedom: Economics, Politics and Culture after Slavery*. Pittsburgh & London: University of Pittsburgh Press, 1992.

Metraux, Alfred. *Black Peasants and Their Religion*. Translated by Peter Lengyel. London: George Harrap & Co., 1990.

Mintz, Sidney and Douglas Hall. *The Origins of the Jamaica Internal Marketing System*. Yale University Publications in Anthropology, no. 57, p. 3–26. New Haven: University Press Department of Anthropology., 1960.

Mintz, Sidney and Sally Price, eds. *Caribbean Contours*. Baltimore: Johns Hopkins University Press, 1985.

Morris, Aldon D. *The Origins of the Civil Rights Movement*. New York: Free Press, 1984.

Morrissey, Marietta. *Slave Women in the New World: Gender Stratification in the Caribbean*. Lawrence K.S.: University of Kansas Press, 1989.

Newton, Velma. *The Silver Men: West Indian Labour Migration to Panama, 1850–1914*. Kingston: ISER, UWI, 1984.

Nicholls, David. *From Desalines to Duvalier: Race, Colour and National Independence in Haiti*, third edition. London: Macmillan Caribbean, 1996.

Orderson, J.W. *Creoleana: Or Social and Domestic Scenes and Incidents in Barbados in days of Yore*. London, 1842.

_____. *Directions to Young Planters for their Care and Management of a Sugar Plantation in Barbados*. London, 1800.

Parry, J. & P. Sherlock. *A Short History of the West Indies*. London: MacMillan, 1956.

Patterson, Orlando. *Freedom in the Making of Western Culture*. Vol. 1. Cambridge, M.A.: Harvard University Press, 1991.

Pinckard, Dr George. *Notes on the West Indies*. 3 Vols. London, 1806.

Pitman, Frank. *The Development of the British West Indies, 1700–1763*. Newhaven: Yale University Press, 1917.

Poyer, John. *The History of Barbados*. London, 1808.

Puckrein, Gary. *Little England, Plantation Society and AngloBarbadian Politics, 1627–1700*. N.Y.: New York University Press, 1984.

Richardson, Bonham. *Panama Money in Barbados, 1900–1920*. Knoxville: Tennessee University Press, 1985.

Robotham, Don. 'The Notorious Riot': The Socio-Economic and Political Bases of Paul Bogle's Revolt'. *Working Paper 28*. University of the West Indies, Kingston: Institute of Social and Economic Research, 1981.

Rodney, Walter. *A History of the Guyanese Working People, 1881–1905*. Baltimore: Johns Hopkins University Press, 1981.

Saville, Julie. *The Work of Reconstruction: From Slave to Wage Laborer in South Carolina, 1860–1970*. Cambridge: Cambridge University Press, 1994.

Schomburgk, Robert. *The History of Barbados*. London: Longman, 1848.

Schuler, Monica. *'Alas, Alas, Kongo': A Social History of Indentured African Immigration into Jamaica, 1841–1865*. Baltimore: Johns Hopkins University Press, 1980.

Scott, James. *The Moral Economy of the Peasant*. New Haven: Yale University Press, 1976.

_____. *Weapons of the Weak: Everyday Forms of Peasant Resistance*. New Haven: Yale University Press, 1985.

Scott, Rebecca. Slave Emancipation in Cuba: The Transition to Free Labor, 1860–1899. Princeton: Princeton University Press, 1985.

Semmel, Bernard. *The Governor Eyre Controversy*. London: Macgibbon & Kee, 1968.

Sheppard, Jill. *The 'Redlegs' of Barbados: Their Origins and History*. N.Y.: KTO Press, 1977.

Shepherd, Verene. Transients to Settlers: The Experience of Indians in Jamaica, 1845–1950. Leeds, England: Peepal Tree, 1994.

Shepherd, Verene, Bridget Brereton and Barbara Bailey. *Engendering History: Caribbean Women In Historical Perspective*. Kingston: Ian Randle Publishers; London: James Currey, 1995.

Sheridan, Richard. *Sugar and Slavery: An Economic History of the British West Indies, 1623–1775*. Eagle Hall Barbados: Caribbean University Press, 1974.

_____. *The Development of the Plantation to 1750*. Kingston: Caribbean Universitiy Press, 1970.

Skeete, C.C. *The Condition of Peasant Agriculture in Barbados*. Bridgetown, 1930.

Spurdle, Frederick. *Early West Indian Government*. N.p., n.d.

Starkey, Otis. *The Economic Geography of Barbados*. N.Y.: Columbia University Press, 1939.

Stern, Steve, ed. *Resistance, Rebellion and Consciousness in the Andean Peasant World: Eighteenth to Twentieth Centuries*. Madison: University of Wisconsin Press, 1987.

Stewart, John. *A View of the Past and Present State of the Island of Jamaica*. Edinburgh: N.p., 1823.

Stewart, Robert J. *Religion and Society in Post-Emancipation Jamaica*. Knoxville, T.N.: University of Tennessee Press, 1992.

Stuckey, Sterling. *Slave Culture: Nationalist Theory and the Foundations of Black America*. New York: Oxford University Press.

Sturge, Joseph & Thomas Harvey. *The West Indies in 1837*. London: Hamilton, Adams & Co., 1968 edition.

Tinker, Hugh. *A New System of Slavery:The Export of Indian Labour Overseas, 1830–1920*. Second edition. London: Hansib Publishing,1993.

Trouillot, Michel-Rolph. *Haiti: State Against Nation.The Origins and Legacy of Duvalierism*. New York: Monthly Review Press, 1990.

Turner, Mary S. *Slaves and Missionaries:The Disintegration of Jamaican Slave Society, 1787–1834*. Urbana: University of Illinois Press,1982.

Turner, Mary, ed. *From Chattel Slaves to Wage Slaves: The Dynamics of Labour Bargaining in the Americas*. London: James Currey; Kingston: Ian Randle Publishers; Bloomington: Indiana University Press, 1995.

Underhill, Edward Bean. *The Tragedy at Morant Bay:A Narrative of the Disturbance in the Island of Jamaica in 1865*. London: Alexander & Shepheard, 1895.

Waddell, Rev. Hope Masterton. *Twenty-NineYears in theWest Indies and Central Africa:A Review of MissionaryWork and Adventure, 1829–1858*. 1863. Reprint. London: Frank Cass, 1970.

Ward, Samuel (Ringold). *Reflections Upon the Gordon Rebellion*. Pamphlet, 1866.

Watson, Karl. *The Civilised Island, Barbados:A Social History, 1750–1816*. Barbados, Barbados: Graphic Prinetrs, 1979.

Watts, David. *The West Indies: Patterns Of Development, Culture and Environment Change Since 1492*.Cambridge: Cambridge University Press, 1987.

Williams, Eric. *Capitalism and Slavery*. London:Andre Deutsch, 1964.

_____. *From Columbus to Castro:The History of the Caribbean,1492-1969*. London:Andre Deutsch,1970.

_____. *Documents of West Indian History*. Port of Spain: PNM Publishing, 1963.

Worrell, Delisle, ed. *The Economy of Barbados, 1946–1980*. Bridgetown: Barbados Central Bank, 1982.

Wrong, Hume. *Government of theWest Indies*. Oxford: Oxford University Press, 1923.

ARTICLES

'An Assessment of the Ideological Position of Grantley Adams in 1937–38, 1948-49'. Paper presented at the 16th Annual Conference of Caribbean Historians, Barbados,1984.

Barrow, Christine.'Ownership and Control of Resources in Barbados: 1834 to the Present'. *Social and Economic Studies*, 32, 3 (1983): 83–120.

Beckles, Hilary.'The Slave Drivers'War: Bussa and the 1816 Barbados Slave Rebellion'. In *Boletin de Estudios Latinoamericanos y de Caribe*, no. 39 (Dec. 1985): 85–109.

'Black People in the Colonial Historiography of Barbados'. In *Emancipation II*, edited by W.K. Marshall, 131–143. Bridgetown : Department of History,1987.

Belle, George.'The Abortive Revolution of 1876 in Barbados'. *Journal of Caribbean History*, Vol.18 (1984): 1–35.

'The Initial Political Implications of Emancipation: Barbados'. Paper presented at the 14th Annual Conference of Caribbean Historians Puerto Rico,April 16–21, 1982.

'The Struggle for Political Democracy: 1937 Riots'. Public Lecture, Bridgetown, March 17, 1987.

Bennett, J.H.'The Problem of Slave Labour Supply at the Codrington Plantations'. *Journal of Negro History*,Vol.36 (1958): 406-439.

Boomert, Arie.'Notes on Barbados Prehistory'. *Journal of the Barbados Museum and Historical Society*.Vol.38, No. 1. (1987): 8-44.

Brathwaite, Edward Kamau. 'The Black Angel'. *Bim*, Vol. 6, No. 22 (1955).

_____. 'Law and Order'. *Bim*. Vol. 6, No. 23 (1955).

Bullen, A.K. & R.P. 'Barbados: A Carib Centre'. *The Bajan and South Magazine*, No.155 (1966): 6-12.

Bullen, R.P. 'Barbados and the Archaeology of the Caribbean'. *Journal of the Barbados Museum and Historical Society*, 32 (1966):16-19.

Carter, Richard. 'Public Amenities after Emancipation'. In *Emancipation II*, edited by W.K. Marshall, 46-70. Bridgetown: Department of History, 1987.

Carrington, Selwyn. 'West Indian Opposition to British Policy: Barbadian Politics, 1774-1782'. *Journal of Caribbean History*, Vol. 17 (1982): 26-50.

Cooksey, C. 'The First Barbadians'. *Timehri*, 3:2 (1912): 142-144.

Drewett, Peter. 'Archaeological Survey of Barbados'. *Journal of the Barbados Museum and Historical Society* Vol. 38, No.1 (1987): 44-81, Vol. 38 No.2, (1988): 196-205. [This was published in two parts.]

Dunn, Richard. 'The Barbados Census of 1680: Profile of the Richest Colony in English America'. *William and Mary Quarterly*, Vol. 26 (1969): 3-30.

Gibbs, Bentley. 'The Establishment of the Tenantry System in Barbados'. In *Emancipation II*, edited by Woodville Marshall, 23-46. Bridgetown: Department of History, 1987.

Hall, Neville. 'Law and Society in Barbados at the Turn of the Nineteenth Century'. *Journal of Caribbean History*, Vol. 5 (1972): 20-45.

Handler, Jerome. 'An Archaeological Investigation of the Domestic Life of Plantation Slaves in Barbados'. *Journal of the Barbados Museum and Historical Society*, Vol. 34, No.2 (1972): 64-72.

_____. 'The Amerindian Slave Population of Barbados in the Seventeenth and Early Eighteenth Centuries'. *Caribbean Studies*, Vol.8, No.4 (1969): 38-64.

_____. 'Aspects of Amerindian Ethnography in Seventeenth Century Barbados'. *Caribbean Studies*, Vol. 9, No.4 (1970): 50-72.

Hunte, Keith. 'The Democratic League and Charles Duncan O'Neal'. Public Lecture, Bridgetown, March 3, 1987.

_____. 'Duncan O'Neal: Apostle of Freedom'. *New World Quarterly*, Vol. 3 (1967).

Innis, F.C. 'The Presugar Era of European Settlement in Barbados'. *Journal of Caribbean History*, Vol. 1, (1970): 1-22.

Johnson, Howard. 'Barbadian Immigrants in Trinidad, 1870–1897'. *Caribbean Studies*, Vol.13 (1973): 5-30.

Lewis, Gordon. 'The Struggle for Freedom'. *New World Quarterly*, Vol.111, Nos. 1-2 (1966 Barbados Independence Issue): 14-29

Lowenthal, David. 'The Population of Barbados'. *Social and Economic Studies*, Vol.6 (1957): 445-501.

Marshall, Trevor. 'The White's in Perspective'. *The New Bajan* (July 1990).

_____. 'The Riots of 1937'. *The New Bajan*. (October 1989).

_____. 'The Termination of Apprenticeship in Barbados and the Windward Islands: An Essay in Colonial Administration and Politics'. *Journal of Caribbean History*, Vol. 2 (1971): 1-45.

Mayers, Richard. 'The Role of the Police in the 1937 Revolt'. Caribbean Studies Paper, UWI, History Department, Cave Hill, 1991.

Molen, Patricia. 'Population and Social Patterns in Barbados in the Early Eighteenth Century'. *William and Mary Quarterly*, Vol.28 (1971): 287-300.

Morris, Robert. 'Slave Society in Barbados'. In *Emancipation I* , edited by A. Thompson, 33-45. Bridgetown: Department of History, 1984.

_____. 'The Rise of the Labour Movement in Barbados from about 1020 to about 1946'. History Department Seminar Paper, UWI, Cave Hill, 1975.

Phillips, Anthony. 'The Confederation Question'. In *Emancipation II*, edited by Woodville Marshall, 7085. Bridgetown: Department of History, 1987.

'The. Political Elite in Barbados, 1880-1914: Aristocracy, Plantocracy, or Bureaucracy'. History Department Seminar Paper, UWI, Cave Hill, 1976.

'The Origins of the Bushe Experiment: A Governor's Eye View'. History Department Seminar Paper, UWI, Cave Hill, 1983.

'The Racial Factor in Politics in Barbados, 1880-1914'. History Department Seminar Paper, UWI, Cave Hill, 1973.

Ramsaram, Ramesh. 'The Post War Decline of the Sugar Economy in the Commonwealth Caribbean'. University of Hull, Conference Paper, Wilberforce Anniversary, July, 1983.

Roberts, G. W. 'Emigration from the Island of Barbados'. *Social and Economic Studies*, Vol. 4, (1955): 287.

Rodney, Walter. 'Barbadian Immigration into British Guiana, 1863-1924'. Paper presented at the 9th Annual Conference of Caribbean Historians, Barbados, 1977.

Rohlehr, Gordon. 'Islands'. *Caribbean Studies*, Vol. 10, No.4 (1971).

Sheridan, Richard. 'The Crisis of Slave Subsistence in the British West Indies during and after the American Revolution'. *William and Mary Quarterly*, Vol. 33, No.4 (1976): 615-641.

Sleeman, Michael. 'The Agro Business Bourgeoisie of Barbados and Martinique'. In *Rural Development in the Caribbean*, edited by P.I. Gomes. New York: St Martins Press, 1985.

Stoddart, Brian. 'Cricket and Colonisation in the English Speaking Caribbean to 1914: Steps Towards a Cultural Analysis'. Seminar Paper, UWI, History Department, Cave Hill, Barbados, 1985.

Vaughan, H. A. 'The Shaping of the New Order: Barbados, 1834-46'. History Department Seminar Paper, UWI Cave Hill No.9, 1981-82.

Ward, J.R. 'The Profitability of Sugar Planting in the British West Indies, 1650-1834'. *Economic History Review*, Vol. 31, No.2 (1978): 197-212.

Watson, Hilbourne. 'Attempts at Industrial Restructuring in Barbados'. Department of Political Science, Howard University: Mimeo, 1986.

_____. 'The 1986 General Elections and Political Economy in Contemporary Barbados'. Howard University: Mimeo, 1986.

UNPUBLISHED THESES

Belle, George. 'The Politics of Development: A Study in the Political Economy of Barbados'. PhD dissertation, Manchester University, 1977.

Davis, Karen. 'The Position of Poor Whites in a Colourclass Hierarchy: A Diachronic Study of the Ethnic Boundaries in Barbados'. PhD dissertation, Wayne State University, Detroit, Michigan, 1978.

Karch, Cecilia. 'The Transformation and Consolidation of the Corporate Plantation Economy in Barbados, 1860-1877'. PhD dissertation, Rutgers University, New Brunswick, 1979.

Innes, Franck. 'Plantations and Peasant Forms. Barbados, 1627-1960'. PhD dissertation, McGill University, Montreal, 1967.

Manyoni, Joseph. 'Social Stratification in Barbados: A Study in Social Change'. PhD dissertation, University of Oxford, 1973.

Will, Wilber. 'Political Development in the MiniState Caribbean: A Focus on Barbados'. PhD dissertation, University of Missouri, 1973.

Index